Spiritual Java

Daily Cups of Inspiration

D1518117

Sally –

May these meditations on ordinary things remind you of the wonder that surrounds us all ... and the one who created it!

w/ love,

Cover art created by Dawn Ashby Caldwell (NewDawningArt.com)

Back cover drawing created by Charlotte Bristol

Scripture quotations are from the New Revised Standard Version of the Bible, copyright © 1989 National Council of the Churches of Christ in the United States of America. Used by permission. All rights reserved. Psalm passages are from the Psalter in *The Book of Common Prayer.*

Spiritual Java

Daily Cups of Inspiration

Chip Bristol

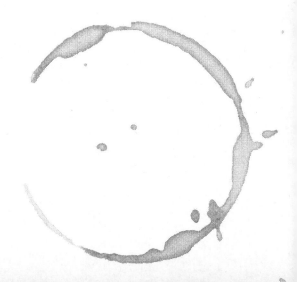

This collection of meditations
is dedicated to our four children:

Wells Usher Bristol

Gregory Hastings Bristol

Charlotte Hanrahan Bristol

McLaren Cunningham Bristol

You show me God's wonder, hope, and grace, daily.

ACKNOWLEDGMENTS

This book began when I arrived at Trinity Episcopal School in New Orleans and was told I'd be preaching every morning. My training continued at Eton College (England), Holderness School (New Hampshire), and Canterbury School (North Carolina), and I'm grateful to all the students, teachers, and parents who encouraged me to offer the gospel in creative ways to the hearts of young and old alike.

My friend, Chris Laney, encouraged me to write a weekly blog years ago, many of which have been edited to fit into this collection, but it was my dear friend, Mike Twilley, and my wife, Louise, who came up with the idea of compiling my meditations into a book. It never would have happened without their support and encouragement.

I'm indebted to my daughters, Charlotte and Clare, for helping with typing, and to Betsy Raulerson, who was willing to read these meditations multiple times and loved them and me despite my spelling, split infinitives, tense shifts, and random capitalization. Richelle Thompson, like a gifted midwife, took it from there and brought this baby into the world. My gratitude to Richelle and her team, Michelle DeMoss-Phillips, designer, Carole Miller, layout and production, and Dave Caudill, proofreading.

These meditations are intended to stir and encourage those who read them. If they help you, please let other readers know, and subscribe to my blog, *Brushstrokes*, found on my website at www.withoutacollar.com.

INTRODUCTION

Her day began with coffee, not the first cup in her apartment but the one at the coffee shop where she met with a small circle of friends each morning before they headed off to work. The group formed by accident on a day when the place was packed, and a few of the charter members, as they now refer to themselves, ended up sitting together and talking. Now, two years later, the group had grown, and the owner had a table waiting for them each morning.

The group was eclectic, a patchwork quilt, one of them liked to say. They were a variety of ages, differing colors, backgrounds, and interests. But when they were together, it just seemed to work.

Sometimes the conversation was about little things like troubles at work or pressures at home, but eventually their discussions moved to deeper things. Some in the circle grew up in church, others did not. Some loved organized religion, others had been hurt by it, but each person was spiritually hungry on some level. The table became their altar and coffee their communion, as they explored the questions and desires of their hearts.

"It's like church," one person said of the group.

"Without all the rules," someone added.

"I'm more comfortable here," said the one gay member of the group who came out during one of the morning gatherings.

"But it's certainly spiritual," one of the charter members said. "At least it is for me."

"I never thought coffee could be spiritual," someone added.

"That's right," said the member who always tried to put a positive spin on things. "It's spiritual java!"

The group laughed as they lifted their mugs in solidarity, then began the morning's conversation.

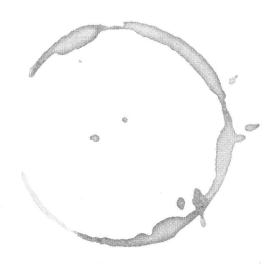

FOLLOW THE YELLOW BRICK ROAD

"It's always best to start at the beginning." —*Glinda*

When I look back on the way I studied for a test in high school, I'm embarrassed. Instead of opening a book or reviewing my notes, I arranged the books on my desk in descending order. I then switched them to ascending order before I sharpened each of the pencils in my drawer. Once I arranged my desk, I moved to other parts of my room. As you might suspect, I rarely got around to studying.

I now know all the arranging was procrastination. Even successful authors face this battle: Steven Pressfield calls it resistance; Julia Cameron calls it fear. Whatever name you use, the phenomenon is known to us all. It may dress up or put on a wig, but its only purpose is to keep you from doing whatever it is you have planned.

When Dorothy was told she needed to see the Wizard of Oz, she was unsure how to start the journey. Glinda tells her to start at the beginning, and that is sage advice for all of us embarking on the journey of a new year. Beginnings can be as exciting as they can be frightening. We can spend so much time arranging things, setting the stage for the days ahead, that we soon find we have taken no steps forward along the way.

There's never a perfect time to start. Preparations are never complete. So, we might as well just get going. "Wherever you are is the entry point," as the Indian mystic Kabir reminds us. May that be enough to get us to put one foot in front of the other this year.

Espresso Shots:

1. *How do you feel as you begin a new year?*
2. *What excites you most? What apprehensions do you have?*
3. *What steps can you take to begin your journey?*

CLEAN BOARDS

He was a fastidious math teacher, both in the content of his classes and the maintenance of his whiteboard. Before introducing a new topic, he always sprayed and wiped the board clean until no traces of past lessons were visible. It took time and effort, and we sat, sometimes patiently, while he rubbed away the most stubborn marks. Other teachers were not so diligent, and the words or numbers left in the corners distracted me.

I always remember this math teacher and his board when moving into a new year. It's a chance for a fresh start, and I am eager to begin again. Sometimes in my excitement, I erase only enough to make room for the new instead of taking the time to erase the entire board. Remnants of past successes and failures remain on the board and distract me from the work about to begin.

It's time to erase the boards of last year and prepare for this one. It takes time and effort to erase the marks from past lessons, but it's worth it. Yes, we can learn from the past, but it can also get in the way and distract us from the present.

Today is as good a day as any to clean the board and make room for what is to come.

Espresso Shots:

1. *In what ways could you erase the board for the new year?*

2. *What are the things that distract you or hold you back from making a clean start?*

3. *Do something physical to erase last year. (e.g., Take a walk or clean out a closet or refrigerator)*

TENDERLOINS AND NEW YEAR'S RESOLUTIONS

The table was set, the wine opened, and everyone gathered, eager to turn the calendar's page. In honor of the special occasion, I bought a tenderloin and cooked it to perfection—or so I thought. It was medium rare when I took it from the grill but well done when we sat down to eat. Someone kindly told me meat continues to cook even after you take it off the grill.

As we ate our overcooked meat, we talked about New Year's resolutions. Some shared that they faithfully made resolutions. Others confessed they quit making resolutions after years of failed attempts.

"I begin the year with good intentions," one person said, "but I never make it past a day or two. Bad habits are hard to break."

"I give up swearing only to curse the next morning."

"I vow to lose weight, but the numbers still go up because of all the holiday parties."

It's like the meat, I realized. Just because I took it off the grill didn't mean it stopped cooking. Bad habits persist, especially in the early days of making a change. Rather than quit or beat ourselves up over failed resolutions, we should be patient and forgiving. We need to give the meat time to stop cooking before we can dig in and start fresh.

It's all about "stumbling in the right direction," as they say in 12-step recovery circles. Looking for progress, not perfection, can make the most outlandish resolution possible.

Espresso Shots:

1. *What's been your experience with New Year's resolutions?*
2. *Has a habit continued to cook after you sought to quit?*
3. *How can you apply the lessons of cooking the tenderloin to your life?*

SPINNING TIRES

We had an unusually big snowfall, and even experienced drivers struggled to make their way on the roads. I enjoy the challenge of driving in snow—but I learned how to drive in New England, not North Carolina. As I watched drivers gun their engines and spin their tires, I remembered one of the essential truths of driving in snow: start slowly. Tires need a chance to get traction so the car can build momentum. If the tires begin to spin, you should remove your foot from the gas pedal, not push it to the floor.

January is a time when the light turns green, and we begin our journey through another year. I need to remember that what is true about cars in the snow is true of people seeking to live intentional lives. We need to start slowly and maintain traction; otherwise, our tires spin, and we end up in the ditch. Resolutions, goals, and to-do lists are all wonderful, but they need to be reasonable. We need to begin the new year slowly, gently putting our foot on the gas. Once we have traction, we can increase our speed, not before.

There are many days ahead. We should plan to use them all as we gradually pull away from the green light and drive into a new year.

Espresso Shots:

1. _Have you ever floored it and ended up in a ditch?_

2. _What would it look like to drive deliberately into the new year?_

3. _Find a moment today or this week to slow down and regain traction._

LIMITED HORIZONS

Limiting one's horizons is a powerful tool. One of the greatest dangers of beginning anything, whether it's a new year, new project, or a new way of life, is looking too far ahead. Just ask someone who's given up drinking. Tell the person that they'll never drink again, and I can almost guarantee they'll be in a bar by night's end. Instead, tell them that they won't drink for the next twenty-four hours, and they have a real chance for success.

As you set out on this year, consider limiting your horizons:

Instead of hiking the entire Appalachian Trail, you only need to reach mile marker seventeen.

Instead of writing a novel, you only need to write that one scene.

Instead of losing thirty-five pounds, you only need to eat well today, at this meal.

Instead of being a perfect parent, you only need to handle this one moment well.

Instead of reading the whole Bible, commit to one book.

Every distant shore can be reached if the horizon is pulled closer, every journey possible if we take it one step at a time. People in recovery circles have been printing bumper stickers about it for years. As we begin a new year, maybe we would do well to follow their lead.

Espresso Shots:

1. *What are you currently facing that seems overwhelming?*
2. *In what way could you limit the horizon?*
3. *What is one thing you could do today?*

EPIPHANY

Today is known in church circles as Epiphany, the day we remember the arrival of the magi (wisemen/kings) to Bethlehem. It is the day they saw Christ, the day they saw God face to face. Although it's often bundled into the Christmas story, I like that the magi get a day of their own.

I've always had a thing for these stargazers. They looked to the stars in search of God. I have the same longing but rarely have the guts to follow the star. Such journeys take an enormous amount of effort. The wisemen traveled a great distance, but I sometimes find it too much work to drive to church, let alone a soup kitchen. I hate to admit it, but I sometimes wish Bethlehem would come to me.

Whenever I hear someone refer to a spiritual journey, I think of those three travelers from long ago. I give thanks for their willingness to look for direction, their perseverance in making the trip to Bethlehem, and their ability to see Christ face to face.

May I have the courage to bring such characteristics to my spiritual journey.

Espresso Shots:

1. *Do you look for God on a daily basis?*
2. *Are you willing to go where God leads you?*
3. *Do you have the perseverance to journey toward God, no matter where you are led or what it requires?*

ARE WE THERE YET?

I would love to have heard the discussion between the wisemen as they followed the star. I'm sure they had doubts along the way, especially as they headed toward a town as insignificant as Bethlehem. Jerusalem would have made more sense, I'm sure, but the star was over Bethlehem, and they obediently followed.

I've come to believe God appears where we least expect to find him. I also believe "Bethlehems" come in all shapes and sizes. We might mistakenly think God is to be found only in churches and cathedrals, but God's undeniable presence can just as easily be found in hospitals, rehab facilities, homeless shelters, soup kitchens, or coffee shops. Where two or more are gathered, we've been told, Christ will be present.

Not only is Jesus found in an unassuming city, but he is also wrapped in swaddling clothes and lying in a manger. It is one more thing for the wisemen to get over. Unlike the robes they are wearing, Christ is in homespun cloth, lying in a trough usually used to feed animals.

Epiphany is just one of countless times Christ challenges our assumptions. Being born in an unimportant city and in a stable, to boot, makes no sense at all—or maybe it makes all the sense in the world.

Espresso Shots:

1. *Have you ever found God in an unexpected place?*
2. *What does the Epiphany story tell us about God being with us?*
3. *How can we stay awake and look for God in unlikely places, wrapped in homespun cloth?*

BRINGING OUR GIFTS

It was the moment of truth. After singing all the usual Christmas carols, we reached the one that always caused me to avoid eye contact with everyone gathered in my great uncle's living room. It was time to sing "We Three Kings," and I desperately wanted to avoid being selected as one of the kings. That meant singing a solo. My gray flannels began to itch, and my necktie tightened. "Let's see," our host began as if he hadn't already made up his mind. "Who should be one of the wisemen this year?"

It's not that I disliked the carol, far from it. I just didn't want to sing by myself. What if I hit the wrong note? What if my voice cracked? People might point or snicker. Better to hide in the chorus.

The same is true with living a life of faith. People sometimes snicker as we look in the sky for a star. They point and mock when we say we believe we're being led. If we can withstand that ridicule, the time comes when we, like the wisemen, present our gifts. Then we face another obstacle of our self-doubt: Is our gift good enough? How does it compare to others? Such thoughts are enough to make clothes itch and ties tighten.

As we pay homage to the three kings—or wisemen, magi, or whatever you wish to call them—may we celebrate their steadfast journey, hopeful search, and inspired arrival. In the light of the star they followed, may we have the same determination and confidence to offer our gifts—our minds and heart, and maybe even our voices.

Espresso Shots:

1. *What gifts can you bring to God?*
2. *What are the compelling fears that keep you from doing so?*
3. *In what way can you offer God a gift, regardless of your fear?*

SPIRITUAL ADD

I have ADD, which means I have a hard time focusing. Like the dog in the movie *Up*, all I need is a squirrel to distract me from whatever I'm doing. There have been times in my career when moving from one thing to another served me well, but usually it torments me. A conversation at the next table and a candy wrapper in a movie theater can whisk me away from the moment, leaving those around me wondering why I seem so distracted.

It has affected my spiritual life, as well. No matter how hard I try to focus and be present each morning, it usually feels like praying in a tree full of monkeys, as the Buddhists put it.

Sitting in my favorite chair each morning with some meditation books gets me started in the right direction, but unopened bills on the counter and a long to-do list draw me away. Scripture tells us to pray without ceasing, but the world is filled with noises and distractions. No wonder it feels like we all have spiritual ADD.

All I can do is continue to try. Rather than fight the distractions, I need to accept them and maybe even make them a part of my spiritual life. Like a child begging for attention, ignoring the distractions only increases their volume. When I acknowledge them, they run off to play, leaving me free to resume my spiritual practices.

Espresso Shots:

1. *What are the greatest distractions for your spiritual practices?*
2. *How can you carve out time to be fully present, spiritually?*
3. *How can you acknowledge the distractions and make them a part of your spiritual life?*

ONTO THE FIELD

"The more often he feels without acting, the less he will be able ever to act."
—C. S. Lewis

I love a good to-do list! I make them all the time. The problem is I put something on a list and then leave it there undone. I read books about personal growth all the time. The problem is I read them and then place them back on the shelf.

I doubt I am unique, but a new year is an appropriate time to look at our propensity to think about things but not act. Spending time each morning reading spiritual meditations is easier than living a spiritual life. Creating a strategic plan is easier than implementing it. Buying an exercise bike is easier than getting on it. Thinking about writing a book is easier than picking up a pen. Thinking about being a caring and supportive spouse, parent, or friend is easier than being one.

Life in the easy chair (pun intended) is more comfortable than taking action. Watching a game from the bleachers is easier than going onto the field, and the more we sit and think, the harder it gets to rise and do something.

Like all these meditations, I write them to myself. I feel convicted as I read C.S. Lewis' *Screwtape Letters* because too often, I think about things and do nothing about them. I convince myself I can do them later. I hesitate because I am overwhelmed by all that's needed to be done. But I now see that any action is better than no action, and any effort only strengthens me for more effort. Now, instead of musing about it, I should get out of this chair and do something!

Espresso Shots:

1. *Name something that has been on your mind for a long time.*

2. *What has kept you from taking action?*

3. *Name one small action you could take.*

Double Shot: *Do that one thing.*

LET'S DANCE!

It was the first writing assignment, and I could feel the anxiety permeate the classroom. The sound of pens scratching and keys clicking seemed particularly loud as the time limit approached. The instructor called us back, and before we shared what we had written, he said something I've never forgotten: "Just remember, everything you're about to read never existed before." It was a simple statement of fact, but it reminded me of one of the most incredible things about being a human being: we get to make stuff!

I grew up being reminded we all were created in God's image. While those images vary, one of the things we have in common is that, like God, we are born creators. Children never give it a second thought. Their days are all about creating pictures, games, and countless other things. They just run to the sandbox and start making something out of nothing. *Ex nihilo* is the fancy word for this approach. No wonder children act like life is more play than work.

Somewhere along the way, all that changed. Creating became something we were allowed to do after we did the real work in school. After school, we were told we needed "real jobs," and creativity was relegated to hobbies. In retirement, some reclaim their creative abilities and wonder why they ever let them go in the first place.

Not all of us were born to sing at the Metropolitan Opera or have art hanging in the National Gallery, but creativity can still be a regular part of our lives. Each of us is a conduit for the creative spirit, which moved over the waters millions of years ago and swirls around us still. I can't help but think the spirit is looking for a dance partner.

Espresso Shots:

1. *What was the most creative time in your life?*

2. *Can you identify one thing you made of which you are proud?*

3. *In what way could you reclaim your creativity and dance again?*

HOME BY ANOTHER WAY

"They left for their own country by another road." —Matthew 2:12

Even as a child, I picked up on the intrigue in Matthew's account of Jesus' birth. King Herod was up to no good, and the wisemen knew it. Instead of returning the way they came and risking another encounter with the inquisitive king, they went home by another way. While this provides another example of how wise they truly were, it also shows the impact Jesus has on people, even as a child in a manger. The wisemen see Jesus, and it changes their lives. They go home by another way.

More than anything else, the greatest evidence that Jesus is who people have proclaimed throughout the ages is the effect he has on the people who have seen or come to know him. Throughout history, there are accounts of people who have met Jesus personally and been transformed by the encounter: the monk in a thunderstorm, the priest at the altar, and the drunk in the gutter all went home by another way after seeing Jesus. While no one knows Jesus in quite the same way, what everyone has in common is the repercussion of the encounter. It changes your direction.

As people on a spiritual journey, we often look at God and argue about who God is and what a person should believe. While I love theology (God-thinking), I'm more entranced by how God changes our direction. God appears to us in countless ways, but the telltale sign of an encounter with God is when one's life heads in a new direction. It happened to the wisemen, and it's happened to countless souls since. Has it happened to us?

Espresso Shots:

1. *Look back and see all the times your life changed direction. What caused the change?*
2. *Did your life ever change directions because of God?*
3. *If so, how? If not, why?*

WALKING THROUGH THE FOG

The storm from the night before combined with a sudden drop in temperature, causing the fog to cover the mountain. My morning hike became more like blind-man's bluff than the inspirational communion with nature I intended.

I heard a stream nearby but couldn't see it until I was right on the water's edge. Even then, I could only see the water and rocks directly in front of me. The far side of the stream was wrapped in fog. I placed one boot on the closest rock and reached out with the other to the rock just beyond. From each rock, I was able to see only the next one, but eventually, I reached the other side.

Later that afternoon, the fog lifted, and I could see for miles. I realized what a gift my morning walk had been. Too often, I want the big view. I want to look out and see miles ahead. The fact is, fog often descends, and I can only see what is right in front of me. Instead of bemoaning the fog, I need to remember how I can make my way across the stream one rock at a time.

Jobs are lost, relationships get cloudy, and illnesses descend. In such times, it's hard to see anything but what's right in front of us. What's right before us, though, is enough to get us to the other side.

Espresso Shots:

1. *Recall a time when fog descended and you were not able to see far ahead.*

2. *How did you reach the other side?*

3. *How can you take the one-rock-at-a-time approach in your life today?*

PART I: BIRTH

He arrived kicking and screaming. Small wonder. He'd left the warmth of a womb where every need was met, and he was safe and secure. It was there he'd become human, then suddenly it was showtime. Out he came, through many contractions, much pain, and countless shouts. What a shock to leave the womb and enter the world! No wonder we all come out kicking and screaming.

I'm sure he'd love to return to the world he knew, but that's not possible. For him to experience life, he needs to make this frightening pilgrimage. He must travel from the place where all his needs are met to a more uncertain place. Such change involves pain and uncertainty, but those are the ticket for admission to this thing we call life.

Like the baby, I often want to stay in the world I've known. When faced with new surroundings, I want to return to where I've come from. But that's not how new life is found.

It wasn't for the baby, and it's not for you and me.

Espresso Shots:

1. *In what ways do you seek to stay in the familiar?*

2. *What fears await you when you contemplate venturing out to new life?*

3. *Why do you think pain often accompanies new life?*

PART II: BAPTISM

I wonder what was going on in Jesus' mind as he descended into the Jordan River to be baptized by John. Hollywood portrays Jesus with head erect, shoulders back, and confidence broader than the stream itself. Since we've been taught Jesus was fully human, I suspect Hollywood has it wrong, and Jesus walked into the water like we would, with hesitation and a good deal of fear.

Jesus' baptism marked the beginning of his public ministry. From here, he traveled into the wilderness, then returned and called his disciples. He taught and healed those around him for three years. In the end, however, he was arrested, tried, and killed. Even his most steadfast followers abandoned him. All of this awaited the man as he knelt in the water to be baptized.

As a child, I remember wanting to shout to Jesus, "Go back! Don't do it!" but my warning wouldn't have carried across two thousand years. I knew what was coming, and now I wonder if he did, too. Perhaps Jesus knew, as he descended into the river, that this was the beginning of the end.

Instead of rattling my faith, such thoughts make me see the story with greater awe. Like all great stories, Jesus' life had a beginning, middle, and end, and to try to separate them is to remove the story's power. His descent into the water was connected to his climbing the hill on Good Friday. The same voice that cried from the cross preached from the hillsides.

The sacred journey begins with baptism. It did for him. It does for us, also.

Espresso Shots:

1. *If you are a Christian, do you see how your baptism is connected to the rest of your life?*

2. *Do you think Jesus knew what lay ahead for him as he descended into the Jordan River?*

3. *Why do you think the church says we are "baptized into Christ's death?"*

THE SYMPHONY

"It is finished," said the composer.

After years of work, his symphony was complete, and it was his *magnum opus*, the work that would define him. He assembled the sheets of music, feeling as if they contained a piece of him. To listen to the symphony was to hear his heart, soul, and voice.

Because music is to be played and listened to, he looked for a worthy conductor who, in turn, would find musicians to form an orchestra. Weeks later, the composer sat off to the side to watch as the musicians entered the music hall for their first rehearsal. The conductor tapped his music stand and lifted his arms to begin. The conductor gasped as his piece came to life. In places, the tempo was quicker than he had imagined, in other places slower. Unexpected instruments were used, and there was even a crescendo he never intended.

It was his piece, but, in some ways, it wasn't. The shape was more pronounced, the tone more subtle, and the emotion more powerful. The piece now belonged not only to him but also to the conductor, musicians, and, eventually, all who heard it.

"It works," he thought to himself after the inaugural performance. "My music has become our music, which, I suppose, was always the point."

Espresso Shots:

1. *Have you ever created something and shared it with others?*
2. *If so, was it difficult to hear or see their interpretation of your work?*
3. *Art only becomes art when it's shared, someone once said. Is that true? Can the same be said of faith?*

ONE STEP AT A TIME

"That's why there are twelve steps, and they're in order," said the wise sage to the newly arrived alcoholic. Like so many of us, the novice wanted to be an expert in a week. He wanted to be airlifted to the summit and not make the climb. He wanted to cross the finish line and not run the race. However you describe it, taking things one step at a time is paramount, not only in recovery but in other areas of our life, including faith.

In my childhood Sunday school, I heard Bible stories that pictured God as a bearded man sitting on a cloud and Jesus as a white man with his arms wrapped around a sheep. When I think back, I saw God as an adaptation of Santa Claus, hoping he would put me on the nice list and bring me gifts.

Fortunately, my understanding of God developed as I grew up. As life became more complicated, concepts of sin and grace helped me navigate the turbulent adolescent waters. In college, I began wrestling with God, and those questions ultimately made my relationship with God stronger and my faith more personal. Having children altered my faith in countless ways, but it was my own personal struggles that gave me a doctorate in theology.

The little boy coloring pictures of Moses in Sunday school could never have understood God like the adult, nor should he be expected to. But the adult is in for a real crisis of faith if God remains a Santa figure.

Just like the newcomer to AA, we are given journeys for a purpose. Yes, they will lead us somewhere, but the only way to experience them is one step at a time.

Espresso Shots:

1. *What was your childhood understanding of God?*
2. *How has that evolved over time?*
3. *In what ways do you need to grow in your faith one step at a time?*

JUST A DRAFT

It's just a draft. Finished, but not complete. Someone once said a painting is never done; it just ends at an interesting moment. Looking at the notebook full of pages, I see a piece that's reached an interesting moment, but because it's a draft, there's more to do.

This draft has just as much to teach me about living as it does about writing. I have a life story I think I understand. It has twists and turns, characters, and themes, all of which leave me wondering whether I even know the theme or purpose of my life. I see a boy driving away from the hospital with all of his father's possessions in a garbage bag who wonders how to be a man. I see a young man with his son on his lap who has no idea what it means to be a father, a nervous man putting on a plastic collar before his ordination, and a chaplain tripping over his fancy academic robes in England. These are but a few of the characters in my story. You, I'm sure, have your own.

Creating a story is hard work. Remembering that it's only a draft is equally challenging. This is as true about the work that sits before me as it is about the one who wrote it. I'm just a draft. We all are. Thanks be to God, who's not done with us yet.

Espresso Shots:

1. Spend time reflecting on the story of your life. List the characters, chapters, twists, and turns.

2. What themes do you see in your story?

3. Because you're only a draft, what work do you think needs to be done to your story?

DIVINE FABRIC OF CHAOS

When asked to describe her church, the pastor replied, "It's a divine fabric of chaos." It was not the most elegant description I've heard, but it was the most lasting.

Depending on the time of day, incense wafts from a meditation group and guitar music echoes down the hall. Smock-clad artists chat as they paint beside one another. A preschool occupies one wing, and a large reception hall hosts daily 12-step recovery meetings and yoga classes. The sanctuary is open for services on Sundays and Wednesdays and for prayer and meditation all other times.

On the surface, it appears unruly. Dizzy from trying to take it all in, I look at the pastor whose broad smile tells me she understands. I ask how she manages it all, and she says, "I don't. I just enjoy the ride."

While walking through the fabric studio on the second floor, she holds several threads as she describes her church. "There are many threads, and when you place them beside one another, a pattern appears, and a garment is created. Layer upon layer, it all seems to come together. It's not one person's doing, one person's idea. Someone greater than any of us, a master artist, is behind it all. It holds together in a profound way I don't understand fully, but I don't have to."

She could have been speaking of our lives as much as her church. We're all divine fabrics of chaos. Thanks be to God.

Espresso Shots:

1. *In what way is your life a series of threads woven into a fabric?*

2. *Do you struggle to manage all the threads?*

3. *How can you celebrate your life as a divine fabric of chaos?*

COFFEE MUGS

Recently, I read the word authentic defined as "bearing the mark of the hands." Such a definition made me think about the collection of coffee mugs in my studio. Collected from my travels, each is a unique work of art. Some are funny looking; all are irregular in shape or coloring, but, together, they are as inviting as the morning coffee they hold.

Handmade mugs bear the marks of the hands that created them, and there's something about the connection I feel with the potter who made the mug that feeds my soul. I can picture the potter throwing the clay onto her wheel and molding the clay into the mug with her hands.

The Bible says that we, too, are made from clay. God's hands took the clay and molded each of us into a unique work of art. We are funny looking and irregular, but each of us bear the marks of God's hands.

Too often, we try to hide those marks. We strive to look like everyone else. Instead of looking like one-of-a-kind works of art, we work hard to look like one of the mass-produced mugs.

The spiritual life invites us to celebrate our uniqueness. Through various practices, we come to know not only the unique works of art we are but also the One who formed us out of clay in the first place.

Espresso Shots:

1. *List the marks or things unique about you.*
2. *Do you appreciate them, or do they embarrass you?*
3. *In what way could you embrace your uniqueness?*

MONEY IN THE ACCOUNT

The furnace went out about two hours before the dishwasher. It was as if they were in cahoots, determined to drive us mad. When the repair services handed us the estimates, I gasped. It was more than I had in the bank. Fortunately, my wife is a saver, and we used some of her reserves to get the repairs done.

It was a similar lesson to one I was taught in rehab. "Make sure you put money in your recovery account, so there's enough when you need to write a check," said the wise old man who taught us on Tuesday and Thursday mornings. What he meant was we needed to go to meetings when we didn't feel like it, pick up the phone to call another person when our schedules were full, and meet with our sponsor when we'd rather be doing something else. That way, when challenges show up, and we want to drink, there's enough reserve in our account to keep us from heading to the bottle.

The same is true spiritually. Our souls are like bank accounts. They need to have resources in them for our proverbial rainy days. Walking, reading, talking with a friend, going to church, or attending a Bible study group are ways to build capital in our spiritual account. We all have different ways of making deposits, but we share the need for the account to be stocked and ready. Challenges will arrive, and doubts and discouragements will sneak in. The question is, will we have set aside enough savings when we need to write a check?

Espresso Shots:

1. *What are three ways you put "money" in your spiritual bank account?*

2. *Has your spiritual account ever been empty when a bill arrived?*

3. *What practices could you take on to begin making daily deposits?*

PLAYING YOUR MUSIC

He was a roadie, the kind of worker Jackson Browne made famous in a song. You know, the first to come and the last to leave, the ones rolling the cases and lifting the amps. He needed a job and was glad to be working for this up-and-coming band with the peculiar name, Lynyrd Skynyrd. His name was Billy Powell.

One afternoon, after everything was set up and he thought he had the arena to himself, Powell sat down at the piano. Trained as a classical pianist, he'd given up hope of ever making money playing the piano. His hands still remembered how to make music, though, and his training came back to him as soon as his fingers touched the keys.

One of the band members stopped by to pick up something and heard the music. Impressed by how good it was, he went to see who was playing and was surprised to see it was one of the roadies. Billy Powell was asked to join the band, and it changed his and the band's life forever. You've probably been the recipient of his talents, including the keyboard solo for the song, "Free Bird."

We have all been given particular talents. There's nothing sadder than not using them, and nothing more remarkable than when we do.

Espresso Shots:

1. *Identify three God-given talents you have.*
2. *Recall a time when you put one of them to use.*
3. *How could you find a way to use those talents fully and more often?*

DRESS REHEARSAL

It was the theatrical equivalent of Christmas Eve. We were handed costumes and told to go to the dressing rooms where people waited, ready to help us prepare for the night's performance. As we dressed, the banter was louder than usual, and it was hard to sit still as they applied our makeup. As the lights dimmed and the overture began, our hearts leaped. "Don't get carried away," the director reminded us. "It's only a dress rehearsal."

His advice was hard to remember that night, and it's been hard to remember ever since. But it still holds true: this thing we call our lives is only a dress rehearsal. Our time on earth is only a tiny moment. Like costumes, our possessions can make us feel important; our successes, like a spotlight, can make us feel it's a one-person show, and the sound of applause can fool us into thinking the approval of others is all that matters.

"Don't get carried away," I hear the real director saying. "It's only a dress rehearsal."

Espresso Shots:

1. In what way do you forget life is a dress rehearsal?

2. What causes you to forget this truth: possessions, success, or applause?

3. How would remembering this is only a dress rehearsal change the way you live your life today?

CREATING

"I like to make shit," replied the carpenter when asked why he chose that particular career. Some of the group touring his studio were taken aback by his reply, but I loved it. In shocking simplicity, he said what I understand in the depth of my soul.

I grew up in a church that spoke of a Trinity: Father, Son, and Holy Spirit. Some describe the Trinity as Creator, Redeemer, and Sustainer. However, one conceives it, I've always been drawn to the first person of the Trinity— the father, the creator. Looking around the world as a child, I marveled at creation. Later, in art class and woodshop, I liked how it felt to make something—like I was participating in creation in some way. That feeling continued when I performed in shows and directed one, when I led committees and we came up with ideas, and when I worked in schools and we built outdoor chapels and taught students how to preach.

I believe we were born to create. We are not creators in the same fashion, all artists who paint, sing, or dance. We may be creators in the kitchen or garden, with words or wood. We may be creators in our vocations as teachers and architects and electricians. To be creators doesn't mean we have to sculpt a monument or write a *magnum opus*. All it means is we participate in creation; we open our hearts and minds to God and then buckle up.

Through us, God can do more, create more than we can fathom. O, that today we would harken to God's voice!

Espresso Shots:

1. *Think about something you created that filled your soul with gladness.*

2. *What was it about that something that made the experience so powerful?*

3. *In what ways can you create more often in your life?*

JUST A DAY

It's just a day. January 25. One of 365 that make up the year, and yet, for me, it's a day unlike any other. It's the day I gave up drinking. Unlike my birthday, which I would rather ignore, I never let this day go by without spending time reflecting and giving thanks.

I won't bore, entertain, or shock you with what led to my decision to get sober, but it was a threshold into a new life for me. On the other side, angels were not singing nor were the people I hurt waiting with open arms to forgive. What awaited me was a new path and a wonderful community of people eager to have me walk beside them, one day at a time.

I am convinced we all have thresholds that await us. Crossing them can seem as overwhelming as not knowing what life on the other side will look like. That's why we, so often, turn around and walk away.

But if today teaches me anything I can pass along, it is that there's life on the other side of whatever door we face. There's a path and others waiting to walk beside you. In my case, God, who was with me on either side of the door, was standing on the other side with a big, wide grin. For that, I am profoundly grateful.

Espresso Shots:

1. *Name a threshold you were scared to cross over.*

2. *If you walked away, why did you do so? If you crossed over, what did you find?*

3. *What threshold do you face today, and how could this become a day you'll never forget?*

MINISTERS

"A dairymaid can milk cows to the glory of God." —*Martin Luther*

In seminary, one of my church history professors told of a gravestone that read, "Here lies Cuthbert Wallace, a devoted follower of Christ who also made shoes." After all these years, I remember this tombstone because it reminds me that anything we do can be a ministry: anything can bear witness to our faith.

I grew up with ministers who were set apart. They were called "father" and wore different clothes. We saw them as different from ordinary people, and we expected them to be so. I never thought much about it at the time, but when I first put on the black shirt and white plastic collar myself, the tension of those expectations was overwhelming.

There's a certain freedom that comes when we pass along being a minister to those who are ordained. *They* can live lives of devotion, *they* can behave in a holy way, and everyone else can go about their business. No wonder we turn to them for prayers and look to them for answers.

But Jesus never expected to get us off the hook; he never thought ministry was for a select few. In fact, his teaching is quite the opposite.

Whether making bread or automobiles, studying or teaching, raising houses or a family, the opportunities to live lives that witness to our faith abound. "Come, follow me," Jesus said. There were no qualifiers, then or now.

Espresso Shots:

1. *What was your view of ministers growing up? How do you see them now?*

2. *Do you think ministry is for a select few?*

3. *In what ways could you serve God in whatever you do for a living?*

WHERE ARE WE?

I drive by the litter-filled stream. I used to play in these waters until the sun set. Now, I mourn that the polluted water is unsafe for children. It shouldn't be this way. Where's God?

Driving by a local shelter, a long line of men, women, and children wait for breakfast. With my belly full, I wonder why so many struggle. How can there be so much need? It shouldn't be this way. Something should be done. Where's God?

Sitting in a wheelchair, never to leave, he watches as friends and family walk to raise money for ALS research. He'll never benefit from such research, and yet he continues to cheer them on. It shouldn't be this way. Something should be done. Where's God?

Maybe I have it wrong. Perhaps I'm asking the wrong question. It shouldn't be, "Where's God?" It should be, "Where's Chip? Where am I in responding to these needs?"

Espresso Shots:

1. *When it comes to meeting the countless needs in the world around you, do you watch from afar or get actively involved?*

2. *Do you write the checks, leaving others to do the work?*

3. *What's one way you can show up to help with a need in your community?*

DAY BY DAY

I grew up going to a small, wood-frame church on the Jersey shore in the summers. It was a place that shaped my heart like no other. On Sundays, a special service was held just for the children. With the minister and organist, the service was appropriately short and sweet. We always concluded the time together by standing in a circle and holding hands while the minister recited the words of a simple hymn before giving each of us a lollipop.

I didn't realize then how much the service and that hymn would shape me. Throughout childhood and even as an adult, I hum (and sometimes sing) the song.

> *Day by day, day by day*
> *O, dear Lord, three things I pray*
> *To see thee more clearly, love thee more dearly,*
> *Follow thee more nearly, day by day.*

I recently looked up the hymn and was surprised by its simplicity. These are the only words, and they're as straightforward as the tune, yet these four lines contain all I need to know about living a spiritual life. Hopefully, in the days to come, I will not only hum the tune but also practice the words.

Espresso Shots:

1. *In what ways could you see God more clearly?*
2. *In what ways could you love God more dearly?*
3. *What would it look like to follow God more nearly, day by day?*

RELEASING THE PEBBLES

Henri Nouwen, one of my spiritual heroes, described a time when he taught a group how to pray. As they sat in the circle, eager to hear his teaching, Nouwen stood and gave each person a pebble. He instructed them to grip the pebble with all their strength while closing their eyes and praying. It didn't take long for them to realize that praying while gripping something tightly is impossible. He encouraged them to open their hands and try again. Prayer was suddenly possible.

I think of this moment whenever I feel cut off from God, or, as they say in 12-step recovery circles, I'm not in the sunlight of the spirit. It usually means I'm holding onto something, maybe even gripping it with all my might. Only when I release my grip is it possible to connect to God and my neighbor.

This lesson is easier to understand than to do. We live in a world that tells us to hold things tightly. Whether to people, places, and things around us, or our sense of purpose and worth, we learn early on to cling tightly. There's a sense of security that comes when holding on, but it's exhausting and, in the end, futile.

When we are willing to open our fists and release our grip, we can talk freely to God and hear what he is saying as well.

Espresso Shots:

1. *What pebbles do you cling to most tightly?*

2. *In what ways does the pebble or your grip get in the way of your relationship with God?*

3. *What would it look like to release your grip?*

FREEDOM

He meant well, but of all the people I have ever worked for, he was the most challenging. He hired me to do a job he had once had, and he couldn't resist the temptation to tell me how he had done it. "I'm just trying to help," he said whenever he saw my frustration with his perpetual advice-giving. I wondered why he had hired me in the first place. Better to hire a clone, I thought, or a robot.

In contrast, my favorite boss was the one who hired me for the same kind of job but approached his leadership in a different way. Once he explained the position, he set me free to do the job as I felt best. At first, the freedom was frightening, but I grew to love the room to experiment and use my God-given creativity. I made more mistakes in this job than in the other, but I was never more alive in my work.

To recall these two jobs makes me appreciate God's freedom. We have been given all the gifts and talents we need just as we have been given opportunities to use them. God doesn't tell us how to do the job. God is not a micromanager. Clones or robots don't interest God. People fully alive are what sets God's heart on fire. It's a risky way to handle things: we make more mistakes this way, but, in the end, we become the children he always hoped we'd be.

Espresso Shots:

1. *Have you ever been micromanaged or given enormous freedom in your work?*

2. *If so, in which did you feel more alive?*

3. *How can you grow in your appreciation of God's freedom, making the most of your gifts and talents in the opportunities before you?*

VOICE RECOGNITION

"Hi Charlie," the man said when he heard the voice on the other line.

"How'd you know it was me?" Charlie asked.

"Because we talk all the time," the man replied. "I recognize your voice."

This brief encounter was not intended as a spiritual illustration, but that's what it became. I couldn't help but wonder if God recognizes my voice when I call, or if I recognize God's. Do we speak to each other enough for our voices to be familiar?

Like most children, I was taught to kneel and put my hands together in a certain way when I prayed. Eventually, I was released from such spiritual shackles when I learned I could talk to God when lying down and standing up, walking or running, in church or on a walk. I still worry sometimes about doing it right, if there is such a thing, but I now believe God is more interested in frequency and authentic conversation than the "right way." The Bible tells us that we should pray without ceasing. For me, that means talking to God throughout my day. It also means listening regularly. If I want the relationship that I say I do, then God and I must speak often enough to recognize each other's voices.

Espresso Shots:

1. *When was the last time you prayed?*
2. *How could you learn to pray without ceasing?*
3. *How could you work with God to develop your ability to recognize each other's voices?*

TAKING A SEAT

I didn't understand the T-shirt when I first saw it. *Sometimes to take a stand, you need to take a seat.* Having recently moved to Greensboro, North Carolina, I didn't know the story about the four students from a local college who went to Woolworth's Drugstore on February 1, 1960, and took seats at the lunch counter. Such seats were for white patrons only, and the black students refused to leave. Their protest began a sit-in movement, which soon spread throughout the South. Students took a stand against racism, and they did so by taking a seat.

In the safety and comfort of hindsight, I commend those students just as I condemn the racist people and system that prevented them from sitting at the lunch counter in the first place. But hindsight is easy. It allows people like me to look back with disdain while not looking at the present with a critical eye. How is racism practiced today? Where are the lunch counters that still divide us?

Looking at our world and ourselves honestly can be painful, and embarrassing. This type of careful evaluation can lead to change, which adds to the difficulty. Too often, we decide it's better to accept things as they are than do the difficult work of changing.

One of my greatest fears is facing God and hearing I played it safe. Instead, I want to have failed because I tried something too difficult. I want to have sat in the company of a few because I cared for many. I want to have squirmed in my own discomfort because I traveled beyond what was familiar, intellectually, spiritually, socially, and financially. In the end, I hope I learn to take a stand. In honor of what happened this day long ago, I hope I learn to take a seat.

Espresso Shots:

1. *In what ways do you prefer the status quo to change?*
2. *Where can you see inequality in the world and discrimination in your life?*
3. *When in your life have you taken a stand—or a seat?*

SITTING IN THE DITCH

I once heard the story of two older gentlemen stumbling home from a festive party. One of the men fell into a nearby snowbank and couldn't get up. His companion, unable to help, simply plopped himself beside his friend while the two waited for help.

Although humorous, the story serves as a vivid illustration of authentic compassion. Having stumbled many times, I've always been moved by the ones who plopped down and sat beside me.

When I was training for the ministry, I spent six months serving as a chaplain's apprentice at a large hospital. Because I was the only seminarian without children, I was assigned the emotionally charged pediatric intensive care unit. It was brutal. The experience was also expensive when I tried to help a family with their enormous hospital bill. Exhausted and broke, I collapsed in the chair at our chaplains' weekly meeting. "Are you done trying to save people?" our mentor asked. I began to understand the power of sitting beside someone and not trying to rescue them.

On the morning of my father's funeral, the minister who would be conducting the service woke me up. "Let's go," he said, and I followed him to a nearby glen with many walking trails. We spoke of many things, none of which was the death of my father, but when we returned to my room, I felt strong enough to handle the day before me. The minister sat beside me in the ditch, and that was enough.

Espresso Shots:

1. *Have you ever tried to save someone or had someone try to save you?*

2. *Have you ever sat beside someone in a ditch or had someone sit beside you?*

3. *Write or call someone who has sat beside you and thank them.*

COMPLETING THE TURN

On a weekend when we were celebrating my stepson's birthday, I found myself in a new role. We were up in the North Carolina mountains, and I became a ski instructor for one of the boys who had never skied before.

I began with the snowplow—or "pizza slice" as it was called when I was taught to ski. I got his skis in the right position, then taught him how to lean toward the outside. He was a quick study. By the third run, he was navigating down the mountain with relative ease.

Excited by his progress, however, he began to rush things. He started a new turn before finishing the one he was in. The result left him lying on the slope, covered with snow, wondering what he did wrong. "Complete the turn before beginning another," I called over my shoulder as I tried to show him what a completed turn looked like.

I realized I was one to talk, not in the way I ski, but in how I live. I often get excited by something I am doing. Maybe it's a painting I've started, a new chapter in a book, or a project at home. I get a burst of adrenaline each time I begin something, but before it's finished, I am eager to start something new. Like my stepson's friend, I begin a new turn before I've finished the turn I'm in, and I, too, often end up lying on the ground covered in snow.

Fortunately, I caught myself in the act when I returned from the ski weekend. Distracted by a new thought, I gently reminded myself what I'd taught the boy: "Complete the turn."

Espresso Shots:

1. *Do you get excited when you begin something new?*

2. *Have you ever begun a new "turn" while in another one?*

3. *How does this lesson apply to your work, relationships, and spiritual life?*

THE WEATHER OUTSIDE IS FRIGHTFUL

The snow came and came and came. For a city used to winter weather, this season had been disproportionately generous. Even the most enthusiastic snow revelers had had enough. The news said more snow was on its way.

A friend in Boston sent a photograph of herself shoveling the walkway outside her house. The snow on either side was above her head. It reminded me of a truth I knew when I lived up north: don't let it build up! Shoveling frequently is a pain, but it's easier than trying to shovel all the snow at once.

It's the same with living a meaningful life. Life's weather is going to show up. Sometimes the storms are light, other times they're heavy, but they're coming whether we like it or not. Snow can fall on relationships, careers, families, physical lives, and spiritual lives. But we have a choice of how to handle the snow. We can wait for all of it to fall, then begin the work, but the lifting will be heavy. Or we can stay on top of the snow and shovel throughout the storm, but that means more conversations, more time on our knees, at the gym, or wherever the shovels are to be found.

We can shovel more often or wait. The choice is ours.

Espresso Shots:

1. *In what area of your life have you waited until the storm passed, and what was the shoveling like?*

2. *When did you stay on top of a storm and shovel more often?*

3. *Where is the snow beginning to gather in your life right now, and which method do you plan to use?*

THE DIVINE ARTIST

It came to me in an instant, as it so often does. The idea filled my heart with childlike excitement, and I quickly went over to my desk and began making notes. There's nothing like the what-ifs of creativity. Everything is possible. Out of nowhere, something new is coming.

I've been at this long enough to know that after euphoric inspiration comes the more mundane—but vitally important—development of a detailed plan. In my experience, every idea evolves through this process, becoming something other than what was first conceived. The trick is learning how to participate with creation and not control it. Like a midwife helping to deliver a child, we are bringing something into the world. It does not belong to us, but we play an essential role in ushering it into the world.

I wonder if this is how God felt when the idea of us first came. I wonder if the idea just arrived and filled God with excitement. What happened when God began to work out the details? As we came into being, did we arrive in a way different than God first conceived? After we arrived, did we become something unexpected? Did God control the creation process to make sure we were exactly as God envisioned us, or did God allow the freedom for the creation to be what it was meant to be?

I like to think of God as a divine artist. Whether a glorious sunset or the exuberant curiosity of a small child, God's artwork inspires me. It brings me to my knees and makes me want to follow God's example.

Espresso Shots:

1. *Imagine a time when you were inspired by an idea.*
2. *How did bringing that idea to life teach you about God?*
3. *In what way is God a divine artist, and how can we follow God's example?*

DANCING IN THE MARGINS

The minister met his trusted friend each Tuesday to discuss his next sermon. After the minister described his intention to speak about living lives of gratitude, his friend asked, "Are you going to remind them to be grateful for the challenges and difficulties of life?" After an awkward pause, the minister answered, "It's not in my outline."

They laughed, knowing how often the important things are not in our outlines. Whether in the pulpit, at a kitchen table, or on a walk, some of the most important things we need to say are not the things we intend to say. Planning carefully, we often end up leaving out what's essential. Neat and tidy outlines are one thing, but the scribbles in the margins need our attention, too.

The same is true in our lives. We spend so much of our time curating our lives so they're Christmas-card ready and social-media worthy that we forget to value the moments of chaos, the times we spend in the margins. Outlines are safer and more predictable. *Tell me what time to pick up which child where, but let's not talk about the state of our marriage. Let's plan that dinner with friends but not talk about my drinking. Let's make sure we have the resources for the prestigious school but avoid the more challenging conversation about whether it's the right school for our child.*

As comforting as outlines are, they can create stagnant, shallow lives. Better to live in the margins, where important things are scribbled, and there's room enough to dance with life.

Espresso Shots:

1. *Do you live your life trying to stick to an outline?*
2. *Have you ever been surprised by something in the margins?*
3. *In what ways could you learn to celebrate the margins?*

PILOT LIGHTS (Part I)

When our father died, my brother and I bought a house in New Hampshire. I think we were searching for a place of safety, a retreat from uncertainty, and space to give voice to our deep sadness. We bought an old stone chapel called the Wayside Chapel that had been converted into a unique home. I remember many things about the place: the wood-burning stove, huge bookcase, and a bathroom located in what had been the bell tower, complete with a stained-glass window.

This morning, however, I am thinking less nostalgically about the place. I'm reminded of how drafty it was. In the winter, the wind blew right through the rocks. When we sat at candlelit meals, the flames more than flickered. We struggled to keep the house warm. The breeze continuously slipped under the furnace room door and blew out the furnace's pilot light, which gave us about an hour before the cold house awakened us to the problem.

I am embarrassed that it has taken me thirty-three years to recognize the lesson that the pilot light and icy breeze were trying to teach me.

I have been born with a pilot light, a small blue flame burning quietly within, waiting to ignite my being and bring warmth to the world around me. It is a primal light, given to me at birth, but it resides out of sight and often goes unnoticed or is forgotten. When needed, though, it is there to bring my true self to life.

Espresso Shots:

1. What is the pilot light in your life?
2. When have you ignored it?
3. What can you do to let that pilot light warm you up?

PILOT LIGHTS (Part II)

More often than I would like to admit, my pilot light has gone out. Breezes of busyness have blown it out. Gusts of upheaval, from unexpected deaths to wrong turns and deadends, have quenched the light. Relentless winds have found their way through rocks and under doors, and the light—unprotected and even ignored—has extinguished.

In time, the cold awakens me to what's happened, and I need to relight the flame. The torches are many: sitting quietly, going to church, talking with a trusted friend, going for a walk, sitting by a stream, looking out at the ocean, listening to music, looking at a piece of art, going to a 12-step recovery meeting, or reading an inspirational work. All of these, and more, are effective tools for relighting the pilot light within, but I also need to be mindful of the cracks and gaps through which the breezes flow. Part of me wants to make my house airtight, but, like the Wayside Chapel, drafts will always find a way inside.

Today, I am grateful to have a flame at all, and I will do what I can to keep it lit.

Espresso Shots:

1. *Describe the strength of your spiritual pilot light.*
2. *What threatens to blow out your spiritual pilot light?*
3. *How can you protect that light?*

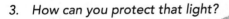

FROST HEAVES

When I moved to New England, I was introduced to frost heaves, a phenomenon of earth expansion and contraction that causes roads to buckle. Like taking a deep breath and popping a shirt button, the earth breathes and contracts, forcing streets to crack and pop up. When you drive over a frost heave, your car shakes, and the wheels fall out of alignment.

It happened to me again on a recent visit. I was traveling down a road lost in thought, and suddenly I hit a frost heave. I jolted back to attention—it awakened and frightened me— and also spilled my coffee all over my shirt. I was suddenly fully present.

I find life lessons in all sorts of places, and on this day, I realized that frost heaves have much to teach us spiritually. Like many others, I've always sought to know where I should head in life. There's great comfort in knowing where one is and where one is going. Such a clearly marked road provides a sense of comfort and security. But we must be ready for the frost heaves to come and disrupt our travels, pushing us out of cruise control.

Like the earth, our lives—including our spiritual lives—are living and breathing things. They expand and contract, with occasional frost heaves that might cause a well-traveled road to crack and buckle. Rather than bemoan the disruption, we might see the spiritual frost heaves as God's way of awakening us, to remind us to not only focus on the destination but also to be present for the journey.

Since my return from New England, I've sought to let my life with God breathe and trust that God will guide me, even when the familiar road cracks and buckles.

Espresso Shots:

1. *Name a time when you have encountered a spiritual frost heave.*

2. *What happened, and how did it affect you?*

3. *In what way did the frost heave serve a fruitful purpose in your life?*

SPOONS AND PIANO STRINGS

The piano in our living room was a source of entertainment and joy throughout my childhood. Only when the room was empty would I venture over and try to play. For some reason, whenever I hit middle C, there was an awful sound, like a musical note mixed in with the cries of a distressed cat. I tried again with the same result. I couldn't figure out what was wrong until I lifted the heavy cover and saw a spoon resting on top of the strings. Earlier, my sister and I had played a game called Hide the Spoon, and I was excited to finally find the spoon that had caused me to lose the game.

I thought about the spoon and the terrible sound when I talked with some close friends about our lives. Each of us had lived, shall we say, colorful lives, and we shared some of the most dramatic stories. Unfortunately, along with the stories of what happened came the things we added, comments about how stupid and inferior we felt when compared to others. Like the spoon resting on the piano string, the stories from our youth sounded different when we added our judgments to them.

We all have spoons that sit on the strings of our lives and change the songs we hear. Knowing this is the first step. Raising the cover and lifting the spoons off the strings is next. It's challenging and uncomfortable work, but in the end, the misleading and hurtful songs fade, and we can hear the sound of our lives again.

Espresso Shots:

1. *Find a story from your past around which other sounds/stories have come.*

2. *Where did the spoon come from, and what does its presence sound like?*

3. *What would it take to lift the spoon?*

THE SAME PEOPLE WHEREVER YOU GO

My father liked to tell the story of two people leaving a small New England town. They met at the post office to forward their mail. The first was distraught. She had lived in the town for years and didn't want to leave.

"The people here have become like family," she said. "I just can't bear the thought of leaving."

"Don't worry," said the postman, "You'll meet the same people wherever you go."

The second was happy to be moving on. He'd never liked the town much and found the people cold and rude.

"Don't worry, the postman said again. "You'll meet the same people wherever you go."

Espresso Shots:

1. *If you had to move from where you're living, how would it make you feel?*

2. *What does that say about the people where you live?*

3. *What does it say about you?*

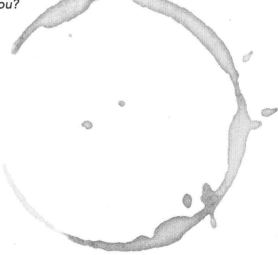

A NEW SONG

In the days when buying a Coke was a treat within an allowance's grasp, we drank from glass bottles. The contents never lasted as long as we wanted, and soon we were left with empty bottles. So we turned them into musical instruments by blowing air across the mouth of the bottle. I can hear the sound, still.

I recalled this childhood memory when speaking to a group of recovering addicts. In the literature of the 12-step program, they speak of "a hole in our soul through which the wind blows." Everyone in the circle, including me, knew the feeling and the sound. Like wind across a Coke bottle, the familiar refrain could be heard: "You're not good enough."

People have tried to fill the hole in their souls so that the wind cannot enter. Some do it with work, others with possessions, friends, or full calendars. Whatever they use, the fix is always temporary. The wind will find a way; the song will return.

I have come to believe we were created with the hole in our soul for a purpose. It serves to remind us that we are incomplete, and the only true fix is to fill the hole with the one who gave it to us in the first place. When we turn to God and let God fill our souls, the wind will blow, and a song will be heard, a new song that we can sing unto the Lord, as the psalmist says.

Espresso Shots:

1. *In what way do you have an emptiness inside?*
2. *In what ways have you tried to fill it?*
3. *What would it look and feel like to fill our souls with God's presence?*

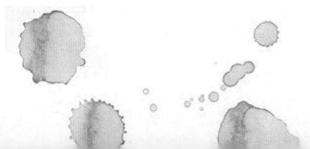

LOSING OUR HEARING

A friend, who was advanced in age, confessed to me that as his hearing diminished, he could not hear certain tones. For example, his wife spoke in a tone that was a real struggle for him to hear. I looked over to see if he was making a joke about the state of his marriage, but he was serious. As I get older, I am beginning to know firsthand what he was talking about.

I wonder if the same is true for our spiritual hearing. Can we hear things in our youth that we can't as we age?

An older couple in our church shows up for everything, participates in many outreach projects, and takes turns leading their Sunday school class. They've not lost their hearing.

A neighbor waved his hands and said, "I just don't want to hear it," when a friend spoke about current political struggles. He was losing his hearing.

"I loved that poem you read in church," one of the church matriarchs said as she greeted the minister. "It's nice to mix things up a bit." She had not lost her hearing.

After a national tragedy, the congregation came to church with heavy hearts, but the minister delivered the sermon he'd written weeks before. He was losing his hearing.

Keeping your hearing intact takes effort and requires an open heart. It's easy to hear only what you want to hear and think what you've always thought, but eventually, we'll grow deaf and miss the people crying out around us.

Espresso Shots:

1. *How would you rate your spiritual hearing these days?*
2. *Are there sounds you would rather not hear?*
3. *In what way can you work to open your ears and listen to the world around you?*

LOVE IS A VERB

The couple sat at a small round table off to the side of the dimly lit, high-end restaurant. They'd known each other for a month, and both felt they were heading toward something serious. They met in aisle seven at the grocery store when he offered to reach something on one of the top shelves. From there, it was meeting for coffee, then walks and some casual dinners.

As the waiter came and poured the expensive wine into the sparkling goblets, the light from the candle flickered. Neither wanted life ever to change.

"I love love," the woman sighed, and the man nodded. They eventually married and had children. They still loved each other, but there were fewer walks and almost no romantic dinners. Their conversations moved from life dreams to family logistics. In church, they noticed an older couple who still held hands. Their children had long since gone, but the couple seemed young at heart.

"How do you do it?" the younger couple asked during coffee hour. "Do what?" the older couple responded. "How do you keep it alive. You look like you're still dating."

"We are, I suppose," the woman replied. "But it wasn't always so." Her husband continued, "I always thought marriage would be one, long, romantic walk, but it isn't." The younger couple looked discouraged until the woman spoke again. "We came to realize that love is not just a feeling. Feelings don't last. Love becomes a verb. When it does, the feelings return as well."

The young couple had no idea what that meant, but, in time, they did. Many years later, as they sat in the pew holding hands, a young couple came up and asked, "How do you do it?"

Espresso Shots:

1. *Describe what love feels like.*
2. *What would love as a verb look like?*
3. *How can you grow to understand love in a new way?*

PLASTER WALLS

My greatest struggle is the discrepancy between the faith I profess and the life I lead. I've never expected perfection, but my imperfections often overwhelm me and cause me to question whether I should even bother to live a life of faith. Maybe faith is for better people, I often say, but I've recently come to see things differently.

I once moved into an old New England home with plaster walls. It was charming, and I was excited to paint the rooms before we moved in. I thought they looked great with a fresh coat of paint—until I turned on the extra lights to focus on my work. Suddenly, the countless imperfections of my work appeared, and my enthusiasm plummeted. A wise friend who had painted plaster walls before reminded me that the walls themselves were irregular, and any attempt to paint them perfectly was futile. "Just look closely and do the best you can," he said.

Like the plaster walls, my irregularities abound. The light of my faith makes my imperfections stand out. Rather than give up because of what the light reveals, I give thanks that I have a faith that reveals opportunities for growth.

My job is to look closely and do the best I can.

Espresso Shots:

1. *Spiritually, have you ever found yourself wanting to give up because of your imperfections?*

2. *Do you sometimes think the spiritual life is only for the perfect (or the really, really good)?*

3. *How can you learn to appreciate seeing imperfections as opportunities for growth and not reasons to feel badly about yourself?*

GETTING WET

I love the story about Jesus standing on the water outside of a boat and Peter wanting to get out of the boat to join him. Peter climbs out and is successful in walking on water at first, but then fear and doubt overtake him, and he plunges into the water.

I remember a classmate in Sunday school saying he thought Peter was silly. Of course, he was going to fall into the water. After all, he's not Jesus. For me, though, Peter was someone I completely understood. His love of Christ and his excitement over the new life Jesus was bringing into the world made him eager to try all sorts of things he'd never imagined. I didn't think he was silly. I thought he was wonderful.

A life of faith involves getting out of the boat—and getting wet. I wish the spiritual life were only about getting out of the boat and walking on water, but it's not. We're going to get wet because we're not Jesus. Fears and doubts always get in our way, but we can't let them keep us from following Jesus out onto the water.

When I recall times that I have climbed out of the boat only to sink, I take comfort in the fact that I'm not alone. Peter's been there, too.

Espresso Shots:

1. *Have you ever climbed out of the boat because of your faith?*

2. *What were the fears and doubts that caused you to sink into the water?*

3. *In what ways can you take comfort in knowing Peter's been there, too?*

ASHES

Sliding between my fingers,
Smooth and coarse,
The ash from what used to be,
Blends until it's carried away in a gust of wind.

Listen closely.
You'll hear echoes of fireside conversations,
Hushed and loving, raised and angry.
Looking closely,
You'll see shards of logs,
Reduced to powder.

Between the fingers of our hearts,
We hold the dust of our pasts.
Successes and failures, hard and heavy,
Made into ash with the flame of time,
Only to be carried away by the wind,
If only we'd open our hands.

One day,
we will be ash, too.
Ashes to ashes, dust to dust,
The past points forward.
Placing them on our foreheads,
They blow away in the wind.

Espresso Shots:

1. *Find some ash and put it between your fingers.*
2. *Think about your past as you move the ashes with your fingers.*
3. *Would you like the wind to carry such memories away?*

THE WELL

There's a story in the Bible about Jesus going to a well in the middle of the day. He meets a woman there, and their encounter transforms her life. I never thought much of the story when I was a child, but then I grew to see the many layers within the story, layers that transformed my life.

At midday, the sun is at its hottest. No one walked out to the communal well at that time. Such errands were saved for morning or evening when it was cool, and the villagers could linger and connect with their neighbors. To go to the well at noon was to ensure no one would be there. As we see later in the story, the woman had her reasons for avoiding her neighbors.

Startled by Jesus' presence, she nonetheless talks with Jesus. With some prodding by Jesus, she shares that she has had many husbands and is presently living with someone who is not her husband. In the day, hers was a scandalous life. No wonder she came to the well at noon. But Jesus doesn't condemn her. He just wants complete honesty. Then, he promises her a living water, which sounds too good to be true.

I once traveled to the well at midday. Actually, it was the supermarket, and I went not at noon but late in the evening, though my reasons were the same as the woman at the well. I had crashed and burned publicly and couldn't bear running into my neighbors and feeling their scorn. I never want to go through that experience again. But I can say that Jesus met me at the well. In the heart of the moment, when I had no choice but to be completely honest, he came and offered living water, and for that, I am forever grateful.

Espresso Shots:

1. *Have you, or anyone close to you, needed to hide because of something you did?*

2. *What was the well where you felt God's presence?*

3. *What do you think living water would taste like, and what would you be willing to do to get it?*

TRYING

The first time I saw the scene, it spoke to a deep place within me. As I walked out of the theater, I was still thinking about the scene and knew I would remember it forever.

In the film *One Flew Over the Cuckoo's Nest*, Randle McMurphy, played by Jack Nicholson, is trapped in a mental hospital and determined to escape. He goes into the bathroom with the other patients following close behind. Bewildered, they look on as McMurphy stands before a large pedestal sink, bends his knees, and tries to lift it from its foundation. He plans to lift the sink and throw it through the window to escape, but it's too heavy. He makes many attempts, and those looking on snicker at his efforts. They think he's crazy. Exhausted, McMurphy walks past the others and says, "Well I tried, didn't I? At least I did that."

McMurphy was crazy to think he could lift something so heavy. His desire to be free was understandable; his effort commendable. It may have caused others to snicker, maybe even point fingers and laugh, but at least he tried.

Like any good movie, this one made me look at life in a new way. I thought about all the people I have known who have tried to free themselves or others in ways that caused the crowd to laugh. I thought about my own unsuccessful attempts to make a difference. Too often, I've measured such efforts by whether they were successful or not. Instead of the laughs, I can now hear McMurphy saying, "You tried . . . at least you did that."

Espresso Shots:

1. *What was a courageous thing you tried but didn't pull off?*
2. *Did others laugh or belittle your efforts?*
3. *What could you try today—not worrying about the success, only the trying?*

FEEDING ALLIGATORS

When asked to describe a moment from his childhood, the recovering addict spoke of living in Florida and wandering to a watering hole near his house where he befriended an alligator. Each morning, he went and fed the beast with bread until his mother found out and put an end to his morning madness.

He met another alligator later in life, one equally dangerous and capable of turning on him at any moment. This other alligator didn't eat bread. It liked cocaine and alcohol. Each morning and throughout the day, the man fed the alligator. No matter how much he fed the beast, it wanted more. Each day the alligator drew closer, and it was just a matter of time before the man was consumed.

Fortunately, he awakened and ran away before it was too late. At a safe distance from the alligator, he learned to play other games. Sleep and exercise were a start, to which he later added prayer and meditation. He found others who knew about alligators, and, together, they read books to help them grow stronger.

He hardly noticed a change at first, but the alligator slowly inched its way back toward the water. In time, it returned to the water, but two eyes still peer above the surface, waiting for him to forget the alligator was there.

Espresso Shots:

1. *In what ways do you feed an alligator that only wants to harm you?*

2. *What would it take to leave the alligator completely?*

3. *What spiritual tools can you use to keep the alligator at bay?*

BACKSTORIES (Part I)

I love a good backstory.

When Mother Teresa died, people read her private journal and realized this venerated soul had spiritual doubts. Some heard the news with horror, but others loved her even more. Knowing the person behind the legend made her real.

Backstories do that.

In an interview with Tom Watson, the famous golfer, David Ferity turned the conversation from golf to something the two had in common, alcoholism. It turns out that Watson, who had been sober for many years, reached out to Ferity when he was struggling, and it changed his life. Knowing their backstories helped me understand the two on a level I hadn't before.

Backstories do that.

His father died when he was just a boy, but he remembered his father with great admiration. People admired his father and said nice things about him to the boy, but when he sat down and talked with his father's roommate from college, it was as if he met his father for the first time. Hearing how he once slept through an exam or helped with a prank on the college president made the boy know his father in a way he never had before.

Backstories do that.

Espresso Shots:

1. *Recall a time when you heard someone's backstory. What was the effect it had on your relationship?*

2. *When have you shared your backstory, and how did it transform your relationship with the person with whom you shared it?*

3. *In what ways can you be more deliberate in sharing your backstory and encouraging others to do the same?*

BACKSTORIES (Part II)

He grew up looking at Jesus' face every Sunday. Located behind the altar, the image of Jesus was a constant companion during the readings and sermons; it made him feel as if he knew Jesus even though the image was a work of art, a stained-glass window.

Many years later, the boy attended classes about the figure in the window. He read the four accounts of Jesus' life written by those who knew him personally, as well as many works written by those who had come to know him well through the years. Slowly, the image in the stained-glass window became three-dimensional. He became more than something to look at—he became a person to know.

In *The Wizard of Oz,* Dorothy pulls away the curtain to unveil the wizard, meeting him face-to-face. We would do well to follow her example with God. Too many of us settle for an image of God. Instead, we should draw close and meet God face-to-face. By doing so, a relationship can begin, one in which we both become three-dimensional. Glass and colors turn into flesh and blood, and paraphrasing the poet Robert Frost, that will make all the difference.

Espresso Shots:

1. *What images or stories about God did you grow up with?*

2. *In what ways did those images or stories hold you back from coming to know God personally?*

3. *In what way can you pull away the curtain and meet God face-to-face?*

TWINKLE, TWINKLE, LITTLE STAR

I don't remember the first time I looked up in the night sky and saw the moon and stars glistening, but this act remains one of the ways I fill my soul. It's like having a progressive work of art hanging above me each night.

I thought I knew what a night sky was like until I went out west. Whether it's the thinner air or the lack of other lights, western nights are the most dramatic I've ever seen. As if the stars, moon, and planets weren't enough, I saw my first shooting star under the western sky.

As a child, I thought the planets and moon were sources of light, but I later learned they simply reflect light from another source, the hidden sun. It took me a while to absorb the concept when I first heard it. I had to change my thinking. Now, when I look up at night, I marvel not only at the canopy of natural art but also the source that makes it all possible.

In time I came to see that we, too, are like the planets and moon. We bring light into the world, but it is not our light. It comes from another source. The Bible says we're created in God's image. I wonder if we shouldn't also say we reflect God's light.

Whether big or small, famous or unknown, nearly perfect or utterly flawed, we all have the light of God shining on us. May we receive that light as the gift it is, and may it shine into the world from each of us and make a glorious work of art.

Espresso Shots:

1. *In what ways do you you bring light into the world?*
2. *Have you ever thought it was your light?*
3. *In what ways do you reflect God's light?*

MEASURING DEVICES

In science class, I was surprised by all the measuring devices: scales, yardsticks, and beakers. In the classroom where we were taught to unravel the mysteries of the world, I learned early on that measuring was an important step.

Once out of school, I learned that there are lots of measuring devices in the world. Buying a house, I was given a form to determine my net worth. When I applied for membership in a club, there were no forms, but there was still a lot of measuring. With each job, there was measuring. First, I was measured to see if I was a good fit and then later, to determine the quality of my work.

I suppose I shouldn't be surprised by all the measuring, but it leaves me grateful God measures us in different ways. Like God selecting David or Jesus calling disciples, it seems God's yardstick has a different calibration than the ones we use.

"I have one yardstick," I can hear God saying with a smile, "and it's called 'grace.' With it, I see you as my beloved child. That's all the measuring I need."

Espresso Shots:

1. *In what ways do you measure the world and those in it?*

2. *Have you ever felt as if you did not measure up?*

3. *What would it do to your view of the world, and your opinion of you, if you truly believed the only measuring that mattered was God's?*

SHOWING UP

"You just need to get your ass in the chair," said the irreverent writing teacher. Rather than soothe us with romantic images of the writing life or filling us with the do's and don'ts of good writing, he plopped his books on the table and uttered that line. I have to say: it was effective. I've never forgotten his words. The most important thing to do as a writer is to show up, get in the chair, and write. Everything else comes after or as a result of doing that one thing.

The same is true of living a spiritual life. We can distract ourselves by spending all our time in preparation, but eventually, we need to get into the chair (or on a walk or in the soup kitchen). The most important thing is showing up. Everything else comes after—or as a result of—doing that.

If we can get ourselves in the chair and do our work on a regular basis, there's no limit to what will happen.

Espresso Shots:

1. *How do you avoid getting into the chair?*
2. *What would it take to stop stalling?*
3. *Do it today.*

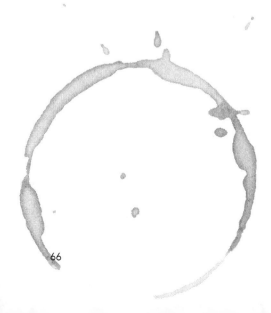

SPIRITUAL HYBRIDS

An increasing number of hybrid cars are on the road these days. Although I'm far from being a mechanic, I understand hybrids operate on two kinds of fuel. When charged, they run on the quiet, clean power of electricity. When needed, the engine switches over to gasoline. The cars get from one place to another with either form of fuel, but how they do so is markedly different.

I suppose I'm a spiritual hybrid. I get where I'm going, but I use different fuels as I travel. When I'm well-rested and recharged, I run on faith. A mixture of my humanity and God's grace, this fuel of faith quiets my engine and expands my love and compassion for others.

The other fuel is fear. A mixture of shame and insecurity, this fuel burns hot and can propel me to warp speed in seconds. Fear always takes its toll on my engine and constricts my heart and ability to see beyond myself.

The question is not whether I can operate on one type of fuel exclusively. I can't. Maybe it's enough to be aware of the two types of fuel. Hopefully, I'll learn how to use one kind of fuel more than the other, but I will always have a choice as to how I get from here to there.

I pray it will be by faith, but fear will always slosh from side to side in my tank, waiting for the moment when the pressures and anxieties of life cause me to switch over my engine. I suppose I should be grateful to have a choice about the fuel I use.

Espresso Shots:

1. *Can you recall a time when you operated on faith? How about when you operated on fear?*

2. *How do the two fuels differ in their effect on you?*

3. *How can you learn to use faith more than fear? Is there a time when fear can be an effective fuel?*

WALKING ON VODKA

"Miracles were all fine and good, way back when," said the man just holding on, "but as for my life, it's all pretty ordinary, at best." I understood but disagreed. I remembered when he first came into the rooms of AA: the glossy eyes and puffy face, vivid stories of excessive vodka drinking, heartbreaking dishonesty, and his slow, fingernail-digging climb out of the depths. I often looked across the room and marveled at how, with God's help, this man was becoming a new creation. On this particular morning, he couldn't see it.

We are so often blind to what God does, I suppose. Like the fog that drifts in and prevents us from seeing the grace-filled landscapes of our lives, we begin to doubt whether God even exists. When the pressure at work squeezes tight, a child stumbles, or the world's ills overwhelm, it's easy to get lost in the fog and, like my friend, no longer see the miracles surrounding us.

I think the blind see and the lame walk every day. It's just that we do not have the eyes to see. My friend bemoaned his inability to walk on water, and I celebrated his walking on vodka.

Espresso Shots:

1. *When was the last time you saw something miraculous?*
2. *Have you questioned whether God still acts in the world?*
3. *What's one miraculous thing that's happened in your life or for someone you know?*

BUCKETS

I carry a shiny, red bucket wherever I go, the kind you play with at the beach with the fancy, white plastic handle. You can't see my bucket, of course, but it's there, and it does what buckets do best: it holds stuff.

Some contents find their way into the bucket by chance. Others are put in deliberately. At times my bucket is light; other times, it becomes so heavy I can hardly carry it. Sometimes it's filled with wonderful things; other times, it carries toxic waste.

As I talked with my daughter in the car the other night, I realized she has a bucket, too. Like mine, it gets filled with all kinds of things. Together, we realized we have a say in what goes into our buckets, what stays, and what gets poured out. She told me about some good things that happened recently, something about a boy and a good grade, and her bucket felt full but light. Later, she shared about a girl who started a false rumor and the teacher who made fun of one of her answers. Her bucket became heavier.

I tried to convince her to pour out the bad stuff and carry only the good, but that's the kind of parental advice that floats away unheeded. I grab the advice before it leaves the car and try to apply it to my own life. Despite my age, I struggle with what's in my bucket as much as my daughter. I cannot control what tries to find its way into my bucket, but I do have a say in what stays in it. Rather than change my daughter, I change myself. Instead of worrying about what's in her bucket, I focus on mine. Somehow, by talking to each other, both our buckets grow lighter.

Espresso Shots:

1. *What do you carry in your bucket?*
2. *Why do you suppose we carry the negative stuff that's so heavy?*
3. *How can you empty your bucket of the heavy stuff and carry more of the light?*

WHERE THE PUCK IS GOING

I've started a tradition of buying my son the jersey of someone famous every Christmas. Whether baseball, hockey, or football, his collection has become impressive. The most recent gift was a Wayne Gretzky jersey. Although Gretzky had retired by the time my son became an avid hockey fan, he knew of Gretzky, one of the greatest hockey players of all time.

When asked about his technique, Gretzky shared that, early on, he learned to anticipate rather than respond. He didn't look at where the puck was but where it was going. The result was he reached the puck before other players, which is one reason he scored so often.

After showing my son highlights from Gretzky's career, I kept thinking about this ability to anticipate where the puck was going. Even though I was never much of a hockey player, I knew it was a technique I could try to apply to my life.

Too often, I've lived my life responding to life. I focus on where I am, not where I'm going. To look up and see ahead would have led to some surprising results, I'm sure. When looking at other people, I've focused on where they are and who they are—never thinking where they are headed. As a husband, father, or friend, I'd like to play the game like Gretzky did. I want to look ahead and see not where people are, but where they're headed. It would be a game-changer for us all.

Espresso Shots:

1. *Do you anticipate where life is going or respond to where it is?*

2. *In what ways have you held yourself or others back by such a focus?*

3. *Try to look down the ice this week, seeing where the puck is headed.*

A NEW LAWN

I live in a neighborhood with neat and tidy lawns. Ours, however, is not one of them. It's a mixture of grass and weeds, but as long as I keep it mowed, it's hard to tell. If I leave the yard unattended for too long, weeds pop up, and it's embarrassing, so I try to keep it cut. That way, you can't tell the weeds from the grass.

We decided to end the charade this year. It meant starting over. We had to kill the weeds and the grass first. The dead grass was unattractive, and more than a few neighbors looked askance as they walked by. It was a necessary step to a new lawn. Just when we began to question our decision to overhaul our lawn, new grass began appearing through the straw. At least for now, there were no weeds, and the fresh start gave us the chance to stay on top of any errant weeds.

As I waited for the transformation of our lawn, I couldn't help but see the parallels between the yard and my soul. There's a healthy lawn within, to be sure, but there are also weeds. Sometimes I have left the lawn unattended, and weeds have appeared, threatening to overtake the grass. It was embarrassing, and, too often, I simply mowed the lawn instead of fixing the problem. Such an approach is effective in the short term, but eventually it stops working. I guess that's what my spiritual practices have been telling me all along: half measures avail us of nothing.

Starting over, or complete surrender, involves a great deal of work. In mid-process, it can look unwieldy to those who pass by, but, in the end, new life will appear. Weeds are weeds—and they will still try to make their way into the mix, but if we stay vigilant, we can better maintain our spiritual lawn.

For me, that is the heart of the season of Lent.

Espresso Shots:

1. *What is the state of your spiritual lawn?*
2. *Have unattended weeds rooted among the grass?*
3. *Do you ignore the weeds or pull them out?*

TRASH AND RECYCLING

On my walk this morning, I noticed two trash cans pulled to the curb, one for recycling, the other for trash. Both were overflowing. I could see items that could not be recycled were in the recycling can, and in the trash were items that could be recycled. While the clear violation of trash protocol tempted me to don my deputy-of-the-universe hat, I continued walking and realized I'm as guilty as the people whose home I passed—I just do it with a different set of cans.

Inside of me, I have two bins: one is for trash, the other for recycling. Like my neighbor, I put the wrong things in the cans. In the trash, I mistakenly put mistakes and experiences that could be recycled, used for other purposes. Recycled, they could hold important lessons for the future, but because of my grief, sadness, or embarrassment, I throw them into the trash, hoping they'll disappear forever.

So, too, I sometimes recycle things that should be thrown away. I retell stories about myself or others that are simply untrue. I recall things I've done and use them to remind myself how worthless or incapable I am. Such trash needs to be seen for what it is and put in the proper can. It needs to be thrown away.

Like my neighbor, I need to learn to sort my trash better!

Espresso Shots:

1. *Name one thing you recycle that you should throw away.*
2. *Name one thing you have thrown away or denied that could be used to grow.*
3. *Try to teach yourself how to use proper containers.*

SAPLINGS

The sapling didn't have a chance. Rising timidly from the earth, it was surrounded by tall and strong trees. The large trees offered protection during storms, but their shadow made it difficult for the sapling to grow. Fortunately, a gardener saw the sapling and reached down with her trowel and moved the sapling to a place with the light and room it needed to grow.

I grew up among giants. Their talent and achievements left me in awe. Like all gifts, however, there was a downside. The very things that inspired me also made me feel less-than. Looking up at big and strong trees can make any sapling feel inadequate. In the shade of others, it's hard to grow.

I am convinced that our sole purpose in life is to grow into the people we were created to be and then offer ourselves to God and the world around us. As simple as that may sound, it's difficult, particularly when we compare ourselves to others and, even worse, try to imitate them.

It reminds me of a Jewish story I once read about a man named Zusha, who was troubled at the thought of meeting God in heaven. All of his life, Zusha tried to be like Moses or King David, when instead God asked, "Why weren't you more like Zusha?"

It's time to grab our trowels and move to a place with light and room to grow into the people we were created to be.

Espresso Shots:

1. *Who were the trees surrounding you as a child?*
2. *In what way did they inspire you? In what way did they intimidate you?*
3. *If you moved to a space with light and room to grow, would you be someone other than who you are?*

JUST A BRUSHSTROKE

It was just a brushstroke. One of many, but this one was different. This brushstroke stood out. It didn't belong. The color, value, and placement changed the nature of the entire painting. She was a better painter than this, she told herself. What was she thinking when she added that stroke to the painting?

Rather than wipe it away or paint over it, she stepped back and looked at the errant stoke. "What gave it such power?" she wondered. "How can such a small stroke dominate the piece?"

Staring, she looked beyond the canvas at the piece of art she called her life. She always hoped her life would be a work of art, one that inspired all those who came across it. She wanted her life to be impressive, to "work," as she said of her paintings.

Like the painting on the easel, however, some brushstrokes didn't fit, ones that changed the nature of the entire image. She wanted to wipe away or paint over such brushstrokes, but she knew that was harder in life than with paintings. "There are no mistakes in art or life," her art teacher once said, but she always doubted whether that was true. "Some things just suck," she sighed.

She awakened as if from a dream and got up from her stool. Lifting the brush and not the rag, she began to incorporate the brushstroke into the piece. It was just a brushstroke, after all.

Espresso Shots:

1. *In what way is your life a work of art?*

3. *Have you ever done something that didn't fit with the life you were living?*

3. *Did you wipe it away or paint over it, or learn how to make it a part of the painting?*

PUTTING DOWN THE STRAW

"I've lived my life looking through a straw," said the wise woman sitting across the circle from me. "I lift it up and peer through its tiny hole and think I can see all there is to see from such a perspective." I am not sure what else was said during the meeting. I became lost in the image of looking at life through a straw.

When we look down the narrow shoot of a straw, we focus on the other end. The problem is that the view is limited. The straw may focus our attention, but it also prevents us from seeing the bigger picture. A limited view can simplify things, but it also keeps us from widening our perspective, taking in the broader context, and enhancing our understanding.

I've used a straw to view those around me. I see them and think I know everything there is to know. I've used a straw to look at my career. I see one job or one moment and think it captures all I've done in my life. I've also used a straw when looking at my life. I see one moment, one success or failure, and think it tells my whole story.

The woman didn't know it at the time, but she helped me see how often I look at life through a straw. Lent is a wonderful season to put the straw down and see life from a new, wider perspective.

Espresso Shots:

1. Have you ever used a straw to look at something or someone in your life?
2. In what way did the straw simplify your understanding?
3. What was missed in the simplification?

LEARNING TO WALK

Down the hall, I saw a group of women surrounding a young child. One had her arms open wide and was encouraging the child to walk to her.

"Come on. You can do it," she said.

The child did his best to comply and eventually made it to the woman while everyone applauded.

I thought about the moment when I reached the sanctuary, and the service began. As I listened to the hymns and lessons, I couldn't help but celebrate that little boy's achievement. Forever, he would be able to say that he took his first steps in church.

Although I have no idea where I took my first steps, I can say the church helped me learn to walk spiritually. The church introduced me to God and lifted up people who could serve as role models. My first steps consisted of coloring pictures in Sunday school classes, but, in time, my steps grew stronger. I remember being able to stay in "big church," as I referred to it and not follow the younger children to Sunday school. It was then I got to hear sermons for the first time. I participated in the youth program and was eventually confirmed, which meant I was a full-fledged member of the church. Many years later, I went to seminary and helped others to take their first steps.

It is a remarkable thing to stand back and look at how you learned to walk, spiritually. For some, the church had nothing to do with it. For others, the church was essential. In any case, our spiritual journey is made up of many steps, and today is a day to celebrate every one of them.

Espresso Shots:

1. What were your earliest spiritual steps?
2. When did your steps grow stronger?
3. In what ways are you continuing your journey, one step at a time?

LEARNING TO WALK AGAIN

He grew up in the church, but he had not been back since his major meltdown. He had made a big, public mistake, and it was all he could do to get up that morning, let alone go to church. He feared the looks. He feared what people would say, to his face or behind his back, about what he did.

"I already feel horrible," he said to his friend, who picked him up. "I don't need the church's help."

Still, the two went to church. He remembers little of the service. As he and his friend walked down the hall toward the car, he noticed the place where he had taken his first steps. His parents had always told him that, surrounded by a bunch of adoring mothers, he had learned to walk in church. Now, he was there trying to learn to walk again. It's one thing to learn to walk, but another to get up and walk again after falling. He saw firsthand how the church loves to teach people to walk but scatters when they fall.

Espresso Shots:

1. *Have you ever fallen in a significant way?*
2. *If so, where did you find forgiveness and encouragement?*
3. *How can you become one of those with arms open wide, not only when someone learns to walk the first time but when they learn to walk again after they have fallen?*

SERVING THE PLOT

Writing teachers are quick to remind you that all things should serve the plot. Whether it's a detail, conversation, or character, everything should point to the plot of the novel. It seems like obvious advice, but writers often get distracted and wander off in directions that confuse or distract their readers. But great writers make sure all things serve the plot.

This advice can apply equally to our lives, but, like some writers, we forget and wander off in different directions. Plot-driven lives are clear, focused, and meaningful. Those living such a life say and do certain things that serve the plot—and they refrain from conversations and actions that don't.

Unfortunately, most of us either do not know the plot, or we get distracted. We wander in one direction or another, distracted by what the crowd wants, our jobs require, and our family expects. Such a life is as confusing as it is frustrating.

Jesus reminds us of our life's plot, and over and over again, he offers examples and instructions for how to live plot-driven lives. Like dropping a centerboard helps a sailboat move forward, a plot-driven life heads in a specific direction. What we say and what we do serves the plot.

I must confess I've not always known the plot for my own life. Even when I did, I still wandered in different directions because of my distracted, scattered heart. Wanting to please others, wanting to make a name for myself and leave a legacy, caused me to wander. While none of those motivations are wrong, they're all external motivations driven by a needy ego. Not until I stood back and asked what would serve God best did I begin to understand the direction I was to take, the plot I wanted to serve.

Espresso Shots:

1. *In what ways do you wander away, and what distracts you?*
2. *Does your life have a clear plot or purpose?*
3. *Does everything you do and say serve the plot?*

GLASSES

"There are only two ways to live your life. One is as though nothing is a miracle. The other is as though everything is a miracle."
—Albert Einstein

I often lose my glasses. I need them to see things at a distance. Unfortunately, when I'm wearing them, I can see things at a distance but nothing nearby. I eventually had to buy reading glasses, which added another ball to my juggling act. (I know: buy bifocals!) There is little wonder why I lose my glasses so often.

My soul wears glasses too. It has two sets: one that sees the world from a spiritual perspective and the other from a secular. When I wear the former, I see all the connections and meaning surrounding me. When I wear secular glasses, the world looks disjointed and haphazard.

Picking up the right glasses for my soul shapes the health of my life, spiritually, emotionally, and physically. *Dear God, help me to choose the right glasses, the right view, day by day. Amen.*

Espresso Shots:

1. *Do you have more than one pair of glasses through which your soul sees the world?*
2. *How do different glasses affect the way you see?*
3. *How can you learn to wear the right glasses?*

DESCENDING

I went to a movie about P.T. Barnum, the great circus creator. I'm not sure how much of the movie was accurate, but I was struck by his inordinate creativity, his unbridled ambition, and his willingness to take chances. These traits helped him establish his business—and almost cost him his dream, family, and life's work. In a confrontation with his wife during a particularly dark period, Barnum confesses he pushed things so far because he wanted to be more than he was.

I felt convicted by his words. I, too, can see times when I tried to be more. Instead of a circus, I used a school. Instead of entertaining, I used education. Instead of a red jacket, I wore a collar. In the end, though, these cost me more than I could have imagined.

One danger of the spiritual journey is that we too often turn it into a self-improvement plan. If I can just do this or not do that, I will be a better person, the logic goes. Like Barnum, our striving to be more can take over. We focus so much on climbing the ladder to a better us that we lose focus and forget that who we are is all we need to be.

This is a time of year that Christians call Lent. It is designed to be a season of reflection and preparation before Easter. Like the spiritual journey itself, Lent often becomes a time when people make an extra effort and seek to climb the ladder to a better version of themselves. Such actions can lead us in the wrong direction. We were marvelously made from the start. What we need is not to ascend but descend. Rather than trying to be more, we're called to live more fully who we already are.

Espresso Shots:

1. *When have you tried to be more than you are?*

2. *What would it look like for you to descend into who you already are?*

3. *In what ways are you marvelously made?*

HEARING THE BELLS

A friend tells the story of going for a run one morning and hearing hymn tunes from a local parish bell tower. "Rock of Ages" and "The Church's One Foundation" kept him company during his run, and the melodies filled his soul and made exercising easier. As he ran farther from home, the sound of the bells became fainter until he could hear them no longer. He turned and ran back into his neighborhood to enjoy the rest of his run in the company of the chimes.

His story speaks vividly of the nature of living a spiritual life. Like the songs coming from the bell tower, God's voice fills the air in which we travel, if we have ears to hear. God's voice can fill our souls and make the journey less lonely. But, like my friend, we can move away from God and find ourselves traveling in silence. Loneliness and uncertainty fill the void, and we begin to question whether we ever heard the bells or if God is with us as we run the race before us. When we can hear only the faintest voice of God, we need to turn around and return to a place where God's voice rings out.

This also means taking time to tune our ears to the bells. I do that by sitting still and listening before I begin my day. I read scripture or something spiritual. I also make an effort to listen intentionally throughout the day. The bells are ringing in the places we go, the people we encounter, and the events of our lives. The key is to listen and to be willing to return when we travel too far from the bells.

Espresso Shots:

1. *In what way do you hear spiritual "bells" during the day?*

2. *Do you sometimes travel too far or too fast to hear them?*

3. *What could you do to stay closer to the bells?*

HOME IMPROVEMENT

The retaining wall outside our house needed repair, so we found someone to do the job. As he and his crew took down stones and reassembled the wall, I noticed our gutters were clogged. Climbing the ladder, I saw two holes in our window screens. You get the picture. Once we started to work on one project, I noticed countless others.

The same is true in my spiritual life. In my reflection time each morning, I become aware of character defects that need attention. No sooner do I begin addressing one character flaw than I notice another, then another. It can fast become overwhelming, which is why so many people give up trying to live a spiritual life. The insights never end. The work is never done.

On more than one occasion, I've wanted to quit. But somewhere along the line, I realized this is a spiritual practice, not a self-improvement program. Taking comfort in the words of the psalmist who says I'm marvelously made (just as I am), I focus on how I can best serve God. The funny thing is, once I accept this premise, I am better able to concentrate on my self-improvement list, pulling out the ladder and getting to work on things within me that stand in the way of serving God.

Espresso Shots:

1. *Is your inner work more a spiritual practice or self-improvement program?*
2. *In what way do you feel you are called to serve God?*
3. *What character defects get in the way of such service?*

Double Shot: *What concrete steps can you take today to address those character defects?*

AIR IN THE TIRES

"Your tires need air," the man beside me said as we filled our cars with gas. Given a financial challenge at work and a disappointing conversation with a friend, I realized my car and I had a lot in common. Perhaps you know the feeling.

We're all busy trying to get from "here" to "there," and our tires inevitably get low. Maybe we realize it, or someone needs to point it out, but when our tires are low, we need air. Filling car tires is easy. Filling our tires is not as obvious or easy.

Most of what I know about keeping air in the tires I've learned from artists. Being an artist requires the courage to be vulnerable and receive reactions of every kind. Such a life can quickly deflate tires. The key is to know how to fill them. A mentor suggests keeping positive reviews around to read when a piece is rejected. Another suggests going on "artist's dates," which are fun excursions when the work of being an artist becomes overwhelming.

Those of us seeking to live spiritual lives can learn a lot from artists. Looking within, facing inner dragons, wrestling doubts, and giving ourselves to others can leave us deflated. When that happens, it's essential we find ways to keep air in our tires for the journey ahead.

Espresso Shots:

1. *Think of a time when your spiritual tires have deflated.*
2. *What is the most effective way to put air in your tires?*
3. *Do one thing today to put air in your tires.*

CLOSER THAN THEY APPEAR

I never thought the words inscribed on my rear-view mirrors, *Objects in the mirror are closer than they appear,* could have theological meaning until a recent writing class assignment. The teacher asked us to plot out the events of our lives, starting from early childhood to the present. As simple as the assignment seemed, its effect was surprising.

I did my best to recall my earliest memories and wrote down every moment from my life that came to mind. The big events were easy and predictable, but the smaller moments, the ones that seemed insignificant, surprised me. Going out to play with friends in my backyard in a new athletic uniform from school and having everyone laugh at me is a memory closer than it might appear. The first time I kissed a girl (badly) seems like my recent past. I can still hear the first time a teacher said I wrote well (despite my spelling).

There's a delicate balance between looking back and looking forward. As we spend time in the season of Lent looking at our lives, we can benefit from looking in the rearview mirror. Like I did during the writing assignment, we might find the little things we remember are closer than they appear.

Espresso Shots:

1. *Make a list of everything you can remember from your childhood.*
2. *What memories made the list that surprise you?*
3. *What is it about those events that make them seem closer than they appear?*

FINDING YOUR BEARINGS

The ship tossed for days. The storm arrived at night and remained for what seemed like a week. Waves crashed against the sides, and wind turned the ship in every direction. All the captain and crew could do was hold on and wait. When the storm finally passed, the crew repaired the damage while the captain got his bearings. Using the stars, his compass, and sextant, he determined where they were now that the storm had passed.

I've always been enamored with the early travelers of the sea. With wooden vessels and primitive equipment, they learned to travel around the globe. Using the stars, they learned how to figure out where they were and how to get to where they wanted to go. While I'm sure a lot of mathematics was involved, the process seems more like an art form to me.

The work of sea captains offes us some lessons as we sail spiritual waters. It's one thing to know where we are and where we are going when the skies are clear and the winds are consistent, but it's only a matter of time before storms arrive. The stars by which we have guided our vessels are hidden, and wind and waves toss us in every direction. We cling to the boat, sure it will capsize, but eventually, the storm passes. They always do, and we can see the sky again and find our bearings. It's essential to know where we are, even if we have been blown off course. That way, we can set sail again.

As one who has been blown off course by many storms and lost his way more times than I'd like to admit, it's nice to know the stars are waiting and the tools are there. All I have to do is make an effort and do the work.

Espresso Shots:

1. *Have you ever lost your way?*

2. *If so, what did you do to get your bearings?*

3. *In what ways can you maintain your bearings on a daily basis?*

DRAGONS

"Hic Sunt Dracones" —*From an ancient map*

Early mapmakers would write "here be dragons" whenever they reached uncharted territory. Unsure of what was beyond the world they knew, they drew pictures of dragons to warn people to avoid such places. People have always been afraid of the unknown. They've drawn pictures and made up stories in an effort to give their fears a name.

I once thought the purpose of faith was to do away with fear, but I quickly learned otherwise. My faith does not eliminate my fear. The dragons are out there in the uncharted territory of my soul; often, all I want to do is sail in the opposite direction.

In my voyages, I've found that fears awaken faith. When fear raises its head above the ocean's depth, I draw the sword of faith and proclaim, "God's got me, and God's got this." The fear is not eliminated, but my faith is transformed. Instead of feeling God's absence, I feel God's presence that is as comforting as it is inspiring.

Dragons come in all shapes and sizes. Walking into an interview, meeting an enraged employer, entering a room of strangers, or making a difficult call can make us want to sail in another direction.

But just as dragons come in many shapes and sizes, so do swords. God is always beside us in ways we may not recognize, causing the mightiest of dragons to slither away.

Espresso Shots:

1. *Where do your dragons reside?*
2. *In what ways do you avoid your dragons?*
3. *How can you use your fears to awaken your faith?*

THE HEDGE

The Bible tells of a man and a woman who live in a garden. They live at one with each other and God until they make a mistake, which causes them to hide. As theologian Henri Nouwen puts it, they hide behind the hedge because of what they have done and the nakedness they feel. Once I stopped worrying about whether the Garden of Eden was a real place or the events actually happened, I could embrace the truth of the story.

I don't believe we are born behind the hedge. It has happened over time. Maybe someone's snicker in class began the journey or a mistake was pointed out for all to see. We eventually sought shelter behind the hedge because of our mistakes or imperfections. While the hedge offers protection, it also serves as a barrier, keeping us from engaging fully with God and others.

The path from the hedge requires courage and vulnerability. Whether it's being willing to have a difficult conversation, admitting a weakness, or confessing a mistake, the journey from behind the hedge is not for the lighthearted. But be assured: there's life on the other side of the hedge. No longer burdened with secrets or shackled by embarrassment, our souls can breathe again, and we feel at one with ourselves, God, and one another, which, of course, is how God intended life to be from the beginning.

Espresso Shots:

1. *What moments have caused you to seek shelter behind the hedge?*

2. *What did it feel like to live hidden in such a way?*

3. *Have you ever tried to come out from behind the hedge? What did the journey require? How did it feel on the other side?*

TO COMPARE IS HUMAN, TO IDENTIFY, DIVINE

"I'm a high-bottom drunk," the woman said with an air of superiority. For those unfamiliar with 12-step recovery expressions, "high bottom" refers not to a plastic surgery procedure, but the fact that she came into the room before hitting the absolute bottom of life. While I was happy she was spared additional pain and suffering, her comment pointed to our propensity to find *something* to make us feel better about ourselves.

Like the poor man and Lazarus, we often confess our sins while looking over at others. "I may be bad," we say, "but not as bad as you know who." No matter our situation, we can always find someone whose situation can make us feel better about ourselves. Such comparisons are like fast food: they may taste good but eventually make us feel awful.

In sharp contrast, I recall a panel presentation where the two speakers sat beside each other. On the surface, the speakers, theologian Frederick Buechner and author Maya Angelou, seemed to have little in common. When the moderator asked about their differences, Angelou pointed out that the two may have grown up differently but shared the same story. Those in the audience remember little else of what was said that day. They heard the most important thing.

Comparing is life-taking. Identifying is life-giving. If we can learn to move from one to the other, my hunch is our souls will breathe easier, as will our world.

Espresso Shots:

1. *How much of your life is spent comparing yourself to others?*

2. *Have you ever found common ground with someone who's lived a different life?*

3. *How can you grow in identifying with others instead of comparing?*

BALANCE

Yoga is hard. Being around people who wear clothes I couldn't fit into in third grade is discouraging. And then there's the intimidation factor of setting my mat beside others who are wrapping their legs around their heads. But for me, yoga itself is the greatest challenge. I'm incapable of keeping my balance. It's only a matter of time before I'm facedown on my mat, shaking my head in dismay. Losing one's balance is part of the deal, I suppose, but it's frustrating and embarrassing, nevertheless. Sensing my frustration, an instructor told me to look for a spot and focus on it. Although I still wobbled, focusing on a spot ahead of me kept me balanced.

Driving from class, I realized I could use the same technique in other parts of my life. Balance has never been a strength. No matter how hard I try, I lose my balance throughout the day. Nowhere is that more apparent than in my spiritual life. I have the best of intentions, but I often find myself facedown on the mat.

Maybe if I focus on something ahead of me, my shaking legs will settle, my distracted mind will quiet, and I can hold the pose. When I look only at me and what I am doing, I always fall. When I look beyond myself and focus on God, I can hold steady.

Lent is a time of refocusing. As with my yoga class, this season is an opportunity to look ahead and focus on someone other than myself. In doing so, I can find balance.

Espresso Shots:

1. *How hard is it for you to focus spiritually?*

2. *What causes you to lose your balance?*

3. *What can you focus on to help steady your shaky legs and quiet your distracted mind?*

LEAVE THE DENTS

After my mother's death, the family divided up her belongings. One of the items that I chose was a gold bracelet with a watch embedded in it. I picked it because I remember her wearing it. Lifting it to my face, I swear I can smell her perfume. It's as if she's just stepped out of the room and will return soon. I wish that were true.

I took it to a jeweler to get an estimate for fixing the watch, and when I heard back, she said it needed only a minor repair but added, "We won't be able to remove the dents."

"The dents?" I replied. "Don't take out the dents!"

The dents remind me of the woman who once wore it. Each dent tells a story. Without them, the bracelet would be just another piece of jewelry.

Our world seems to have an aversion to dents. Both in the things we own and the lives we live, we seem determined to remove (or hide) the dents, when, in fact, it's the dents that tell the stories of our lives. The dents make us unique. They make us real.

I plan to give the bracelet to one of my daughters one day. Hopefully, she will add dents of her own.

Espresso Shots:

1. *In what ways do you hide your dents?*
2. *Remembering someone you loved, which dents made them special?*
3. *In what way can you embrace your dents and encourage others to do the same?*

RUNNING WITH GIRAFFES

"Look!" My friend pointed to a herd of giraffes running on an open plain in Kenya. I had learned how to shuffle cards and was practicing. I almost missed the giraffes, but I looked up in time to see the unforgettable sight thanks to my friend.

The more I read about the spiritual life, the more I hear one refrain: Wake up! We are so often distracted by trivial tasks that we miss wonders outside our windows. Sometimes trivial tasks keep us from seeing unforgettable moments. Other times, regrets about the past or worries about the future make us miss the present.

I remember looking down at my phone and almost missing my child's performance.

I remember my financial worries almost keeping me from participating in a groundbreaking ministry.

I remember being distracted by poor service at a restaurant and missing what my son was trying to tell me.

I know I'm not alone, but being in the company of equally distracted people doesn't diminish my regret over missing what matters. Rather than mourn the loss, I'm using my past to awaken me. I've had years of slumber; now, it's time to wake up to what is right outside my window. I want to put down the playing cards that distract me and look out at the world around me. Better yet, I want to stop the car, get out, and run with the giraffes.

Espresso Shots:

1. *How present are you in your life?*

2. *What are your most significant distractions?*

3. *In what way can you wake up—or get out of the car and run with the giraffes?*

SQUEAKY DOORS

There once was a man who had a squeaky door. He went to the hardware store, bought some WD-40 lubricant, and placed the can in his toolbox. Much to his dismay, the door continued to squeak.

It's an absurd little tale, but it also reveals an important truth. In the season of Lent, many set out to solve their squeaky doors, but we don't use the tools we have and so we give up before we've even started. Like the recovering alcoholic who starts drinking again because she didn't go to meetings, find a sponsor, and work the steps, we often don't do the very things we should in order to grow in the ways we desire.

A person wants to get in shape but never unpacks his gym bag. A couple wants to grow closer but continues to have dinner in front of the television. A person wants to get a new job but never finishes her resume.

The same is true with those of us who seek to grow spiritually. We could make time for prayer and meditation, but we don't. We could go to church but find countless reasons why it's too inconvenient. We could read the Bible or another spiritual text, but the pile of books beside our chair is dusty.

In AA, they talk of a toolbox. The first step is to acquire the tools. The second is to use them. We all have plenty of tools. We just need to use them.

Espresso Shots:

1. *What are some of the squeaky doors in your life right now?*
2. *What tools do you need to help you grow?*
3. *Use one or more of those tools for a month and see if you notice growth or change.*

PEOPLE PLEASING

"If we're such people-pleasers," said the recovering alcoholic, "where are all the pleased people?"

The room erupted in laughter as everyone shared the sentiment. Many in the circle had spent their lives trying to please a father, mother, or significant other to no avail. The lack of success was not from a lack of effort. Whether because of a difficult parent or an unquenchable thirst to feel good enough, the room was filled with people who had climbed off the people-pleasing carousel and were trying to reclaim their balance.

In college, a dear friend once gave me a Zen quotation that said something like: Once you decide to be great, you hold yourself captive to those who make that decision. The quotation has stayed with me for the rest of my life, even though I have been incapable of living a life based on its wisdom. Like many others, I've been held captive by the opinions of others.

Jesus seeks to free us from the judgments of others. He knows that the only opinion that truly matters is God's. We are to play to an audience of one, said a famous pastor, but that is easier to say than do. Applause and recognition can be as addictive as any drug, the chains equally binding, but God wants us to be free, and now is as good a time as any to take him up on the offer.

Espresso Shots:

1. *List three people who you sought to please in your life.*

2. *In the end, were they pleased? Did you become who you were created to be?*

3. *What would it take for you to live free of others' opinions or expectations?*

THE BRIDGE (A parable for those in therapy)

There once was a village tucked away in the mountains of Nepal. On three sides, mountains protected the village; on the fourth was a broad, fast-flowing river. Across the river was a bridge, which was the only way in and out of the village. Built years ago by villagers who were long gone, the current villagers did all they could to maintain the bridge. When a plank got loose, they reattached it. When the paint peeled, they added a new coat. It was as if the bridge was a part of the village, which only made it more devastating when they learned it was beyond repair and needed to be replaced.

"The bridge has served us well," one person said. "But the time has come to replace it with a new one." Another asked: "Can't we repair it like we have?" Someone added, "It was always good enough for our ancestors."

"No," came the resounding response. "The foundation's rotted. No maintenance can help that." So the villagers agreed to tear down the bridge and replace it, but as the work began, many began to have second thoughts about the plan. When half the bridge was taken away, they approached the village leaders again.

"Why'd we decide to do this anyway?" someone asked. "Can't we put it back the way it was? At least we could walk across its wobbly planks."

"The problem is," began one of the village elders, "you're only seeing the bridge that's being taken apart. Try to see the bridge that's coming instead."

"But how can we see that?" someone asked. "It doesn't exist."

"Yes, it does!" said the elder. "We just haven't built it yet."

Espresso Shots:

1. *When have you decided to make a change in your life but then had second thoughts?*
2. *Have you focused on what's being taken apart rather than what is going to be built?*
3. *Do you believe the future you already exists but just has to be built?*

TRANSACTIONAL GIVING (Part I)

I began working in the fundraising department for public television, where I was introduced to transactional giving. "If you give at this level, you get a tote bag," we would say, "but at this level, you'll get not only the tote bag but the CD as well!" It wasn't about giving to a worthy cause; it was about what someone would get in return for giving.

Since then, I've seen other forms of transactional giving. A donor gives so his name will be listed with the other wealthy people from the community, a child receives a new bike because he did well in school, a donation is made more to be invited to the fundraising event than to support the cause. The list is endless.

Generosity is one of the gifts of the spirit. As such, we are called not only to be generous but to do so in a way that is in keeping with our faith. Do we support people and organizations trying to make a difference in the world? Do we make gifts expecting something in return? (e.g., a tote bag, recognition, a special seat)

Giving to make the world around us a better place is terrific. Doing so with no thought of what we might receive in return is divine.

Espresso Shots:

1. *When have you given transactionally?*
2. *When have you given with no strings attached, and how did it feel?*
3. *How could you grow in your giving without receiving?*

TRANSACTIONAL GIVING (Part II)

"I go to church to hedge my bets," the outspoken retired naval officer proclaimed. He wasn't sure about all the God mumbo jumbo, as he called it, but wanted to be sure he had a ticket to heaven when he died.

When I heard him, I realized transactional giving had made its way to religion. No longer were people worshiping God because of all that God was, and is, and always will be. Now, people expected something in return. *If I do this, God will like me. If I give this, God will return the favor and bless me.* Transactional giving is central in television evangelism, but it's in the pews in our neighborhoods, too.

I'll never figure how this whole faith thing works, but when it comes to giving, I know that when I give freely, the gift means more. When I give anonymously, it's as if I've been given a gift. Whenever I seek credit or something in return, my gift becomes tarnished.

God is not into transactional giving. In fact, God's all about giving with no strings attached. God is generous without expectations. He blesses us all despite the many reasons he shouldn't.

Sitting here as the sun is coming up, I marvel at the beauty. I did nothing to deserve such a thing. Maybe that's the point. Perhaps I should learn to follow God's example.

Espresso Shots:

1. *In what ways is there a bit of transactional giving to your faith?*

2. *In what specific ways has God given to you with no strings attached?*

3. *What would it mean to follow God's example?*

DECREASING AND INCREASING

Early in the Gospel of John is a scene with John the Baptist and his disciples. His followers are confused when Jesus arrives. Which one was the prophet, which one the Messiah? John explains that his role was to prepare people for Jesus and adds one of my favorite lines in scripture: "He must increase, but I must decrease."

No better words describe the spiritual journey. No better standard exists to measure one's spiritual life.

I'm embarrassed to look back and see all the times and ways I have sought to increase, rather than decrease. What's worse is that I have often done so in the name of Christ. Delivering an inspirational sermon, wearing a fancy robe, processing in a momentous service, and building impressive chapels have too often been ways to advance my career and increase my standing in the communities I was hired to serve.

There have been other times as well, times when I did things no one knew about, times when there was nothing in it for me. Those were the times when I decreased so that God and God's kingdom could increase.

The spiritual journey is one of progress, not perfection, and I take comfort that we are all works in progress. Sometimes we get it right, sometimes we don't, but the hope is that we are stumbling in the right direction, to use a phrase from 12-step recovery circles.

As John pointed out years ago, that right direction is one in which we decrease and God increases.

Espresso Shots:

1. *How much of your time and effort is spent so that you can increase?*
2. *Can you identify a time when you decreased, and God increased?*
3. *In what specific ways can you decrease so that God can increase?*

RIDING DONKEYS

"They brought the donkey and the colt, and put their cloaks on them, and he sat on them." —*Matthew 21:7*

When was the last time you rode a donkey?
When was the last time you apologized to your child?
When was the last time you stayed after a meeting and stacked the chairs?
When was the last time you admitted you were scared?
When was the last time you did the dishes?
When was the last time you watched a movie someone else wanted to watch?
When was the last time you cried openly?
When was the last time you wrote a note by hand?
When was the last time you tried something for the first time?
When was the last time you prayed with someone outside of church?
When was the last time you told someone you love them?
When was the last time you volunteered?
When was the last time you listened patiently?
When was the last time you sang even though others could hear?
When was the last time you faced someone mad at you?
When was the last time you spoke of your faith?
When was the last time you rode on a donkey?

Espresso Shots:

1. *Pick two or three of these questions and answer them.*

2. *Read the story of Jesus' entry into Jerusalem in Matthew 21.*

3. *What would it mean for you to ride on a donkey?*

WASHING FEET AND WASHING HANDS

Water appears in the Holy Week narrative in two significant places. The first is when Jesus washes the disciples' feet, and the second is when Pilate washes his hands. The two events stand in sharp contrast to one another. Jesus kneels like a servant and washes his followers' feet, all of them, even Judas. Pilate stands proudly and washes his hands of Jesus and all the controversy surrounding him. It seems we have a choice in how we will use water in our lives. Will we use it to honor or dishonor others?

I would love to have been in the room when Jesus washed the disciples' feet. The look on their faces (and his) must have been priceless. It made no sense according to the social customs, yet it's what he chose to do in his final hours. Pilate, on the other hand, did exactly what one might have expected. He wanted nothing to do with this controversial figure, so he washed his hands of Jesus and and distanced himself before the crowd turned on him.

I have seen the church use water in both ways. Defying social pressure, it has knelt and honored unexpecting children of God. So, too, it has washed its hands of those who challenge the depth and breadth of God's grace. Like the church, I, too, have used water both ways. When I followed Jesus' example, my heart was filled, and my passion for life ignited. When I was like Pilate, the memory haunted me and made me feel spiritually sick.

That should tell me all I need to know.

Espresso Shots:

1. *When have you washed someone else's feet?*

2. *When have you washed your hands of another?*

3. *In what way can you use the events of Holy Week to grow in your discipleship?*

DANCING WITH SHADOWS

"You must forgive me, I am confused by shadows," says the somewhat delirious but endearing character Don Quixote in *Man of La Mancha*. After a life full of chasing windmills, he struggles to find his home between the world he sees and the one he dreams. In the end, like us, he is confused by shadows.

To make this point in a sermon one morning in my school's chapel, I had a teacher turn on a spotlight as I preached. I spoke of living life as if there was a spotlight shining. It makes us bright and easy to see, I pointed out, but it also casts a shadow. Moving my arms and legs, I watched as the children connected what I was saying with the shadow on the wall behind me. I reminded them that with light comes shadows. The shadows may scare or confuse us, but they also have much to teach us.

Peter Pan had a shadow, but he lost it. He knew it was part of him and went looking for it—he even had Wendy sew it to him so they couldn't be separated again. Once they were reunited, Peter danced with his shadow.

This is as good as any image when trying to understand the season of Lent. We are called to turn from the spotlight and face our shadows. We need to work through our fears and confusion until we learn to dance with our shadows.

Espresso Shots:

1. *In what ways do you try to ignore or avoid your shadow?*
2. *What could you do to turn and face your shadow?*
3. *What would it look like to learn how to not only face your shadow but also dance with it?*

RECALIBRATION

A garage is an unlikely place for a Sunday school lesson, but I take them wherever and whenever they come. A friend gave me a tour of his three-car garage that he and his sons had turned into a NASCAR pit stop. In one bay, they were restoring an MG sports car; in another, they transformed a regular car into a race car and a classic SUV to its original condition. They had installed a hydraulic lift and possessed every tool one could imagine. I felt like even I could fix a car in such a place!

As we walked back to the house, my friend described their work. I was struck by the time, attention, and patience. It was a constant recalibration. Adjust this, tighten that, and then adjust a little more so the car could run smoothly.

My friend had recently lost his father, which was why I'd come to visit, and I realized he was now going to need to recalibrate his life. It would be difficult and time-consuming work, I pointed out over dinner, but he knew what to do. He would need specific tools. He would need to make adjustments and change settings, but there was new life on the other side.

I realized after my visit how much of our lives involve recalibration. The reasons for recalibration are many. Whether coping with a loss, struggling in a relationship, or facing a sudden health change, we all need to be able to adjust and adapt. Because the only constant is change, the most important skill we can learn is how to recalibrate.

Espresso Shots:

1. *When in your life have you had to recalibrate?*
2. *What was the hardest part of doing so?*
3. *What were the tools you used, and what were the skills you developed by doing that work?*

Double Shot: *What needs recalibrating now? Begin adjusting.*

FOOLS

Too often, I've lacked the self-confidence to be foolish in public. My children and some of my friends might disagree, but I spend an excessive amount of time and energy worrying about the crowd and what they might think about me. Such concerns are paralyzing. They keep me from being my true self, and I know that's not how God wants me, or you, to live.

There's a man who organizes an annual parade in his neighborhood. The only rule is everyone must participate. No one can stand at the curb and cheer. He's a fool, and I think God loves him.

There's a talented painter who gives away his artwork. He could make a good living selling his paintings, but he can't help it. If someone likes a painting, he wants them to have it. He's a fool, but I think God loves him.

She has three degrees but left her job at a major company to work at a nonprofit that serves single mothers trying to improve their lot in life. She's a fool, but I think God loves her.

There are as many ways to be a fool as there are to be a human being. The key is not to be a fool for its own sake. We are told to be fools for Christ's sake. It's tempting to applaud those in the fool's parade from the safety of the curb, but God wants no spectators. We need to put on our funny glasses and carry our balloons, and when you hear someone say you're such a fool, reply, "Thank you so much!"

Espresso Shots:

1. *In what ways do you strive not to stand out, not be considered a fool?*

2. *When was the last time you did something wonderful with no regard for what others thought?*

3. *What would your life look like if you were more foolish, for Christ's sake?*

SOMETHING ABOUT A MEAL

On his last night with his friends, Jesus shares a meal. They sit close to one another and talk about their hopes and dreams, their families, and all they have been through. When the meal is almost over, Jesus takes bread and wine and gives it to them. Never have they felt his presence like this night.

There's something about a meal.

The son had really messed up. He knew there would be consequences for what he'd done, but first, the father needed to have a frank, come-to-Jesus conversation. Instead of meeting in his office, the father and son went out to dinner. Something changed as they sat down. Instead of racing headlong into the fight, they buttered their bread and began talking about how hard it is to do the right thing sometimes. The father spoke from his own experience rather than focus on his son's. The two felt closer to each other than they had ever before.

There's something about a meal.

As they sat at the table, the couple made small talk while they waited for their server. They were both exhausted from a difficult week at work but sitting at the table restored their spirit. Soon they moved from work woes to all the wonderful things they could do on vacation next month. Soon, they were laughing and reaching for each other's hand. Before the meal was over, he reached in his pocket for the ring.

There's something about a meal.

Espresso Shots:

1. *Have you experienced a meal that became sacred?*

2. *What made it feel so special? Setting, people, conversation?*

3. *Describe a moment when you felt God's presence among the bread and wine.*

THE LORD'S PRAYER

The two groups gathered every Friday morning down the hall from one another. Other than that, they had little in common. One group was made up of men, the other co-ed. One was full of professionals; the other had many who were out of work. One met to share their struggles in living spiritual lives in a secular world, while the others shared their struggles with alcohol. But at 8:55 a.m., they both had something in common: they said the Lord's Prayer.

Like these two groups that meet just down the hall from one another, we live in a divided world. Whenever two or more are gathered, we focus on our differences. This one's a banker, that one's an artist; this one's a Christian, that one's a Jew. This one's a pillar of the community, that one's not to be trusted.

It's easy to find the things that divide us, but another thing to discover what unites us. No matter who we are, we're God's children. No matter who we are, we long to believe life matters, that we matter. We hunger for food, both literal and spiritual, and we are fully aware of all the ways we fall short of who we were created to be. None of us wants to make mistakes, but we hope, in the end, we will be forgiven.

These are the things we have in common. These are our prayers, whether we're in one room or the other down the hall.

Amen.

Espresso Shots:

1. *When you are in others' company, do you focus on what you have in common or what you don't?*

2. *Have you ever met someone different but realized that you share many of the same hopes and fears?*

3. *In what way can you say and act out the Lord's Prayer in your life as you walk beside people who may or may not appear like you?*

THE WHOLE STORY

I recently attended a revival of *Godspell*, one of my favorite musicals. For those unfamiliar with it, *Godspell* is a musical based chiefly on the Gospel according to Matthew. It retells the parables of Jesus in a lively and entertaining way and contains many memorable songs. The show takes a theological turn in the second act as it heads to the finale, and the crucifixion and Easter always bring the show to a full, emotional conclusion. Just as Judas arrived to betray Jesus, a woman across the aisle grabbed her daughter's hand and escorted her out of the theater. I could tell it wasn't because they had somewhere else to be. It was because she wanted to spare her child from the pain and suffering to come.

I've thought about their abrupt exit ever since. I understand the desire to avoid the end of the story and spare one's daughter (and oneself) from the pain and suffering, but the pain and suffering are part of the story. Without it, the story is incomplete. You need to stand at the foot of the cross to be able to kneel at the empty tomb.

The woman who left the show was not unique. Thomas Jefferson cut out pieces of the Bible he didn't like. Churches pick and choose what parts of the story they read. It may make it easier to read only the parts you like, but it's not the whole story.

We also do it with our own stories. We tell people some of our story, usually the good parts, and we leave out the rest. Just like *Godspell* without the ending, or the Bible selectively edited, our stories lose their power when we pick and choose the parts we like. It's not easy to look at the hard or bad parts, but that's the only way to reach the ending. It never ends at the cross but at the empty tomb. That's the whole story!

Espresso Shots:

1. *What parts of your story do you ignore or deny?*
2. *How could you learn to embrace your whole story?*
3. *Is there anything in your story you think God cannot redeem?*

THE VASE

The vase sat proudly above the other wedding gifts. It was a gift from the bride's great aunt, and everyone who passed by marveled at its shape and colors. Aunt Beatrice, known to have a particularly good time at weddings, asked a young man to dance for a lively number toward the end of the evening and spun out of her partner's arms into the table of gifts. The vase toppled over and crashed on the floor. Everyone was horrified and came running over. The minister assured the bride it would be okay as he swept up the countless shards. On their first anniversary, a package from the minister arrived on the newlyweds' doorstep: he reassembled the vase, gluing all the pieces together.

"Don't mind the cracks," the note read. "It's how the light gets in."

It has taken years and many falls to the floor to understand the truth of that note. So often, I bemoan the falls and am embarrassed by the cracks, only to be reminded that God's light can only reach my soul through the cracks.

Espresso Shots:

1. _When have you fallen to the floor?_
2. _Did God's light come to you through the cracks made from such falls?_
3. _What would it look like to allow more light to shine through such cracks?_

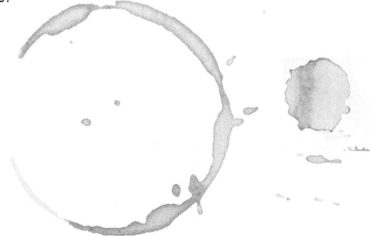

CLIMBING DOWN THE STAIRS

"Almighty God, Father of all mercies...give us such an awareness of your mercies, that with truly thankful hearts we may show forth your praise, not only with our lips, but in our lives, by giving up ourselves to your service, and by walking before you in holiness and righteousness all our days."

—*Excerpt from "The General Thanksgiving," The Book of Common Prayer*

Whenever our babysitter was with us on weekends, she took us to the Princeton University Chapel for worship. The pulpit was as captivating as the building itself. Looming high above, the minister began the ascent during the hymn and reached the top of the twenty-three steps as we closed our hymnals. The pageantry said as much as the sermon. When the sermon was over, the minister descended the stairs, and this, too, was dramatic. Ever since, I've reminded myself of the importance of both climbing up and climbing down the stairs, spiritually.

Giving voice to our faith is essential. We may not ever find ourselves delivering a sermon, but each of us has opportunities to climb the stairs and give voice to what we believe. Hopefully, we won't use the time to put on airs or sound like someone else but rather speak in a voice that's uniquely ours.

But that's only half the work. We must also walk back down the stairs and live out what we profess. For me, this is a more challenging journey. It's easier to say we believe in God than it is to live out that belief, easier to profess loving our neighbors than actually doing so.

One of my favorite prayers includes the phrase, "not only with our lips but in our lives." It reminds me of the stairs in the chapel. It's paramount to climb up and use our lips to profess our faith, but it's just as important to climb down and live out that faith with our lives.

Espresso Shots:

1. *Do you give voice to what you believe?*
2. *Do you live out what you believe in a meaningful way?*
3. *Which of the two is harder for you?*

SOMETHING NEW

"What's happened to you? You've got a new look," the woman said, trying unsuccessfully to hide her disdain. It wasn't my button-down shirt, khakis, or shoes but my necklace, a rope with a ring made of wood. My son made it while he was camping in the wilderness of Utah, and I treasure it because it connects me to him.

The woman was right. Such a necklace was new. It didn't fit with my usual attire, but whenever I wear it, I'm reminded of the one who made it, and I celebrate my "new look."

One of the great gifts of life is being able to change, but many of us are frightened of changing or doing anything that might make us stand out to those who have established notions of who we are. Change takes courage and effort. It's easier to stay the same and go through life without drawing attention to yourself.

But I think God created us to change. We were molded out of clay, and I think the hope was the clay would stay moist so the molding could continue throughout our lives. When someone changes a career because of a yearning inside, I think God gets excited. When someone takes up art in their older years or takes a class in their free time, God dances. Change is such a part of what it means to be a human being, yet we try hard to avoid it.

God created us unique. How dare we dilute God's creation with uniformity? How dare we let our fears and insecurities distract us from living our unique lives to the fullest? How dare we let people make us second-guess doing or wearing something new?

Go ahead! I dare you. Make someone wonder what's happened to you.

Espresso Shots:

1. *When did you make a change that someone noticed and made you question doing such a thing?*

2. *When was the last time you followed a yearning within and made a change?*

3. *Who would you be—what would you do—if no one was watching?*

Double Shot: *Now, go and be (or do) that thing!*

IT'S WHAT I DO

I worked on a cattle ranch the summer between high school and college. It was a vast property, with many people working hard to keep it running successfully. Of all the people I came to know, the one who meant the most to me was the most unassuming. His name was Leonard, and it was his job to keep all the ranch equipment in running order. He rarely ventured beyond his shop in the barn and always seemed to be fixing something. I loved to visit Leonard and watch him work. He was a master at repair.

During haying season, it was my job to drive the tractor and trailer through the fields. I didn't notice the flat tire on the trailer and drove all day until the rim was dented in the shape of a flower. Mortified and embarrassed, I brought it to Leonard, who lifted his eyebrows and said, "That's not good." He didn't say anything else before getting to work on the rim. When I returned the following morning, the trailer was restored and ready for work.

"I don't believe it," I exclaimed. "How on earth did you fix it?"

"It's what I do," is all he said with a grin as he returned to his shop.

Whenever I think about Jesus, I think about Leonard. When I become mortified and embarrassed by all the mistakes I've made, I hear Leonard's voice saying, "That's not good." When I think about Good Friday and Easter and how the disciples must have been beside themselves with what happened, I hear Jesus saying what Leonard did when he presented me with the restored trailer. "It's what I do."

Espresso Shots:

1. *Have you ever been mortified and embarrassed by a mistake?*

2. *Has anyone come and helped restore you—and the mistake?*

3. *If so, how did that feel, and how does that help you appreciate God's ability to restore?*

MELTING SNOW

It was like waking up on Christmas or a parent telling you there would be no school, but I was a grown man traveling out west. An unexpected snowfall arrived and covered the mountains and valleys, as well as all the trees. It looked like a winter wonderland ... in April. By the day's end, most of the snow had melted, except at the higher elevations, and I heard someone comment that the snow was gone.

Was it?

Yes, the white blanket to which we had awakened was gone, but the snow had only melted. Now it was living on as water for the streams and creeks, trees, and dry soil.

My spiritual life has undergone a similar transformation. Perhaps yours has, as well. Some days, I experience God as particularly close, as if it's Christmas. I celebrate such moments and want them to last, but they don't. Life starts to look normal again, as if the snow—and God—have gone.

But God has not gone. God is always there but has begun the descent to less-noticeable places, filling the streams, creeks, and dry places of my soul.

Espresso Shots:

1. *Think of a time when you experienced a spiritual high and felt God's presence.*

2. *How did you react when life returned to normal?*

3. *In what way can you see the spiritual high make its way to less-noticeable places within your soul?*

MEETING A STRANGER

"You will meet a stranger...and it is you." —*Anonymous*

I once participated in a guided meditation in which I was led through my childhood home. With eyes closed, I walked through the front hall, climbed the steps, and made my way down the hall to my bedroom. I was told to open the door and take a seat beside the young boy sitting there. The young boy was me, the instructor said, and I remember the intense feelings that came as I imagined sitting beside myself as a seven-year-old.

Ever since then, I have tried to engage in similar time travel. I have wanted to sit beside not only that young boy, but the older boy in high school, starting college, the one who just had a son, the one living abroad, the one who had it all, the one who lost it all, and the one who learned to pick up the pieces and carry on. With each, I've tried to sit and listen to what life was like and what that boy was feeling.

It all may seem a bit strange to some, but I'm more convinced than ever that such time travel is remarkably relevant and important to our spiritual lives. The joys and pains of our past are part of our present story. Each chapter has molded us into the person we are today. A spiritual life is about a relationship with God, but any relationship involves two people. To come to know ourselves, not just who we are but who we've been, is as important as coming to know God. To sit beside ourselves at specific moments in our past can be like sitting beside a stranger, a stranger who is us and who has much to say.

Espresso Shots:

1. *Close your eyes and walk through your life, from today back, and see if there's a moment to which you feel drawn. Sit beside yourself at that moment and strike up a conversation.*

2. *What is he/she feeling right then? What are his/her concerns, sorrows, pain? What are his/her joys? In what ways can you grow this relationship?*

3. *Repeat (with you from other moments in your life).*

WORDS

"Then God said..." —*Genesis 1:3*

One way I've tried to make people feel comfortable with my being a minister is to out-swear them. I pepper my sentences with colorful words, so they don't think I'm a goodie-goodie or too spiritual to be real. I now see the strategy as a quick fix, one that may have worked occasionally but failed most of the time. It's left me with a bad habit that's hard to break, but the importance of words makes it worth it.

Words are powerful. They can bring life or take it. They can build or destroy. They can inspire nations, communities, or families, but they can also divide, diminish, and destroy.

When I look back, I see times when I have used words well and moments when I haven't. I can see when my words have added light to the world, and when they've brought darkness. I can see when they've comforted and when they've hurt. There's no doubt that I would like to use words well, but changing is extremely hard, at least for me.

We are intimately connected with our words, but we often use them with little thought, which leads to our using them poorly. Our intimacy with our words makes it hard to separate what we say from who we are. It also makes change exceedingly hard.

God used words to bring creation to life. As we seek to grow spiritually, we would do well to look at how we use words.

Espresso Shots:

1. *When was a time someone built you up with words? When did they tear you down?*

2. *How do you use words? (To entertain, to distance, to inform, to comfort, to encourage?)*

3. *In what way would you like to change the way you use words?*

OLD BOOTS

Standing before the doctor, the man described his chronic back pain. Listening carefully, the doctor tried to determine the problem. The patient's back looked healthy, but then the doctor saw a pair of old boots clumped together by the patient's clothes.

"Tell me about those," the doctor instructed.

"Those are my work boots," the patient replied. "They belonged to my father, and I've worn them every day since he died. They're the most comfortable boots you can imagine, completely broken in."

The doctor picked up one of the boots and noticed the soles were completely worn down. "The problem isn't your back," the doctor said. "It's these boots."

The patient left the doctor's office with a heavy heart. He loved his boots. Each time he wore them, he thought about his father, but the pain in his back wasn't worth it. It was time to let them go, so he went to the store and bought a new pair of boots.

Espresso Shots:

1. *Have you ever tried to walk in shoes that belong to someone else?*

2. *Have you ever struggled or felt pain living a life that doesn't belong to you?*

3. *Why would you wear such shoes? What would it take to buy shoes of your own?*

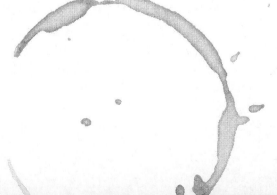

THE GOSPEL ACCORDING TO A MOBILE

I once worked in a building beside a mobile maker. The woman cut and bent pieces of wire, then added colorful butterflies or silver circles. The finished mobiles were remarkable pieces of art, but they became extraordinary when the wind blew. Suddenly, the pieces of art came alive, swirling in the breeze, and I watched with childlike delight.

I bought one of her mobiles and put it beside a window in my daughters' room. I sometimes wander in and blow on the mobile, just to watch it come to life. As I watch, the spiritual implications are not lost on me.

I believe we are all works of art. I also believe whatever we do is also a work of art, whether we care for a family, work at a bank, or collect the trash. While this is worthy of praise and gratitude, the magic is when the wind blows, and our lives become living works of art.

Such moments are to be celebrated. When the spirit blows through us, and we become more than we ever imagined, we should give thanks and praise God.

Espresso Shots:

1. *Have you ever felt God's breeze blowing through you or seen it blowing through someone else?*

2. *What was your reaction when you or someone else became a living work of art?*

3. *How can we place ourselves where the wind is more likely to blow?*

BOXES

I was raised to believe there were two kinds of emotions, good ones and bad. Emotions like love, happiness, excitement, and hope belonged in one box. Into the other went emotions like anger, fear, sadness, and resentment. I was encouraged to open the first box and share the feelings contained in it as much as possible. The second was to be closed tight.

It has been a struggle, but I have slowly learned that both boxes need to be open—the emotions in each need air. Feeling joy and happiness and hope is healthy, but so are the other feelings. As one person taught me, anger and resentment are useful tools to discover the hurts and fears they seek to hide. We need to take the lid off the boxes and feel the feelings, even if they are difficult or dark. We needn't take up residence in box number two but give it the light of day it needs.

Like a child clamoring for attention, emotions will act out until they get attention. Once we open the lid and feel the feelings, they calm down. In the end, there are no good or bad emotions. There are just emotions, and emotions are made to be felt. Then, we can get on with living our lives.

Espresso Shots:

1. Were you raised with boxes for your emotions, one marked "good" and the other "bad," or were you taught to accept all emotions?

2. What is to be gained by selecting which emotions to feel? What is to be lost?

3. In what ways can you learn to give your emotions attention but not let them run the show?

TAXES

"Render unto Caesar the things that are Caesar's and unto God the things that are God's." —*Mark 12:17*

As followers of Christ, we reside in the uncomfortable space between two worlds—the secular one and the spiritual one. Unlike the woman who declared she didn't vote because she lives only for God, most of us walk between the world we live in and the one we believe in. The line between the two can get blurry, but like so many things, it is not about one or the other. It's about both at the same time.

Today is one of those days when the world in which we live comes knocking with a bill in hand. No one likes taxes. They didn't in Jesus' day, and they don't now. Yet taxes are a reality we must face, particularly today.

Taxes remind me that I have a stake in the country in which I live. After all, I'm one of the millions who fund it. That's why I vote and look for ways to participate in our democracy.

But I also need to be equally deliberate and vigilant about the other world to which I belong. I need to participate in God's kingdom, as well. That means supporting it financially and getting my hands dirty in its work.

I'm embarrassed that I don't participate in both worlds equally. I render unto Caesar more than I do to God. Today is a vivid reminder of that fact and an open invitation to balance the scale.

Espresso Shots:

1. *What do you do to support the country in which you live?*
2. *What do you do to support God's kingdom?*
3. *In what way can you balance your participation in those two worlds?*

UNDER CONSTRUCTION

My mother always reminded me to look not at the person standing on center stage—but the one standing beside him or her. It was a lesson she taught not only with words but also with how she lived her life. I was reminded of her advice when I traveled to Charlotte, North Carolina, to visit the Billy Graham home and library. I've always been interested in the man, but I have been equally fascinated by the woman who stood beside him for all those years.

It's heart-warming to walk through Billy's childhood home, and inspirational to walk through the doors at the base of the glass cross in the barn wall, but my soul was filled not by the home, the library, the legacy, or the man, but by the woman buried beside him.

Outside the library, off to the side, are Ruth and Billy's graves. On his, there's a cross above his name, as I expected, but over hers was a Chinese symbol. Surprised, I found out it was a symbol (or letter) that she had seen when living in China. It translates as, "Under construction, thank you for your patience." When she first saw it and learned what it meant, she said it was what she wanted on her gravestone.

I'm not sure there's a better message for any of us because no matter how hard we try to hide it, we're all under construction and can thank God for His infinite patience.

Espresso Shots:

1. *In what ways are you under construction?*
2. *Are you tempted to hide the work in progress?*
3. *In what ways would patience help? (From others? From yourself?)*

ONE MATCH

I only had one match. Fortunately, the wood was dry, so with plenty of paper placed strategically, I lit the match. I could only watch and hope the one small flame could spread. As it struggled to grow, there was smoke, then a flicker, then a flame, and then another. Once I heard crackles, I knew the wood was taking over, and a robust fire was on its way. To think it all happened because of one match made me try to apply the same lesson to life.

Some of us only have one match, but with it, we can light a fire. If the wood is dry and placed strategically so there's enough air, one match can lead to smoke, flickers, and flames. More importantly, a single match can warm an entire room.

She may not be able to cure cancer, but she can teach children who will do their part to change the world one day.

He may have wanted to be a doctor, but for a variety of reasons, he never completed high school. As a mechanic, he fixed the ambulance that saved a child's life. That child is now the leading surgeon at a renowned medical center.

She always wanted to be a missionary but needed to make enough money to support her growing family. After work each Wednesday, she serves meals to the homeless in the city and delivers a meditation. She never knew it, but more than a few of the guests point to this woman and her work on Wednesday nights as the reason they became Christians.

We often figure that one match isn't enough— imagine what we could do if only we had more! We forget: we only need one match.

Espresso Shots:

1. *What is your wildest dream for your life?*
2. *What is one small thing you could do related to that dream?*
3. *How could you encourage someone to see that one match is plenty to make a difference in the world?*

SIDE STREETS

I've always had a thing for side streets. No matter how impressive a city may be, how shiny its storefronts, I've always been drawn to the streets and shops off to the side. People walk slower on the side streets. Pinstriped suits give way to blue jeans, and people often sit on the steps and are willing to strike up a conversation. Side streets have more trash than the main streets, but that adds to the character that makes me feel more at home.

I have the same preference spiritually. There was a time when I walked on the main street and tried to walk as fast as those beside me. I dressed to fit in and behaved like I belonged, but it was exhausting. Keeping up appearances and trying to be like others can wear a person out.

Eventually, I found my way to the side streets. They're not as wide nor as flashy as the main street, but they have a charm of their own. People walk slower on side streets. They're willing to strike up authentic conversations. There's more trash in the side streets, but even that makes me feel more at home.

When I look at the gospels, it seems Jesus had a thing for side streets as well. He was always wandering into neighborhoods others feared. He struck up conversations with unlikely characters. He didn't seem to mind the trash.

Sometimes I look out at the main street and am tempted to return, but then I remember what it felt like out there and what it feels like off to the side. Given Jesus liked side streets, I figure I'm in pretty good company.

Espresso Shots:

1. *Do you live on the main street or the side streets?*

2. *What is it that is appealing about the main street, and what do the side streets offer?*

3. *In what location and in whose company, are you most at home, spiritually?*

JOINING THE GAME

I recently visited a school with no bleachers. I thought someone might have forgotten to set them up, but I learned it was deliberate. The school was small, and they needed every student to participate. As a result, there was nowhere to sit, nowhere to look on.

I was surprised by how uncomfortable the bleacher-less field made me feel. On the one hand, I thought it was a wonderful statement, but my palms began to sweat when I imagined going to such a school. I've always liked to pick and choose when I participate. Sitting in the bleachers is so much safer than getting onto the field.

Teddy Roosevelt spoke eloquently of those who are brave enough to enter the arena, the ones with sweat, blood, and more than a few skinned knees. Author Brené Brown built on his words by encouraging us to dare greatly in her amazing book, aptly called *Daring Greatly*.

We live in many fields —work, relationships, creative pursuits, social gatherings, and faith. In each case, there lies the temptation to climb into the bleachers and watch. But we were not created for the bleachers. We were made for the field.

May we suit up and go into the game today.

Espresso Shots:

1. *When have you chosen the bleachers over the field?*
2. *What was it about getting on the field that intimidated you so?*
3. *In what way can you climb from the bleachers and onto the field in a relationship, at work, or in your faith?*

THE ARTIST IN THE PARK

The artist sat on a bench overlooking a neglected vacant lot. Sitting there each afternoon he got an idea because that's what artists do. He had spent his life painting and had made more money than he ever thought he would, so he decided to put some of that money to good use. He bought the vacant lot and hired a crew to transform it into a wonderful park.

"You must not tell anyone," he instructed the workers, and they didn't.

When the work began, people were curious. When they heard it was going to be a park, they grew excited. They wondered who was turning it into a park, but mostly they were eager to enjoy it. When the day came for the park to open, a line of parents and children were waiting. Everyone wanted to be the first to slide down the slide, swing on the swing, and play in the sandboxes.

From his bench, the man looked on with great satisfaction. Everyone seemed so happy, and they treasured the park and treated it with love and respect. After all, it was a gift. It pleased the artist to hear parents say they wished they could thank whoever gave the wonderful park, but, in time, the children and parents forgot the park was a gift. They behaved as if it belonged to them.

"It's mine," one child shouted and none of the parents corrected him.

Brokenhearted, the artist got up from his bench and walked back to his studio.

Espresso Shots:

1. *Do you see creation as something that belongs to us or as a gift given to us?*
2. *Do your actions reflect your answer to the first question?*
3. *How would the way you live change if you saw the world and all you have as gifts?*

ENOUGH IS GOOD

Does anyone feel good enough? I'm just wondering. Even the most successful or self-confident among us must have some lingering doubts. For some, it could be about whether they've achieved enough; for others whether they've been good enough. Some wonder if they've been a good enough mother or father, friend or partner, daughter or son. It's a slippery slope, as people like to say, because there are always ways in which we could have done better.

What adds to the challenge of feeling good enough are the images placed before us. Advertisements and movies present certain ideals, and it is hard not to measure ourselves against them. No wonder so many of us feel like we're not quite good enough.

Fortunately, I once heard a minister say, enough is good. She was speaking to her congregation on Homecoming Sunday and wanted everyone gathered to take a deep breath. Like the people in the pews, she was overwhelmed with the amount of money needed for the next year's budget and the list of programs and initiatives the parish wanted to instigate.

"We're just a bunch of human beings," she reminded them, "doing the best we can. It is wonderful that we want to do so much good, but I fear we're trying to be good enough for each other, for this city, for God. Perhaps it's time to stand back and remember that whatever we do is enough, and our enough is good."

I believe she was not only talking to her parish but you and me, as well.

Espresso Shots:

1. *How much do you struggle with feeling like you, what you do, or who you are is good enough?*

2. *How much of your "good enough" is based on the opinions of others?*

3. *What do you think God thinks of you?*

CORE WORK

If I hear another thing about core work, I'll scream! The newest exercise focus, core work, is designed to strengthen the "muscles beneath the muscles," the ones that stabilize us. We need and use them all the time, so gyms and trainers make a concerted effort to get their clients to strengthen their core. Not as dramatic as lifting weights with barbells from a bench press, strengthening core muscles involves holding poses while standing or sitting on an unstable surface. To maintain balance on such a surface, a person must activate his or her core muscles. It doesn't sound difficult, but it becomes challenging within seconds. Even though I get frustrated, I can see that there are many benefits to a strong core.

I've often thought of spiritual work as a kind of exercise program. There's a routine or rotation I follow to strengthen my spiritual muscles. I carve out time for prayer and meditation. I add into the rotation reading and quiet reflection. Some may find helpful exercises such as journaling, walking, or specific spiritual disciplines, but the exercises that I like least are the ones that happen when ordinary life has shown up and challenged me in some way. I am away from my comfortable chair with my neatly arranged books. I am off-center or feeling as if I'm standing on unstable ground. I may need to have a difficult conversation with someone, face a crisis at work or home, or grapple with uncertainty about a project. Whatever the reason, I have to work to maintain balance, and it can be excruciatingly difficult at times.

I suppose this is spiritual core work. But I don't like it any more than the other kind of core work.

Espresso Shots:

1. *What spiritual exercises do you do?*

2. *In what ways does life challenge you to develop your spiritual core?*

3. *How can you use the instability of life to grow stronger, spiritually?*

NO PLACE LIKE HOME

"My heart is restless until it finds its rest in thee." —*St. Augustine of Hippo*

When it comes to longing for home, I make Dorothy look like an amateur! I have no ruby slippers, but I've tried to click my heels all my life, hoping they would bring me home.

If I could just have those friends…click, click, click.

If I could just have that job…click, click, click.

If I could have that house…click, click, click.

If I could have that bank account balance, that spouse, that award…the list is endless and my heels have blisters.

If you've ever clicked your heels, you know home is as elusive as it is seductive. "Home" puts on many costumes and wears many masks, but ultimately it's the place for which we all long. And it seems so often just beyond my reach. Some people are content right where they are; others search endlessly. Some people settle for false homes because they can't find a place where they are known and loved for who they truly are.

I once read that if you look for happiness, you'll never find it, but if you do the next right thing, happiness will be the natural result. I think home is similar. When we search for it in the people, places, and things beyond us, we never find it, but when we live authentic lives connected to the One who gave us life in the first place, we feel at home wherever we are.

Espresso Shots:

1. *List three places you've searched for home unsuccessfully.*

2. *Describe a moment when you were home.*

3. *What can you do to resist the temptation to click your heels?*

THE NEXT BENCH

I went to a remarkable retreat center where the grounds were as inspirational as the facilities. During the first of many walks through the woods, I stopped at a bench with a particularly pleasing view. There was a small creek with enough water and rocks to make the sound one craves when sitting and thinking. I thought I'd found *the* spot and planned to spend most of my time on that bench.

After a while, though, I stood and continued walking on the trail and was surprised to find an even better bench around the bend. *This* is the spot, I thought to myself. The trail then led up a steep hill, which I did not particularly want to climb, but at the top was another bench overlooking the best view of all. The bench was surrounded by massive boulders, an altar, and a cross. Sitting there, I thought about the progression of benches.

Throughout my life, I've searched for just the right place. Whether it's a place or job, I stake my ground and plan to remain there forever. I fool myself into thinking I've arrived, that things can never get any better than this. Then the situation changes, and I am forced to move on. Such changes are difficult. I mourn having to move on, but I've always found another bench waiting.

I've been given such a wonderful life, for which I often give thanks. Sometimes I think my life can get no better, but I would have missed so much if I'd sat on the same bench all my life. I get fooled into thinking this life is as good as it gets. When I do, I cling to this world with clenched fists. But there's another bench around the bend. It's just out of sight, and it will put this one to shame.

Espresso Shots:

1. *Have you feared moving from one bench to another?*
2. *Have you ever grieved such a move but been surprised by what was around the bend?*
3. *Do you believe there's another "bench" waiting when you leave this mortal life?*

STORYTELLING

Whenever someone uttered the words, "once upon a time," I sat up and paid attention. I loved stories. I still do. Stories teach and entertain. They also endure. Stories can say things in a way a person can remember for years.

Over the years, I learned that there are stories that delight and inspire and stories that hurt. People tell both kinds, and nowhere is that more apparent than in the stories we tell ourselves.

Listening to interviews with some professional athletes, I can hear how disciplined they are to tell themselves positive stories. When they recount their performance, they put a positive spin on what happened to build on their success or loss. We are not so disciplined. Too often, telling ourselves negative stories comes more naturally.

One of the most important spiritual skills we can develop is questioning the stories we tell. Is it true? Where did I first hear that story? Why do I continue to tell it? What if I were to tell myself another story?

Stories carry enormous power. It's important we use that power for good and not harm. Life is tough enough without making it harder with the stories we tell ourselves.

Espresso Shots:

1. *What's your favorite story about you?*
2. *What story do you tell yourself that isn't necessarily true?*
3. *Where did it come from, and why do you keep telling it?)*

Double Shot: *What would it look and sound like if you were to tell a different story?*

HINGES

The doors of our new chapel were massive, but they needed to be, given the size of the church. The wood had to be specially ordered and required the finest woodworkers. In the end, the doors were things of beauty.

"But they won't be worth a thing without these," said the contractor as he held the metal hinges. "They may look insignificant, but without them, these beautiful doors won't be able to open or close."

I watched as the hinges were attached, and doors were installed. Because of the hinges, just the lightest of effort could sway the towering doors. On the day we dedicated the chapel, everyone marveled at the doors, but no one noticed the hinges.

The contractor helped me see how something small can make all the difference. Whether it's refusing to give up your seat on a bus, posting 95 theses on a door, or throwing tea in a harbor, small moments and unknown people can open doors and change history.

Given that the new chapel is on a school campus, I hope the students learn the importance of hinges.

Espresso Shots:

1. Identify someone or some event that was small but had the power to open or close a door.

2. Look back and see if you had a "hinge" that changed your path.

3. In what way could you become a hinge for a person or cause in your life?

THE FINISH LINE

"I'll see you at the finish line."

The words stirred me in a place so deep I gasped. The young girl was giving the final meditation before the assembled group ran a marathon and was speaking about the conclusion of our upcoming race. But, for me, her final sentence spoke of a different race.

Maybe it was because I was nervous about the run or because I had just been through a tough year or because I was getting older and had become more reflective about life, but the power of her words stirred me, and they have stuck with me ever since.

What if there is a place? What if there's a finish line? What if we will reach that place one day and feel the elation that comes at the end of a race? Will there be a moment when we look down the way and see our journey's end and, like the marathon, see people holding signs and cheering? Who will we see standing there? Heaven is the only word for such a place. Just the idea of it changes how I look at my day-to-day struggles.

God has never spoken to me in a distinct, clear voice, at least not in a voice or moment that has been utterly recognizable. Whether through a particularly beautiful place, intimate moment with a child, or through a comment made by a young girl standing in front of a bunch of nervous runners, God's voice comes to me as a whisper, a glimpse caught out of the corner of my eye. I fathom the messages in bits and pieces, but they're enough to get me to lace up my shoes with renewed enthusiasm, profound gratitude, and, most of all, deep hope.

Espresso Shots:

1. *If you imagine your life as a race, who do you hope to see at the finish line?*

2. *In what ways do you hear God speaking in whispers?*

3. *How could you run the race set before you with renewed enthusiasm, profound gratitude, and deep hope?*

FIRES

In middle school science class, our teacher set two identical cups on fire. Over one, she placed a glass globe that filled with smoke before the fire extinguished. The uncovered cup continued to burn. It was her way of teaching us how fire needs oxygen. It was a vivid lesson I've remembered ever since.

Most of my life has been spent in school communities. I've always loved watching individuals come together and become something more by living and working together. When it goes well, it's inspirational. Not only does the community become more than anyone thought possible, but so do the individuals.

But, like any good thing, there's a downside. Individuals can go against the community, its leadership, or other members. It might appear harmless at first, but the spark that comes from gossip or divisive criticism ignites a fire that can quickly destroy a community.

My science teacher taught me that all fires need air. With a good breeze, a fire can spread rapidly, but without air, it goes out almost as quickly as it began. Fire starting often looks innocent at first: "Did you hear about …" "I don't mean to be negative, but …" "I always thought they were a *good* family …" Spreading honey doesn't put out a fire; it just hides the flame.

I'm no paragon of virtue. I've blown on emerging fires, just as I've stood back and done nothing when I've seen smoke, but the spiritual life is about progress, not perfection. It's made up of countless choices, and this is one of them: Will I start fires today, or put them out?

Espresso Shots:

1. *When were you in a situation when you started or spread a fire within a community?*
2. *Why is gossiping such a temptation?*
3. *How can you develop the spiritual discipline of not spreading gossip?*

KNOWING THE FATHER

I didn't know his father. Although we had been friends for years, I had never met his father. Still, when I heard of his father's death, I knew I had to attend the funeral out of respect and love for my friend.

The church was packed, and the stories told were as colorful as they were entertaining, as heartbreaking as they were inspirational. People spoke of his quick wit, which made me think about his son's innate sense of humor. They spoke of his uncanny ability to say just the right thing, which made me think of the time his son captured a moment perfectly when the rest of us looked on tongue-tied. They spoke of his talent as an investor in startup companies, and it reminded me of his son's entrepreneurial spirit. And when they spoke of the father's kindness, I couldn't help but think about how his son always refrains from saying negative things about people.

As I left the funeral, I realized I *did* know the father. I knew him through the son.

Only later did I come to see the spiritual lesson in the moment. In church, I was taught I would know the Father through the Son. Now I understand. When people speak of the grace, love, and forgiveness of the Father, I can know that because of his Son.

The lesson also speaks to our own lives. Who do people know through us?

Espresso Shots:

1. *In what way can people know your father by meeting you?*

2. *In what way can people know you by meeting your father?*

3. *In what ways can people meet Christ by meeting you?*

HEARING GOD

My room shared a wall with my parents' room. I could hear them talking but couldn't understand what they were saying. I heard a word or two and could tell which voice belonged to which parent, but that was about it. It was comforting hearing their voices, even if I couldn't understand their words. I was tempted to draw closer, maybe put a glass up against the wall to hear more clearly what they were talking about, but I never did. Of course, I could have walked down the hall and asked them directly, but I didn't do that either.

Thinking about my connection to God this morning, I thought about my room beside my parents. I believe in God, and I believe God speaks, but I've always struggled to understand what God says. At times, I think I can make out a word or two, but mostly it sounds like a muffled voice. Just hearing that sound gives me comfort, but I envy the people who have close personal relationships with God and can hear God clearly.

If I want to hear God, I need to draw closer. Maybe I should put a glass up against the wall. Maybe I should trust the people who tell me I can walk down the hall and speak to God directly.

I'll never know unless I try.

Espresso Shots:

1. *Do you believe God speaks?*
2. *If so, are you able to hear God's voice, or is it muffled?*
3. *In what way can you draw close and make an effort to hear God more clearly?*

BEING THE STREAM BED

I had the stream to myself. Finding a smooth boulder, I sat and listened as the water bubbled past. I marveled at the way the water flowed over and around the rocks, and I closed my eyes to listen to the intoxicating sound. Reaching down, I cupped some of the water in my hand and took a sip.

Such moments make me particularly reflective. On this particular day, I thought about how my life was like the stream. I cascade over rocks and dance my way downstream and shout with glee for others to hear.

Thanks to a friend, I realized I had it all wrong. She's a painter, and she pointed out that we are not called to be the water but the stream bed. "When I paint like I'm the water, the work is usually contrived and awful. When I paint as the stream bed, surprising things flow through me, and it's magical."

She was only talking about painting, but it was easy to see how her insights applied to the spiritual life. When I see myself as the water, it becomes all about me. When I'm the stream bed, I open myself to letting God flow through me. This spiritual enterprise always leads to wonderful, surprising moments. Today, I pray to be the stream bed and not the water. May I open my arms and heart and let the water flow.

Espresso Shots:

1. *In what way have you seen yourself as the water and not the stream bed?*

2. *What does it look and feel like when you allow God to flow through you?*

3. *Look for an opportunity to allow God to flow through you today.*

REPORT CARDS

My sister sent me three boxes stuffed with keepsakes from our mother. One of the boxes was full of things about me—programs from shows I'd performed, notes and letters I'd written, and every report card since third grade. I'm not sure why she kept my report cards. They were not things of beauty.

In third grade, I was diagnosed as dyslexic, and the grades and comments spoke of my significant struggle in school. I didn't need such reminders. The memories and the lifelong feelings they instilled have been companions ever since.

His spelling is atrocious.

He does his best with what he has.

What he lacks in ability, he makes up with a pleasant attitude.

When I finished looking through my report cards, I was deflated and full of self-loathing. Sometimes voices from the past can do that.

There are other voices to listen to, however, but they are harder to hear.

You are marvelously made.

God's power is made perfect in our weakness.

What you meant for evil, God used as good.

Countless biblical figures and people through the ages expressed these messages of life and love, but as Julia Roberts's character says in the movie *Pretty Woman*, "The bad stuff is easier to believe."

Just like a drunk must discard a lifetime of bottles, we need to discard the messages that hold us back. Whether these are report cards or echoes of things said, it's time to put them in the trash and start listening to new voices.

Espresso Shots:

1. *In what way do you keep reading report cards and voices from the past?*
2. *What do you think God wants you to hear?*
3. *What would happen if you threw away all of the report cards?*

A MIGHTY WIND

If I hadn't known better, I would have said it was a calm, clear day. From inside a mountain home, looking out at the beautiful view, it looked that way. The flags on the deck, however, danced wildly. Because of them, I knew there was a wind. Like the dust that reveals a ray of light, the flags helped me see the wind.

I experience a similar situation in spiritual life. I look out and think I see things as they are, but, with some help, I can see wind all around me. The Hebrew people called such a wind, *ruach*, and believed God was with them in the wind. Christians also believe God is present in the wind. We call it the Holy Spirit. This wind swirled around the disciples long ago and continues to do so today.

I don't see the wind, which can sometimes lead me to question whether there's any wind at all. But then something, or someone, is placed before me, like flags on the deck, and I'm able to see the wind. It might be an unexpected phone call, visit, or comment, but the wind causes the flag to dance.

The mighty wind makes itself known through the most unlikely flags. Because of them, we're able to see the wind and know we're not alone.

Espresso Shots:

1. *Name a time in which you thought there was no wind and that you were alone.*

2. *Identify a flag that blew in the breeze that made you aware of the wind.*

3. *Spend the day looking for flags blowing.*

Double Shot: *Be the flag for someone else.*

WHAT'S IN YOUR BIBLE

A popular advertising campaign asks: "What's in your wallet?" Recently, I thought of an interesting twist: "What's in your Bible?"

The idea came as I visited my mother, who spoke of a special note she received from a beloved nephew. "I'll show it to you," she said as she went over and picked up her Bible. Placed between the pages were countless notes and pictures. These were the things that mattered to her most. I wondered if any of the notes I'd written her were stored in her Bible.

Does the place where something is stored matter? What's wedged between the pages containing the Beatitudes? Psalm 23? The Book of Job? In the end, however, I was moved the most by the simple fact that she stored treasured things in the pages of her Bible.

I began wondering what I would put in the pages of my Bible. The diplomas I worked so hard to receive? The few awards or citations I've received? What about prestigious job offers or impressive bank statements? The answer to all these questions was, "No."

For me, the hand-drawn birth announcements for each of my children would be tucked inside, probably near Psalm 139. The note my father wrote me to say how proud he was of me would be stored near the father's greeting of the Prodigal Son. The letter my goddaughter wrote to me while I was in rehab would be folded near where Jesus spoke of having life and having it more abundantly.

Bibles, while thick, have limited pages. We'd have to select carefully, but I suspect the exercise would remind us what really matters.

What's in your Bible?

Espresso Shots:

1. *Do you have a Bible?*
2. *Do you ever open it, or is it for display?*
3. *If you were to place important things from your life within its pages, what are three things you'd put there?*

A WONDERFUL WORLD

The groom went to his sister and reached out a hand for a dance. "What a Wonderful World" played, and they clung to each other, swaying back and forth. I knew enough about their stories to know the poignancy of the moment. The blending of music and backstory was beyond anyone's full comprehension.

They had lost both parents to addiction and suffered from it themselves. The brother had been to prison, and they had both endured many other hardships. On this day, though, they held each other tight on the dance floor.

I once thought belief in God would make life go my way. I thought an all-loving God would fill my days with rainbows, but I now see this perception of God was of my own making. Life, whether you have faith in God or not, can be a struggle. The miracle comes when you hold onto that faith while also struggling.

After the music was over, the brother and sister clung to each other for a moment longer. They said nothing but spoke volumes.

Yes, it's a wonderful world.

Espresso Shots:

1. *When you were young, what did you think faith in God meant for your life?*

2. *How do you see that faith now?*

3. *In what ways have you come to see it's a wonderful world despite the struggles?*

BALL MARKS

On my dresser is a tool for repairing ball marks on the surface of a putting green. It was given to me while I was playing golf the other day. Undoubtedly, the giver hoped I'd use the tool to leave no trace of having been on the greens. Printed on the tool was "X 2," which I thought might be the logo. I then realized it was there to encourage me to repair my own ball mark and the mark of another. Therein lies the sermon, I thought.

What a different world it would be if we repaired our ball marks—and those of others. No matter how talented we may be, we leave marks. Over time, careless words and selfish actions have left their marks on our friends, neighbors, and loved ones.

The question that awaits us now is about how we will repair our ball marks. There are a variety of tools to do so. We can apologize, correct something we did wrong, or learn from our mistakes and live differently. We can do much to repair the marks we've left, and, while we are at it, repair another's mark too.

Espresso Shots:

1. *Identify a place you have left a ball mark.*
2. *Did you repair it, or leave it behind?*
3. *In what way could you repair one ball mark you've made?*

Double Shot: *Repair the ball mark left by another.*

THE BLESSING OF A LIMP

There is a vivid story from the Hebrew scriptures about a man named Jacob who wrestled with an angel throughout the night. He planned to reconcile with his brother in the morning, having acted shamefully in his past. The angel awakened Jacob, and the wrestling match began. Jacob came to recognize his opponent was an angel and refused to stop wrestling until he received a blessing. When it was given, Jacob's name was changed to Israel, which means one who wrestles with God. He was also given an injury that caused him to limp for the rest of his life.

Although I loved the story as a child, it's meaning has captivated me as an adult. Once I had wrestled with an angel and been given a limp of my own, I came to understand the importance of the story.

Because of my wrestling match, I no longer drink alcohol. The first time I stood at a party with sparkling water instead of a cocktail, I wanted to hide. I felt like everyone was staring at me as I crossed the room like I had a limp. At the end of the evening, a woman came up to me and whispered she'd like to meet sometime to discuss her husband's drinking, which was becoming a problem. Earlier that day, I'd met with my daughter, who wanted to talk. She didn't focus on how hard it was to face her friends after they heard I'd gone to rehab. Instead, she said how proud she was of my decision and felt like she had her father back.

As I went to bed that night, I gave thanks for my limp. It's been a blessing.

Espresso Shots:

1. *Name a time when you wrestled with God.*
2. *In what way did that struggle lead to a limp?*
3. *Has the limp become a blessing?*

INVISIBLE FENCES

Driving past the lawn with the little yellow flags around the perimeter, I knew another "invisible fence" had been installed. Poor dog. What looks like an open, spacious yard is now a deceptive cage. His collar will use electric shocks to teach him where not to go; ultimately, if he's like most dogs, he will make peace with the invisible border.

I relate to the dog. Don't you? Sometimes I see open spaces but forget about the invisible fence. I am not sure who installed them—parents, teachers, or events in life—but I sure know when I cross the line. Each time I get close to an edge, I feel the shock and pull back. We've all been there, right?

Just ask the obedient child who tells a family secret.

Just ask the wife who shares she wants to go back to school.

Just ask the churchgoer who admits doubts.

Just ask the child who has come out of the closet.

Just ask the artist who paints in a new style.

Collars come in all shapes and sizes, as do the shocks that compel us to fall back in line. Most of us decide the potential freedom is not worth the discomfort, but others accept the pain as the price for new life. For them, the yard is not enough. The promise of new life outweighs the pain it will take to get there. That's easy to say, but the shocks and discomfort are real.

So is the freedom that lies beyond.

Espresso Shots:

1. *What was an invisible fence in your yard when you were growing up?*
2. *What fences remain today?*
3. *What would it take for you to go beyond the fence?*

FINDING OUR PURPOSE

The clay was molded as it twirled around the wheel. With the hands of a master moving inside and out, the lump of clay took shape. Once in the form of an urn, the clay was placed on a rack to dry. When the potter wasn't looking, the urn marveled at what it had become. It gave thanks for its creation and the skill of the potter. The feelings of gratitude gave way to sadness as the urn sought to serve a purpose other than sitting on a shelf.

"What good is it just to sit here?" it asked. "I'm here to carry things, not sit empty."

A week later, an excited servant arrived searching for seven urns for an upcoming wedding. The disgruntled urn was one of the urns selected and was pleased to be filled with water in anticipation of the wedding feast. In time, though, water was not enough. The urn longed to carry something more.

Just then, the urn heard the servants discussing the fact that all the wine was gone. They searched but found no more wine. Without wine, the wedding would end. A servant passed by the urn and smelled the unmistakable scent of wine. He discovered seven urns full of the finest wine he had ever tasted. He called out to the other servants, and the urn swelled with pride as they marveled at the wine it was carrying.

No one knew how the water had become wine, but the urn only cared that it was now doing something important. Now the party could continue.

Those who have ears to hear, let them hear.

Espresso Shots:

1. *In what way do you seek to have an important purpose?*
2. *Have you ever imagined yourself as a vessel capable of holding wine or something special?*
3. *What can you bring to the party?*

BUMPER-TO-BUMPER THEOLOGY

I was recently in bumper-to-bumper traffic, trying desperately not to lose my temper. I understand traffic caused by an accident or debris falling in the road but not the kind I experienced today, the kind caused by nothing at all. Instead of acting out and letting the other drivers know how I felt, I tried to see what the moment could teach me.

While I waited for some profound insight, I decided to put space between me and the car in front of me. When he or she put on the brakes, I allowed time before I put on mine. In some small way, I felt absorbing the slowdown would make it easier for those behind me. Every time I didn't put on my brakes, the car behind me didn't have to either, and we slowly chipped away at the traffic jam as a whole.

I realized I have the opportunity to respond the same way in the rest of my life. When someone says something offensive, or I hear gossip or a person cuts in line, or whatever the challenge may be, I can try to absorb the "traffic" and not add to it.

It's not easy to drive smoothly in traffic, but there would be less traffic if we all tried. It's not easy to live smoothly in a volatile world, but if we all tried, things might calm, if only within us.

Espresso Shots:

1. *What creates traffic in your life? (Comments, behavior, gossip, politics)*
2. *In what way could you absorb the traffic that surrounds you?*
3. *What effect do you think it could have?*

MOVING THE CHAIR

With an afternoon all to herself, she headed to the patio to enjoy time in the sun. She took her place, closed her eyes, and let her heart and mind wander. Before long, she fell asleep, and when she awakened, she was in the shade. Rather than move the chair, she decided to return to the house.

Her afternoon describes the way many of us live our spiritual lives. We're given moments when all seems right with the world, the joy of life surrounds us, and we close our eyes and let our hearts and minds relish the blessings of our lives. Such moments don't last, though. Like the woman on the patio, we fall asleep, the sun moves, and we find ourselves in the shade. To remain in the sun, we need to move our chair.

It's often said that the only constant is change. In our individual lives, relationships, businesses, and spiritual lives, the sun is always moving. The challenge is to be aware of the shade as it creeps closer and to move the chair when darkness comes.

When our knee hurts, we see a doctor. When relationships struggle, extra effort and sometimes professional help is needed. When sales drop and competitors innovate, it's time for the team to meet and dream as they once did when the company was young. So, too, when we feel ourselves drifting away from God. It's not enough to sit in the sun and hope the good, warm feelings will last. We need to move the chair.

Espresso Shots:

1. *Are you presently in the sun or shade, spiritually?*
2. *What could you do to return to the sun—or remain in the sun?*
3. *What spiritual practices could you use to keep your chair in the sun?*

FOLKS OFF TO THE SIDE

Friday nights at a club were called "informal night." It was intended to lighten the otherwise stodgy atmosphere of the place, and many attended. At the end of the evening, the staff relaxed in a room off to the side. One of the club members decided to join the staff. Conversations about sailing and tennis gave way to the Yankees and funny mishaps from work that night. It was genuinely informal, and the member finally felt like he belonged.

****

The Science Center had become a centerpiece of the city's cultural resurgence. Because of dedicated staff, committed volunteers, and well-attended fundraisers like the one he was attending, the center enjoyed great success. The patrons feasted on BBQ and beer while strolling among the animal exhibits and danced through the night to lively music. Out of the corner of his eye, he noticed the staff dancing off to the side, almost out of sight. He knew many of them personally, so he strolled over and joined in. It was the same music, just a different dance.

****

It was one of New York's premier churches, and they were proud to host the Archbishop of Canterbury. After the 8 a.m. service, while standing at the doorway greeting the congregants, the archbishop noticed men and women entering a door off to the side. "They're part of our homeless ministry," the rector told the archbishop. He asked if they could visit the others in the homeless ministry before the next service. After joining them for breakfast, the archbishop celebrated communion using toast and juice. "At which communion do you think our Lord was more at home?" he asked the rector as they returned to the church.

Espresso Shots:

1. *Have you ever noticed people off to the side?*
2. *Have you ever joined them?*
3. *Are you willing to see those off to the side—and join them?*

OLD WINE

On the night before we moved, I couldn't sleep. I imagined each room and what I needed to do to get it ready for the movers. We were downsizing, so much of the work was deciding what should be taken to the new house and what should be thrown away.

Stored in the basement was an extensive wine collection, bought when I could still drink. Many of the bottles were quite valuable, which is why I did not get rid of the wine when I got sober. I let the movers handle the furniture. I moved the wine, but as I heard the bottles clink against each other, I realized the time had come to get rid of my old wine. As confident as I may be that I will not drink again, having such a collection in the house was too dangerous.

I decided to divide the collection and deliver it to friends who would enjoy the wine. Unannounced, and usually under cover of darkness, I went and left each box at someone's doorstep. I grew more excited with each delivery, and by the end of the evening, I was almost giddy.

Not only was I getting rid of old wine, but I was also making room for something else, new wine if you will. It turned out to be one of the most powerful nights of my life. It was a celebration of friendships, a recognition of a meaningful life choice, and a clearing out that allowed my soul to breathe and grow in new ways.

Espresso Shots:

1. *What do you cling to that belongs to the "old you"?*
2. *How can you clear your house and heart of old wine?*
3. *What new wine could await you if you could make room?*

HANDS

Even though I knew it would happen at the end of the service, I was surprised by how much it moved me. This was the Sunday when new elders were ordained into our church, and after answering a series of questions, past elders were invited to come and place their hands on the newest ones. From all over the church, men and women stood and made their way toward the front. Hands were placed on the new elders, and when the crowd grew big, hands were placed on the elders who had their hands on the newest elders. It was like watching a chain of connection, and it made me think of all the other hands, the ones throughout the centuries who have been part of this apostolic succession.

The moment was about more than hands, however. It was about passing along a blessing. Watching the crowd before me, I was reminded of the many hands that have reached out and rested on my shoulders. They, too, offered God's blessing. I left the church with a grateful heart, knowing that the opportunities for blessing others don't just happen in church. God's blessings are ready whenever we dare to reach out and place our hands on the shoulder of another.

Espresso Shots:

1. Think of some of the hands that have been placed on your shoulders. If you have the opportunity, thank the people who have blessed you.
2. How has God's blessing come to you through others?
3. How can you extend your hand and bless someone today?

PLAYGROUND GATES

I attended a conference on a seminary campus down the road from my childhood home. My mother moved after my father died, but so much of heart and soul are still in the old house. I can picture my bedroom, smell the old wood floors and oriental rugs, and imagine games with my sister in our great backyard.

During one of our lunch breaks, I made the short walk to the property's edge and looked across the front lawn. The driveway was smaller than I remembered, and the new owner had changed the color of the place. I wanted to ring the doorbell to see how things looked, but I didn't. I could tell it wasn't our house anymore, nor was I the little boy who once lived there.

Back at the conference, a speaker told of a trip to England he and his wife took recently. They made a point of visiting Kensington Gardens, the hometown of J.M. Barrie, creator of *Peter Pan*, and they went to the park where Barrie reportedly sat most afternoons. They heard the sound of children playing on the other side of the nearby wall; a passerby explained the Peter Pan Garden was on the other side. The couple wandered toward the entrance gate only to be told by a guard that they were not permitted to enter. "No Grown-Ups Allowed," the sign said, and the couple left, disheartened.

Sitting in the comfort of my conference seat, I understood exactly how that couple had felt. I had felt it only moments earlier.

Espresso Shots:

1. *Have you ever tried to return to your childhood home or a place that once meant the world to you?*

2. *Were you able to go there, or were you prevented from crossing the threshold?*

3. *Write a description of that place with as much detail as possible and share it with someone.*

A MODERN LITANY

These are your opportunities…seize them.

These are your challenges…face them.

These are your successes…celebrate them.

These are your mistakes…learn from them.

These are your gifts…use them.

These are your weaknesses…embrace them.

These are your friends…treasure them.

These are your enemies…understand them.

These are your questions…ask them.

These are your wounds…show them.

These are your words…value them.

These are your arms…open them.

These are your hands…loosen them.

This is your life…live it.

Espresso Shots:

1. *At which of these are you best?*
2. *Which one challenges you the most?*
3. *How can you address the challenges?*

SODA BOTTLE THEOLOGY: MAKING ROOM

In a fleeting effort to be like his brother, the young boy blew over the top of the soda bottle. Instead of a breathy whistle, soda sprayed all over his face. "It needs to be empty," the others said, rolling their eyes. Once he finished his soda, the boy tried again and heard the sound he'd been searching for.

Mark Nepo, one of my favorite spiritual writers, points out that for an instrument to make music, it needs to be emptied. A drum, violin, flute, and countless other instruments need space inside if they're to make music. The same is true with you and me.

So much of life is about getting full, not empty. We learn more and do more until there's no more room inside. No amount of wind can make our bottles whistle because they're full. Too often, I've done the same spiritually. I've tried to learn more and do more, and the result left me full. There was no room for the wind to enter. No song could be made.

While learning and doing both have a place in spiritual living, so does the practice of emptying ourselves. We need to make an effort to make room within so that there's space for God.

Espresso Shots:

1. *Take a deep breath and hold it. Now, try to take another breath without letting the air out.*
2. *How is that similar to your spiritual life?*
3. *In what ways can you empty yourself (your calendar, your to-do list, your spiritual routine) to make room?*

SODA BOTTLE THEOLOGY: A HOLE IN THE SOUL

The first time I heard it, I gasped. Someone was reading from the Big Book of Alcoholics Anonymous and described "a hole in the soul through which the wind blows." I knew such a hole in the soul, and I knew what it felt like when the wind blew through it. Like an empty soda bottle that whistles when you blow across its top, there's a sound when wind blows across the hole in our souls.

What that sound says to each of us varies, but for those sitting in the circle that morning, the sounds were all about our shortcomings and the mistakes we had made. No wonder we drank to fill the hole. No wonder others fill the hole with packed calendars, work, sex, food, exercise, you name it. There are as many fillers as there are holes, but none can fill the hole, not completely and not forever.

Some say we should fill the hole with God, but I have a slightly different take. I think we should keep the hole empty so that God can make music out of our emptiness. It's hard and humbling work to empty the holes we've filled for so long, but if we're able to do so, we can hear the magic as God's wind, which many call the Holy Spirit, blows across our emptiness. Suddenly the imperfections and incompleteness we've tried to fill become music for others to hear.

Espresso Shots:

1. *In what ways do you feel like there's a hole in your soul?*

2. *In what ways have you tried to fill it?*

3. *What would it look and sound like if you stopped filling it and allowed God to blow through your emptiness?*

ROLLERBLADING

I'll admit it. I was one of the many people who took up rollerblading when it first became popular. There was a park near our home, and its wide trail allowed me to play music and skate away!

One of the things I learned (the hard way) was that coasting is never a good idea. Resting on both skates at the same time leads to a fall. When both skates hit debris, you're going down. It's much better to always have a skate in the air so that when the skate on the road hits something, the other can take over.

Gamblers call it "covering your bets." Investors call it "diversifying." But whatever name it's given, the truth that one should always be prepared for bumps in the road is sage advice. Coasting is tempting, particularly when you have been making a significant effort and are out of breath, but a rock can come when you least expect it and put you on the ground before you even know what happened.

There's a flow to rollerblading, a back and forth that can move you forward smoothly. There's a flow to the spiritual journey, as well. We seek to move forward and make efforts to do so. Sometimes, when we get tired and need a break, we decide to coast and place both blades on the road, but rocks remain where we least expect them. Better to keep moving from one side to the other so that when we stumble, there's another skate on which to rely.

Espresso Shots:

1. *Have you ever coasted and been surprised by a sudden piece of debris?*

2. *In what way can you skate with one foot on the ground and the other in the air?*

3. *What are the various skates you can use as you journey spiritually?*

PREPARING THE HOUSE

When the ranch owner assigned our weekly duties, I was given the job of painting a small house on the property. Given the demanding duties at a large ranch, painting a house seemed like a gift. I was eager to get started. I entered the barn to get the paint, but the foreman handed me a scraper, sandpaper, and tools for repairing the house.

"You don't start by painting," he said. "First, you need to inspect the entire house, wash it, scrape and sand the places where the paint is chipped, and then repair any damage before even thinking about picking up a paintbrush."

The job wasn't the gift I hoped it would be. The house was old and needed a lot of repairs. I didn't get started on painting for weeks, but it taught me a valuable lesson about painting—and spiritual work as well.

I'm always eager to buy a new book or journal, set up space, and establish a routine, but that's like picking up a can and starting to paint before preparing the space. Spiritual work begins with looking at our lives closely, scraping away old paint, and repairing damage. It's not as sexy or satisfying as a new book or candle, but it's every bit a part of the work. Without preparation, any work we do will not last long.

The rewards of spiritual work await, but preparation is the first step.

Espresso Shots:

1. *In what way can you stand back and look at your life for a few days?*

2. *Do you see chipped paint, cracks, or rotted wood, places that need attention?*

3. *Can you grow to see how such preparation is as much a part of the work as the painting?*

SPLIT LOGS

He was a friend of a friend, but after years of meeting on Friday mornings in a spiritual support group, he became a friend of mine. Well-traveled, he spoke of terrain I had not yet reached, described views I had not yet seen. As if standing on the side of the trail clapping his hands, he encouraged me to travel on, to see within what I couldn't see on my own.

You can do this.

You can rise up and carry on.

God loves you more than you know.

If you don't believe me, read the Bible.

Today I received word he died, and my thoughts are not only of my appreciation for his friendship but also my dismay over letting our opposing political views come between us. Like a wedge in a log, his love and my hatred for the same politician split us apart.

Things that divide us sometimes seem to overtake the things that unite us— as neighbors, Christians, Americans, and citizens of the world. How you vote, which news channel you watch, what team you support, what state or region you come from, how you worship, if you worship, are all the wedges that can split us apart. Maybe it's always been this way, but it seems worse than ever.

In all my self-righteous indignation, I sit here mourning not only a friend but the lost days of friendship because of the wedges that divided us. I cannot change things with him, but I can with others.

Espresso Shots:

1. *What are some of the wedges that get between you and others?*

2. *In what ways have those wedges split you apart from others?*

3. *Are the wedges worth it?*

THE CRIB

A dismantled crib leans against the curb,
waiting to be taken
with the trash.
Worn out and dated,
it speaks of a season past.
A truck comes to carry it away,
taking with it
wakeful nights,
heartbeat close,
fluffy hair and infant smell,
and whispered dreams.
"Wait!"
the mother cries,
running in her bathrobe to stop the truck,
"I've changed my mind."
Unable to hear her,
it drives on.

Espresso Shots:

1. *When have you put something from your past at the curb (literally or metaphorically)?*

2. *Recall a moment in your past. Use all your senses to bring it alive.*

3. *What have you let go of that you regret?*

DANCING TREES

One windy day, I passed by a magnificent magnolia tree holding court at the top of a hill. Having stood there for countless years, the tree's trunk and branches demanded respect, if only for longevity, but it was the way they danced in the breeze that took my breath away. Swirling along with the wind, the branches twisted back and forth. The branches clacked against one another, while the leaves made the sound of applause.

It would be easy to look at the sight and marvel at the tree, but the performance was not a solo act. The tree, impressive as it was, would have stood stationary if not for the breeze. With the wind, the tree came to life and danced for all to see.

I live in a grove of trees, I suppose. Some are old, others are saplings, some grand, others easy to overlook, but when the wind blows through our community, the dance begins. One tree sways this way, another swirls in a different direction, and the leaves applaud in delight.

When trees are dancing, it's easy to forget the wind, just like it's easy to forget the Holy Spirit when the preacher is preaching, a volunteer is serving, or a painter creating.

It's the wind—always the wind—that inspires the dance.

Espresso Shots:

1. *When have you seen someone full of life or dancing in the wind?*

2. *Were you able to see not only the person but the wind blowing them into a dance?*

3. *In what way can you spread your branches and allow God's wind to blow through you?*

DEFAULT SETTINGS

I'm not technologically gifted, but I know enough to get the computer to do most of what I need. Where things get frustrating is when I rub up against my computer's default settings. Whether it's a particular font or preferred email address, my computer goes to its default settings. If I want something different, I need to change the setting manually, and if I want that change to be permanent, I need to change its default settings.

I was doing battle with such technological matters recently, bemoaning my computer's inability to read my mind, when I realized how similar we are. I, too, have default settings. I think they were set in hopes of making it easier to navigate life, but they can be a source of real problems and frustrations. For example, if my wife brings up finances, I automatically get defensive. When something my child is doing scares me, I get angry, and when someone laughs at something I did, I feel useless.

These are only a few of what I've come to know as my default settings. Recognizing them is the first step. Once I see them, I can manually change my reactions. In time, I might even be able to change my default settings, but that takes time and effort. Default settings are, by their very nature, stubborn.

When Richard Niebuhr wrote, "God, grant me the serenity to accept the things I cannot change, and the courage to change the things I can," he was talking about discerning our default settings. What can we change, and what is beyond our control? Too often, default settings appear permanent. They're not. We can change them over time.

Espresso Shots:

1. List five of your default settings.
2. Identify ways in which you would like to change them manually?
3. How could you change one or more of your default settings permanently?

HOW GOD MUST FEEL

The two awakened without the need of an alarm and spoke only of joyful things over coffee. "The doors to graduation open in an hour," she reminded her husband, so they dressed quickly and were among the first to stake a claim over their seats. They didn't want to miss a moment and were pleased by their third-row selection.

As they waited for the ceremony to begin, they reminisced about their child's life. In a rare moment of visible affection, the husband reached for his wife's hand and squeezed. An announcement was made, the music began, and the couple stood as the faculty and graduates processed. It was only a matter of seconds before they were both in tears. This is it, the moment we've been waiting for, they thought.

Unfortunately, the people sitting behind them were not as moved by the occasion. With phones in hand, they talked throughout the ceremony. Oblivious to the events on stage, they shared videos and scores from the night before and counted the minutes before they could leave.

The man grew increasingly irritated. He looked back at the troublesome group, but they didn't care. He let out an audible sigh, which had no effect.

"For God's sake," he sighed.

"Exactly," replied his wife. "Now we know how God must feel every Sunday."

Espresso Shots:

1. *When it comes to living spiritual lives, are you more like the couple paying attention or the crowd who are busy with other things?*

2. *How could you grow in your appreciation for all God has done in the world?*

3. *In what ways could you learn to pay attention?*

THE POWER OF PINK

Things in this country are sometimes overwhelming. Regardless of one's political leanings, we can all agree that divisions abound, anger burns, and people on all sides are acting like spoiled children. I've recently had to turn off the news and look elsewhere for the country I love. Little did I know I'd find it on a cloudy morning, surrounded by hundreds of pink shirts.

It was an annual Women's Only Run fundraiser for breast cancer research. I stood on the curb, looking out at a sea of pink shirts. The pink shirts came in all sizes, but there were two shades: one for those who ran in support of someone and the second for survivors. Some runners had no hair; others had no breasts. One could only walk, and another was pushed in a wheelchair.

But the morning was filled with enormous joy and hope. There were no Democrats or Republicans, no Christians or Jews, no rich or poor. Just human beings standing, running, and walking beside one another.

For a few hours, the world was a beautiful place. As I walked to my car, I watched a mother and young daughter walking ahead of me, each wearing a different shade of pink. Hand in hand, I could see strength being passed from one to another. It was the power of pink. May the world learn from and find more of this power.

Espresso Shots:

1. *Where do you find hope and strength when you're discouraged?*

2. *Reach out to someone you know who's been touched by breast cancer and offer encouragement.*

3. *Think of one or two ways you can cross the many lines that divide us. Then act.*

I KEEP FORGETTING

As I rode in the car with one of the men from the rehab community, he spoke of his daughter and how he dreamed of being with her again. It had been a long time since they'd been together, and it was clear he thought about her all the time.

In the silence that followed, I thought about his daughter. Does she think about her father? Does his absence make it easy for her to forget about him? I felt like finding his daughter and telling her about her father, not only about the courageous efforts he is making to get and stay sober but also about his deep and abiding love for her.

It made me think about my relationship with God. The silence and distance I sometimes feel make me forget about God. I wonder if God is there and if God thinks of me, let alone cares for me.

In many ways, I'm like the man's daughter. I know her father thinks about her all the time and wants nothing more than to be reunited with her, but she doesn't know that. Maybe this is the way it is with God, too.

Like I wanted to do for the girl's father, it would be great if someone came and told me that God thinks about me all the time, that God loves me and longs to be with me.

Wait a minute. That's already happened. Oops. I keep forgetting.

Espresso Shots:

1. *Are you and God close?*
2. *Do you feel God's presence? Do you hear God speak to you?*
3. *Does God feel your presence? Does God hear you speak?*

HOBBITS AND ADVENTURES

"Hobbits don't like adventures" is how the graduation speech began. What followed was a message about finding the courage to leave the shire and trusting that the adventure of the unknown will outweigh the comfort of the familiar. Yes, there will be mountains and valleys, companions and dragons, but in the end, the hobbit will be changed in dramatic and wonderful ways.

It would have been a good graduation speech on its own, but it came from a boy who, two years earlier, was curled up in the safety of his bed. Diagnosed with Asperger's Syndrome, he did not know if he wanted to live anymore, and yet, in that very dark place, his mother found a special school far away. He would have to leave the familiarity of his "hobbit hole" and go on an adventure into the unknown. However, because of Asperger's, his fears were larger, the mountains higher, woods darker, and dragons more ferocious.

But somewhere, somehow, he rose from his bed and got in the car. He survived the first day, then the second, before realizing there was hope. In two years, that lost child was found, or as the Bible puts it, "He was dead and is alive again." Now he stood before his classmates—faithful companions and dragon-slayers one and all—and delivered a commencement address I'll never forget. I give thanks for the courage he found, the companions he walked with, and the opportunities he seized.

He was forever changed because of the adventure, as were his parents.

Espresso Shots:

1. *When have you been stuck in the familiar but afraid of the unknown?*

2. *When did you find the courage to go beyond the familiar, and what did you discover by doing so?*

3. *In what ways are there adventures calling you? What would it take to answer?*

ROOM 325

Walking down the once familiar hallway,
I travel somewhere between then and now.
Rooms with unfamiliar names,
Call forth echoes of residents past.
The corridor is smaller, or I'm larger.
Time travel makes me dizzy.

Room 325 hasn't moved,
And I stand feeling as if I should remove my shoes.
The same hand grasps the same handle,
Thirty-five years later,
And sees a familiar sight:
A carpet of discarded clothes, a towel strewn upon a chair,
And a bed ravaged by the sudden departure for a first-period class.
Unopened books sit on the desk.

The room is mine, but the clothes are not.
I'll loan it to others, I suppose,
Forever,
And depart as if an intruder.

My headmaster is now a portrait.
Teachers archived in frames.
The acned youth walk by unimpressed.
"In my day …" I want to say,
But it's no use,
The bell rings to call us to the passage of time.

Espresso Shots:

1. *When was the last time you returned to a place of your youth?*
2. *What were your feelings and thoughts in such a space?*
3. *List three things you know now that you wish you'd known then.*

THE TRINITY

My sister is an artist who uses a needle and thread to create works of art that adorn many houses. She began with needlepoint but eventually moved to quilting. One of her quilts lies at the foot of our guest room bed. It's a masterpiece of intricate colors and patterns. If I stand back, it's one beautiful quilt. If I draw close, it is many small pieces of colorful fabric.

It's not unlike my sister, herself. Standing back, she's a woman sewing a quilt. If I draw closer, she's a daughter, wife, mother, and grandmother creating works of art for the people she loves. Like the quilt in her hands, she is made up of many colorful pieces sewn together into a wonderful creation.

I remember the first time a minister tried to explain the Trinity in a sermon. She began well but then got tangled up in the three in one and one in three. I've entangled myself whenever I've tried to figure out God. So, I draw near and celebrate God as the creator. I look over and appreciate God's love and redemption in Jesus, and I dance with God's continuing presence in my life through the Holy Spirit. These are the three ways in which God is known to me. When I stand back, I'm unable to see where one ends, and the other begins. I see one God.

It can make me feel spiritually dizzy if I think about it too long, so I decide to nap in the guest room under my sister's beautiful quilt.

Espresso Shots:

1. *In what ways do you know God?*

2. *Have you ever tried to figure out God?*

3. *If you were to draw close and stand back, how would your view of God change?*

CALLUSES

My childhood summers began when my shoes came off on Memorial Day and ended on Labor Day when I reluctantly put them on again. I remember the freedom of walking barefoot on the sidewalk and comfort when my feet were buried in the warm sand. My shiny white feet were sore at first, but within a week or two, the color of my feet matched my legs, and a layer of protection grew on my soles. By the end of summer, my calluses rivaled the sturdiest construction boots.

Looking back, I'm grateful for nature's way of protecting my tender feet, but I've come to see that calluses are not always good things, particularly when they form on our hearts. Like my shiny white feet, there was a time when my heart was soft and exposed to the world. I don't remember it, but I'll bet I could feel the world and people around me like the first few days of summer when I walked gingerly on the sidewalk and sand. I can only imagine some of what caused the calluses to grow, but I can also point to specific things that made me put a layer or two around my heart for protection.

I'm grateful for that protection, I suppose, but sometimes the layers grow too thick. With each layer comes more distance between us and our lives; eventually we must try to scrape at least some of the protection away. It's not pleasant work, but we were created to feel. While our bodies try to protect us from pain, our souls long to be set free. It may mean more hot sidewalks and stubbed toes, but it will be worth it.

Espresso Shots:

1. *How thick are the calluses around your heart?*
2. *What do you recall happening that made the calluses form?*
3. *What would it take to remove some of the calluses, and what do you think the benefits would be?*

THE CAMERA LENS

"Watch your camera lens," my writing instructor said. She wanted me to focus on a single detail, one moment, then broaden the scope. It's advice I hold onto when writing. I also need to remember it when living.

To focus one's lens on a small detail can be powerful. A child's hand placed in yours, a spouse's light touch when you're emotional, or an encouraging note or comment just when you need it are moments we should slow down and focus with as tight a lens as possible.

But keeping our lens tight can be overwhelming and destructive. We can lose sight of the bigger story, and small moments can dominate the narrative. Instead, we need to learn to widen and tighten our lenses. I suppose that's why I make a point of walking on the beach and hiking mountains. Both activities right-size me. It's also why I go to church and AA meetings.

Summer is a great time to adjust our lens. We have many opportunities to focus on time with family. We can also widen our gaze and see a larger horizon. The key is to be mindful of the camera lens. It can make a story, as well as our lives, come alive.

Espresso Shots:

1. Take a moment to focus on one specific aspect of your life. Study it.
2. Now widen your lens and see your life from a larger perspective.
3. Develop an intentional practice of adjusting your camera lens each day.

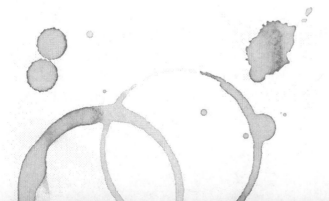

NOT MUCH OF A CARPENTER

I'm not much of a carpenter, but that's not the point. Despite spending hours of my youth in my brother's workshop in the basement, I never got past the basics. Still, when I decided to build a container for the trash and recycling cans, I awakened with the excitement of a child on the first day of summer vacation. Over coffee, I made my plans and figured out everything I'd need and drove to the hardware store. I set up a workstation and determined the order in which I should proceed. I cut the supports and screwed them together.

While correcting several errors, I marveled at my friends who make this kind of work look easy. The sides were next, then the hinges and the top. In the end, I pulled it off, but anyone who looked closely would see many imperfections. Putting away my tools, it was clear I wasn't much of a carpenter, but that's not the point.

My efforts to construct a life of faith are not unlike constructing such a container. I awaken every morning with high hopes and spend time getting ready before I begin. I make plans, but either the day itself or my scattered heart usually gets in the way. Mistakes are constant, and I need to stop and correct them. There are those who make such spiritual work look easy, but I push on. Whether it's a day that feels like a disaster or one that's not so bad, I am fully aware of the fact that I'm not much of a carpenter, but that's not the point. I can get lost in judging my work, comparing it to that of others, but this is a fruitless endeavor. Instead, I need to see that I showed up and cared enough to try. Even though I'm not much of a carpenter, that's the point.

Espresso Shots:

1. Recall a time when you joyfully built something. What was it and how did it make you feel before, during, and after?

2. Compare that experience to your efforts to live a spiritual life. How are they similar? What can such a comparison teach you?

3. In what ways can you help remind yourself that it's not about being a good carpenter but about showing up and trying?

CHANGING OUR SWING

He went to see a golf instructor to get help with his game. He was a functional golfer, as he liked to put it, but wanted to improve his game. The instructor identified a number of things he could improve. Shift your grip, he said. Widen your stance, and focus on your rhythm. Under the instructor's watchful eye, the man was successful, but when he went off by himself to practice, it was as if his entire game unraveled.

I smiled as he told me his story, not because I took delight in his struggle but because I knew what it was like to try to improve something and watch as things felt like they were coming apart. Most recently, it happened in my personal life.

I am working with a wonderful therapist. She's a pro, and I'm eager to address things that are getting in the way of living an authentic, meaningful life. After listening to my story, she makes suggestions and challenges long-held beliefs. She questions stories I've been telling myself and pokes and prods me in uncomfortable ways. In her office, things make sense, but each time I leave to practice what we've talked about, it's as if I am losing my mind. Forgotten emotions resurface, thoughts swirl in my head, and it feels like my inner life is unraveling.

"That's what getting well is all about," she told me. "It begins with the courage to try, continues when you make changes, then it's about weathering the uncertainty of living life in new ways." During a particularly rough day, I clung to her counsel and trusted that the way I was feeling was a part of getting better. I was tempted to return to my old, familiar ways, but reminded myself that I, like my friend, wanted to change my swing, so I carried on

Espresso Shots:

1. *When have you tried to make changes in your life (at work, in a relationship, in your spiritual life)?*

2. *Did things feel like they got worse before they got better?*

3. *Did you weather the storm, or return to the way things were before?*

ADJUSTING THE KNOBS

I drove across the country with a friend before my senior year in high school. Back when radios had knobs, we listened to music the whole way to California and back. One knob was for volume, the other for finding a station. It was the job of whoever was in the passenger seat to find a good station. I remember finding a great station outside St. Louis and sat back to enjoy the music, but it wasn't long before we heard the first bit of static and then more. Eventually there was so much static, I had to adjust the knob. When the static returned, I had to find another station.

I think our experience in the car is similar to living a life of faith. It can be a wonderful adventure, but it's hard to keep the radio tuned to the right station. As we travel, static arrives. It's not too bad at first, but the noise increases as we travel farther from the signal. Eventually we need to adjust the knobs—and maybe even change stations.

Adjusting the knobs and changing the stations is part of the spiritual journey. The good news is there's a signal. It just needs to be found. It doesn't move: we do. Our job is to adjust the knobs so we can hear the music as we travel.

Espresso Shots:

1. *In what ways is your spiritual life like tuning into a radio?*

2. *In what ways does static get in the way of hearing the signal?*

3. *What are the ways you can adjust the knobs?*

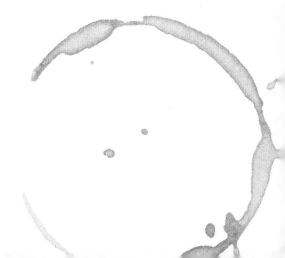

HAPPY PLACE

This week, I received a number of Instagram posts showing pictures of beautiful places with the caption, "My Happy Place." Pictures of beaches, camps, mountain sunsets, and even a pilot looking out above clouds made a fascinating collage. Such places filled friends' souls, but it made me wonder if everyone has such a place.

There are many places in which I've been happy. Sitting beside a waterfall, walking beside a dramatic sea, and watching a colorful sunrise or sunset are among my favorites. I once went to such a place and was filled with a happiness the likes of which I'd never felt. It made such a lasting impression, that I went back to the exact location so I could feel the same elation. Much to my surprise and disappointment, I felt nothing, despite sitting on the very same rock and looking out at the very same view. It was still beautiful. It just didn't stir my soul as it once had.

I remember a *New York Times* wine critic being asked about the best bottle of wine he'd ever had. Given his access to priceless vintages, his answer surprised everyone. It was a bottle anyone could find in a grocery store. He had opened the bottle while rowing on a lake on a misty evening with the woman who would eventually be his wife. Years later, they returned to the same lake and opened the same wine on one of their anniversaries, but it wasn't the same. It had nothing to do with the wine, they learned.

So it is with happy places. Happiness comes from somewhere beyond mountains, sea, or wine. Certain places can open our hearts in wonderful ways, but the happiness lies elsewhere. It cannot be manufactured, manipulated, or bottled. Happiness is a gift, wrapped in many packages. When given, we should receive it with grateful hearts. We should give thanks not to the gift, but the one who gave it, our true happiness.

Espresso Shots:

1. *Where is your happy place?*
2. *When you are there, what is it that fills your soul?*
3. *Is it the place that makes you happy—or where your heart goes when you're there?*

THE RHYTHM OF THE BEACH

The first day at the beach is always an adjustment. Travel is over, and I awaken to different air, sounds, lighting, and scenery. Being at the beach is more than arriving. It doesn't just happen. I have to slow my pace and quiet my mind.

Walking on the shore with my glistening white feet, I let the water wash away another year's toil. The waves come onto the shore, then recede, like a heartbeat, and I encourage my breathing to follow along. My mind, however, is not as quick to comply. Thoughts about yesterday's travel and the work I left behind distract me. I've brought more books than I can possibly read, a list of calls I should make, and an overstuffed beach bag of concerns I'm determined to figure out while on vacation. The seagulls laugh at my plans.

My pace slows as one foot after the other sinks into the wet sand. The waves and the birds go about their business, and the present moment waits for me to arrive. Like a child wrestling with a blanket and protesting they are not tired, I fight slowing down. Still, I carry on, knowing my heart and mind will eventually find the rhythm of the beach. It's a familiar first-day-at-the-beach liturgy, and I comply to the call to worship.

Espresso Shots:

1. *When was the last time you slowed down?*

2. *What's the hardest part of getting your heart and mind to join you on vacation?*

3. *Is there a way to slow to the rhythm of the beach even when you're not there?*

SAILING UPWIND

I'm not a sailor, although I have enormous respect for those who are. I have never figured out how a boat can travel upwind. Sailing downwind is easy to comprehend; upwind is a mystery. My brother has tried to explain the physics of it all, but I still don't understand.

As I navigate through life, I can sail two directions. I can go downwind, which takes little effort or thought. All I have to do is open my sails and let the wind take me where it will. The other choice is to sail upwind, which requires thought and effort. Both trips use the same wind, but depending upon which tack I chose, I'll end up in different places. One is easy, the other difficult, but I'm convinced the thought and effort required in sailing upwind is the "more excellent" way Paul refers to in 1 Corinthians.

To open our sails and let the breeze blow us downwind is easy and takes little thought, but we will likely end up where we'd rather not. Heading in the other direction is more difficult but leads to a better place. One is about sailing by our own wind, the other with God's. I still don't understand sailing, but I see how it can teach me about life.

Espresso Shots:

1. *When have you sailed downwind, and where did it take you?*

2. *Have you ever made the effort to use the wind in another way and head upwind?*

3. *What would it take to turn your life toward God's will?*

SWIMMING POOLS

This is the season of swimming pools. The air is filled with the sound of splashing and shouting. It's also a time for adults to sit at the water's edge and unwind. Whether dangling feet in the water or sitting in a chair, staring out at the water can allow our minds and hearts to wander and souls to breathe. Pools have much to say. Their clean, cool water is an invitation to remember the need for refreshment, but there's also something more.

At one end the water is shallow, the other deep. I remember as a child walking from the shallow end to the deep, feeling the water rise above my bathing suit, up my chest, over my neck, lips, and eventually eyes and hair, until I was completely submerged. It was at this point I had to begin swimming. My feet went from standing to kicking, my arms from floating to moving from side to side, keeping my head above the surface.

Small children play in the shallow end, where they belong. Eventually they'll long for deeper water. At the other end, adults swim. Some challenge themselves by diving for objects. Others leap from the diving board, trying to make a big splash or perfect dive.

In which end of the pool do we live? Do we live where our feet can touch the ground or where we need to swim? Do we like the security of the shallow end or the adventure of the deep? Are we willing to look for things below the surface, or are we focused on making a splash for all to admire?

Sitting by the pool, watching and listening to summer at its best, can remind us about our lives away from the pool. Maybe it's time we look at how we swim.

Espresso Shots:

1. *Did you favor the shallow or deep end of the pool as a child? Why?*
2. *Which end of the pool do you prefer now? Why?*
3. *Is God inviting you to swim in a new way?*

LOWERING THE CENTERBOARD

In my creative pursuits, I sometimes flounder. Dizzy with ideas, I don't know where to start or what to do next. With such abundance, you might think the progress would be plentiful, but it isn't.

My spiritual life can be the same way. My desire to go deeper increases, and I start to read several new books. Suddenly I am lost among too many possibilities. Whenever this happens, I'm reminded of something that happened one day when we were sailing. There was plenty of wind, but we couldn't get the boat to go forward. We tried adjusting both the mainsail and jib, but the boat didn't respond. Then we realized the centerboard was lifted out of the water. With one simple push, the boat glided forward, and we were on our way. It was such a silly thing to forget and such a simple thing to do. With the centerboard down, the boat moved forward.

I try to look for some small gesture in my creative life that will cause me to move forward. It doesn't have to be anything grand. It can be as simple as pushing the centerboard down and experiencing a surge forward. When I am lost in possibilities, I look for something specific I can do to move me ahead.

Author and writing coach Julia Cameron has made a name for herself working with blocked creatives. She advises creatives to do one small thing when we feel stuck. For writers, craft a sentence or paragraph; for painters, pick up a brush. She knows from personal experience that a small gesture can get an artist back on track. The same is true for our spiritual lives as well. All we have to do is lower the centerboard.

Espresso Shots:

1. *Identify a time when you were stuck.*
2. *How could you have lowered the centerboard and begun moving forward again?*
3. *What small gesture could you do today to make progress?*

YOUR SOUNDTRACK

In anticipation of a big birthday, I compiled several songs that had meant something to me throughout my life. This life soundtrack was as exciting as it was revealing. Certain songs were integral to specific chapters of my life. As each song played, I could tell you who I was with and where I was.

Like my life, my soundtrack was eclectic. It went from sappy to rock, from showtunes to classical. Some songs reminded me of fun times, others of dark days. In the end, the soundtrack provided a musical landscape, capturing the highs and lows and twists and turns of my life.

Sometimes spiritual work involves looking back, recalling people, places, and moments from your past. Getting in touch with who we were at different chapters in our life can help us understand our journeys and the people we've become.

What song do you remember from middle school? Was it a happy time in your life? Who was your best friend?

What was the song you listened to when you first fell in love?

What song did you play when you needed to let your soul breath?

What song did you dance to at your wedding?

What was a song you remember introducing to your child?

What was the first song to move you, spiritually?

What hymn was played at (fill in the blank)'s funeral?

Espresso Shots:

1. *Make a twenty-five-song soundtrack of your life.*
2. *Add another twenty-five songs.*
3. *Play it and talk about the songs with someone to whom you're close.*

HAVING FAITH

One of my mentors used to tell the story of taking his boat to the local marina for repairs. When he arrived, a man was sitting on the dock smoking his pipe. My friend explained the problem he was having, and the man stood and began working on the boat. It took a while, but the man fixed the problem. As he was putting the engine cover back on, the owner of the marina arrived. Confused, my friend asked who was fixing the boat. It turned out the guy was just someone who stopped each morning to shoot the breeze.

"So, you're not a mechanic?" my friend asked. "How'd you fix my boat?"

"You thought I could, so I figured I should give it a try."

This story always reminds me of the power of faith. My friend believed the man could fix the boat, and the man responded by doing just that.

Hopefully we've all had people who believed in us. Sometimes, they had faith when we didn't, but because of their faith, we responded by doing things we never thought possible.

When I look at the New Testament, I see Jesus believing in people. His faith in them caused them to be and do things they never thought possible. So often we talk about having faith in God. Sometimes it's important to see God's faith in us and how it can empower us to become more than we ever thought possible.

Espresso Shots:

1. *Think of one person who had faith in you.*
2. *What did that person's faith inspire you to do or be?*
3. *Write and thank that person, if possible, or pass on their faith in you by believing in someone else.*

CLOUDY DAYS

I expect too much of life. I first suspected it in high school when I thought my classmates should behave a certain way. It was confirmed when I started dating and again with every job. This morning, as I awaken at the beach on a cloudy, rainy day, I'm reminded of it once again.

There is little better in life than a sunny day at the beach. Looking out at waves breaking, birds swooping, and fish leaping can fill my soul like nothing else. Watching as children make sandcastles and play tag with the sea can turn back the years, if only for a moment.

As an adult, I have learned that sandcastles wash away and games end. It is tempting to expect life or people to remain a certain way, but that's like wanting it to be sunny at the beach every day. When I accept the cloudy day as an invitation to give my sunburned neck a break and use the time away as an opportunity to explore, the day is suddenly transformed.

The lesson, of course, is not about inclement weather. It's about accepting changes and finding new life in that acceptance. Whether with work or homes, each other or ourselves, the cloudy days will come, but so will the sunny ones. Accepting whatever weather comes our way is to accept life on life's terms, and that always leads to brighter days.

Espresso Shots:

1. *When was a time your expectations got in the way?*

2. *When did you find new life through accepting people, places, and things as they were?*

3. *What would acceptance look like at work, at home, for yourself, and for others?*

WALKING

I prepared for the run for weeks. I worked up to long distances, then tapered off the week before the race. Standing with the other runners, waiting for the start, I felt ready. With unbridled excitement, I set off faster than usual. I tried to keep up with the runners who looked like they knew what they were doing, but I soon ran out of steam. I ran at a pace that was not mine, and I knew I wouldn't finish if I didn't slow down to my own pace. Consumed with reaching the finish line, I did not look at the scenery or converse with the other runners. I made it, but most of the miles were simply endured.

Behind me, my stepdaughter and her close friend made their way along the course. They decided to walk the 13.1 miles instead of run, and they held hands and sang songs most the way.

They waved to the crowd cheering them on and shouted encouragement to the runners beside them. For them, it wasn't a race at all.

I hardly said a word at breakfast the next morning, but the two girls laughed and joked. I limped to the car to drive home, but they skipped. I doubted I would ever run such a race again, but they were already making plans for next year.

Espresso Shots:

1. *How often are you so consumed with the race that you miss the scenery or people around you?*

2. *When was the last time you walked, held hands, or sang?*

3. *When have you finished a race but never wanted to run again?*

A SPIRITUAL NOMAD

"How can we sing the songs of the Lord while in a foreign land?" —*Psalm 137:4*

Elmer Picket was a creature of habit. He awakened every morning at 6 a.m. and did his chores between his first cup of coffee and breakfast. He wore the same boots he'd worn for years and always hung his coat on the hook to the right of the kitchen door. Routine gave him a sense of comfort, which is why he was so disturbed when he came in one morning and realized his coat hook was gone.

"What am I supposed to do with my coat?" he asked his wife, who explained she was redecorating the entrance way.

"You'll just have to hang your coat on another hook," she replied.

Espresso Shots:

1. *Where do you hang your coat, spiritually?*
2. *How can you be flexible about finding another hook?*
3. *When have you felt like you were praising God in a foreign land?*

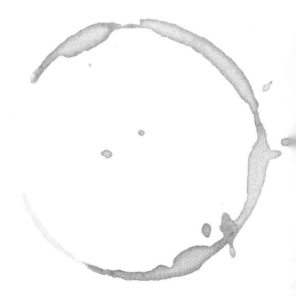

SEARCHING FOR HOME

What do you do when something you've relied on and been comforted by and expected is taken away? That's the question so many of us have been asking as we try to adapt to life during the pandemic. Some of the changes have been small, others significant, but all of them have left us off-center and out of sorts.

For me, the biggest adjustment has been finding a spiritual home. I love and rely on church to ground me and connect me with God and others. Going to church on Sunday—hearing the organ, singing the hymns, listening to the lessons and sermon, and seeing others—feeds my soul. It's a routine I enjoy, but it's been taken away, and I've struggled more than I thought I would without it. Our church, like many others, has worked hard to offer alternatives, but virtual church just doesn't do it for me.

I've taken walks, listened to music, subscribed to inspirational podcasts, sat in solitude with candles, but none of them has taken the place of going to church.

I know the church is not a building. There are other places I can feed my soul, but I miss my church!

Espresso Shots:

1. *Besides church, what spiritual disciplines connect you to God?*

2. *What practices connect you to others?*

3. *What do you like most about going to church?*

TOO SMALL FOR YOUR BRITCHES

"You're too big for your britches," my mother would say whenever I was overly focused on myself. It was an effective reprimand, one that burst my bubble like a needle against a balloon. Inevitably though, the balloon (and my ego) filled up again.

When I think about living a spiritual life, committing to a life aligned with a purpose, I think we have the opposite problem: we're too *small* for our britches.

We are raised to do more, achieve more. As a result, we try to climb as high as we can. Sometimes the result causes us to become inflated, too big for our britches, and life finds a way to right-size us. However, when it comes to our spiritual life, many of us are reticent to climb; we reach only for what is well within our grasp. In other words, we remain too small for our britches. We write a check instead of giving our time to a cause. We are quick to give voice to our faith but slow to live it out. We care about those in need and think a bag of donated cans will be enough.

Can you imagine if we were as bold with our faith as we are in our careers? Instead of giving canned goods, we would bring our full selves to work to eradicate hunger in our community. Instead of writing a check here and there, those with the resources could give a largesse from their portfolios. Instead of complaining about politicians, we would run for office. When it comes to living out our faith, being too big for our britches would be a welcomed change.

Espresso Shots:

1. *How does your professional effort compare with your spiritual one?*
2. *Have you ever done anything bold spiritually?*
3. *What would it look like to be too big (or bigger than you are) for your britches, spiritually?*

PERFECT PITCH

"It's the place about which I have perfect pitch." —*Reynolds Price*

When Wendy arrived for her audition, she was asked to sing a song other than the one she had prepared. It was a familiar song, but not in her range, which caused her to struggle on the high notes. Before crossing her name off the list, however, the director asked her to sing a song of her choosing, which revealed her significant talent. He heard her perfect pitch.

***

He was not like the other fathers. He couldn't throw a football, was incapable of going camping, and was completely uncomfortable at father-son nights at his child's woodshop class. But he could play any song on the piano by ear, perform on the organ with both hands dancing across the numerous keyboards and feet on the pedals, and, most impressive of all, compose music while sitting on the beach, not hearing a single note. Music was his home, the place he had perfect pitch, literally and figuratively.

***

She and her husband questioned having children. With emerging careers, and a love for the freedom of being child-free, they seriously considered remaining so. However, children arrived, and suddenly she found a part of her heart she didn't know existed. The determined professional gave way to the enthralled mother. Never looking back, she embraced motherhood fully. She found her true self, her perfect pitch.

Espresso Shots:

1. *Have you ever tried to sing a song that was not yours, or not in your range?*

2. *Have you ever sung your true song with perfect pitch?*

3. *What would it take to sing only the songs meant for you?*

DOWN TO THE STUDS

On our way to Disney World, my family and I stopped for the night in Beaufort, South Carolina, where my wife's relative lives in an antebellum home overlooking the waterfront. The owner, an architect, has worked continuously on the house, stripping it down to the studs and repairing the plaster walls. He's brought it back to its original charm without adorning it with excess decorations.

Disney was a culture shock after visiting his home. With everything designed to be magical, the litter-free streets, pristine architecture, and piped-in music made me long for the rustic old house in Beaufort. It's not that Disney World isn't impressive—it's just not real. Given the long lines at the amusement park, I could see there's a great hunger for make believe.

There was a time when I was enchanted by Disney and all things neat and tidy. I took comfort in television shows that showed perfect families, successful friends who seemed to have it all together, and a church that promised, with Jesus, everything would work out well.

Now I know there's no such thing as a perfect family. No matter how things appear on the surface, there's more to the story than meets the eye. This is not to say that life is not enchanted. It is. It's just not make-believe. In the imperfections, there's real life. Even in the not-working-out-the-way-we-would-like, there's magic.

You might need to look a bit harder, have more faith, but when life is stripped down to the studs, it's often an enchanted kingdom.

Espresso Shots:

1. *When were you drawn to something that was perfect but not real?*

2. *In what ways do you care more about the outward appearances than the solid foundation?*

3. *How can you find and celebrate the messy real life found behind or beneath a person's appearance, including yourself?*

FEAR

I'm afraid of fear. I know that's redundant, but it's also true. I'm not sure whether I was born this way or if I learned it, but the fact is, I run the other way whenever fear arrives. I sometimes act as if fear doesn't exist, so I appear confident and brave—but that's just fear wearing a costume.

I'm in a program that speaks of living life surrounded by a hundred forms of fear. We share how we've coped (badly) with our fears and learn from one another about better ways to live. Self-help author Elizabeth Gilbert says fear is often in the car with us; the trick is not letting it drive.

There's nothing a person can do to keep fear from showing up, but we have much we can do once it's in the room. We can acknowledge it. We can listen to what it's trying to say. Best of all, we can use fear to help us grow. Through her book, *The Artist's Way*, Julia Cameron taught me to see fear as a road sign, letting me know when there's danger or a sharp turn ahead.

For me, fear always points me to faith. It's not that faith will eliminate fear; it's just stronger. Fear makes me feel alone. Faith reminds me I'm not. God's got it. God's got me, fears and all.

A classmate in seminary once told the story of teaching his son how to jump off a diving board. With knees shaking, his son stood at the edge of the diving board paralyzed with fear as he looked down to the water. His dad was in the water below with arms opened wide, calling out, "I've got you."

Whenever I'm fearful, I think of that boy at the end of the diving board. More than the shaking knees or the water below, I try to focus on the father with his arms open wide, saying, "I've got you."

Espresso Shots:

1. *What is your greatest fear?*
2. *To what do you think it is trying to point?*
3. *In what ways could you keep fear from driving the car?*

NEW FRAMES

I recently decided to tackle some long-neglected home projects. I filed paperwork, put new batteries in the smoke detectors, and returned each bicycle to operational form. As is so often the case, one project led to another, and I turned my attention to the many photographs displayed throughout our home. Some needed to be replaced with more current photos, but others just needed new frames. It's remarkable how much better a picture can look when it's put in a suitable frame.

Because of the time of year, I began to think about Father's Day as I moved photos from one frame to another. Father's Day is a wonderful celebration for many, but there are those for whom it's not an easy day. "It's complicated," said a friend when he spoke of Father's Day, and I couldn't agree more. Listening to many songs about fathers has shown me what a common struggle Father's Day can be.

Like New Year's Eve, when people put on silly hats and drink too much all in the name of forcing a good time, Father's Day can feel a bit orchestrated. Like midnight on January 1, we wait for the band to play only to see all the ways we haven't been the fathers we hoped to be. This year I'm going to fight such morose thoughts and let the day be what it is. I'm going to accept my fatherhood for what it is. I'm going to look at Father's Day anew, giving thanks for the many blessings rather than bemoaning the many shortcomings. In other words, I'm going to take all my old thoughts and images out of their frames and replace them with new ones.

Espresso Shots:

1. Which relationship in your life needs a new frame?

2. What is wrong with the current frame?

3. How could you see the relationship in a new way if you put it in a new frame?

WALKING THE TRAIL

There it was, the actual Appalachian Trail. The sign beside the road said so. With great excitement, I pulled over and walked a portion of the famous trail that leads from Georgia to Maine. I've read countless books about the trail and always hoped I would hike it from one end to the other.

With reverence, I approached the small, unassuming entrance into the woods. Without the sign, I would have missed it. I knew in my mind it was just like any other trail, but because it was the Appalachian Trail, I felt like I was processing down the aisle of a cathedral.

Until that afternoon, I had only read about the Appalachian Trail. Now, I had actually experienced it, if only for a mile or two. Part of me wanted to choose which was better: firsthand experience on the brief portion I'd walked or books describing the entire trail.

I live in that same tension spiritually. Surrounded by books and creeds, I have learned much about God and the spiritual life. I've also had a few moments when I have ventured out and tried to live a spiritual life, if only for a mile or two. Like so many other situations, I am tempted to pick one over the other, but the fact is I need both. I need to hear about the journey from those with greater experience, just as I need firsthand experience.

Fortunately, the great cloud of witnesses took the time to map out what they saw, who they came to know, and to record their successes and mistakes. Their work makes it possible for me to get out of the car and walk on the trail. It's not an either/or thing, but a both/and. So, with book in hand, I will carry on down the trail.

Espresso Shots:

1. Are you more a reader about or an explorer of the spiritual life?
2. In what ways do books and the experiences of others feed your soul?
3. In what ways do you avoid the trail by only reading about it?

CHANNEL MARKERS

Much of my childhood summers was spent on the water. It was there I learned, sometimes through error, the importance of channel markers. Green on one side, red on the other, they provide navigational clues through narrow or shallow passages. I always thought of the two markers as separate—one was green, the other red, one was on the left, the other on the right—but I've come to see how connected they are.

We live in a world that likes to see differences. The clarity we feel when one thing is this way and another is that prevents us from seeing connections. To see how seemingly opposites are connected is to find channel markers through which we can sail.

The need for love is connected to a fear of getting hurt.

The drive to be successful is connected to weak self-esteem.

The desire for certainty is connected to persistent doubts.

Theologian Richard Rohr, one of my favorite writers, cautions against either-or thinking. This approach, he says, thwarts all theological, social, and political growth. Identifying extremes is the first step of healthy navigation; understanding their connection is the second. The channel markers help us find a passage between. Whether sailing on a bay or walking through a day, such navigational wisdom can lead to safer, deeper waters.

Espresso Shots:

1. *In what areas of your life do you fall into dualistic, either/or, thinking?*
2. *Can you see the connection between seeming opposites?*
3. *How can you learn to navigate between them to deeper waters?*

AUTOMATIC PILOT

He had purchased a new boat and was eager to show it to his friends. He waited with the engine running at the dock at the lake's edge, and he couldn't wait to show his friends what the boat could do. They were impressed with the seats and comforts of the boat, but once they were out in open water, he showed them the feature of the boat that truly set it apart.

"Look at this," he said. "It has an automatic pilot feature. When I push this, the boat heads in whatever direction I tell it to, so I don't have to think about it."

After all the ooo's and aah's of the passengers, one person asked how the automatic pilot knows where the rocks are. The owner of the boat hesitated. "It doesn't," he said, and he turned their attention toward something else.

It took me years to understand the dangers of traveling on automatic pilot. The ease of travel and not having to think outweighed the danger. Being able to travel hands free means you are able to do other things while traveling.

Then there are the rocks. No matter how sophisticated our automatic pilot may be, it cannot navigate around the rocks. It cannot discern, anticipate, or react. All it knows is how to head in a certain direction. It's only a matter of time before it plows into the rocks.

Espresso Shots:

1.   How often in a day do you travel on automatic pilot?

2.   When has doing so served you well, and when has it not?

3.   How can you learn to travel intentionally, with hands on the wheel and eyes looking ahead?

IMITATING

When it comes to our spiritual lives, who are we imitating? Who do we admire and want to be like? Is it a father, mother, or some other mentor? In a world that emphasizes the importance of being unique, we've lost sight of the value of imitation. Like a child trying to be like a parent, imitation can point us in a certain direction. Paradoxically, we then use our gifts to become unique imitations.

For Christians, the one we are to imitate is clear. Scripture tells us we are to seek to be Christ-like—to imitate him in his words and deeds.

I'm embarrassed by how little I've imitated Jesus. Too often, I've focused on being independent and unique. I've picked a few characteristics of Jesus I like but ignored others. I've tried to follow some of his teachings but have never "put on the mind of Christ," as Paul put it.

To fully imitate Jesus would mean focusing on him and then heading in his direction. It would mean spending time getting to know him. Then it would mean trying to be like him in my own way. For me, that would require a lot of changes. Certain behaviors would need to cease while others would need to begin. Certain longheld views would need to be released and new ones adopted. The words I say should sound like him. The actions I take should be like his.

I'll never be more than an imitation, but that, at least, would be a step in the right direction.

Espresso Shots:

1. *When it came to your spiritual life, who have you imitated?*
2. *In what ways does your life reflect the God you claim to believe in?*
3. *What would it mean to be an authentic (and unique) imitation?*

VIA NEGATIVA

The art instructor gathered the class for a demonstration. With a piece of charcoal and a large sheet of paper, she drew a picture of the still-life arrangement set out before the class. Unlike her other demonstrations, this time she drew everything that was *not* the still life. She drew the spaces between the apple and the banana, the space between the bowl and the fruit. Her drawing looked strange at first, but then the class began to see the drawing come to life. By drawing everything that was not the still life, she drew a vivid picture of a bowl with fruit.

The churchy term for this is, *via negativa,* which means coming to know something by seeing everything it is not. It is a powerful tool in art and theology—and also in life.

If you go to the self-help section at your local bookstore, you'll find countless books on how to know your true self. They vary in methods, but what they have in common is directing readers to look closely at themselves so they can be happier, thinner, or more successful.

Like staring at something for too long, we can lose sight of ourselves if we stare too much. Sometimes, we need to see ourselves from a different perspective. Instead of looking at who we are, we should look at who we aren't. It's strange and awkward at first, but, like the art demonstration, we begin to see a vivid picture of ourselves once we identify all the things we are not.

Espresso Shots:

1. *Make a long, specific list of all the things you are not.*

2. *Look at the list and see what it shows you about yourself by identifying the person you aren't.*

3. *How can you use the via negativa tool to better grow into the person you are?*

CLIMBING THE FAMILY TREE

While reading the opening chapter of Matthew's Gospel, I can't help but hear the question once asked of me by a Richmond, Virginia, socialite when I was applying for a job: "And who are your people?" I didn't understand her question, just as I have no idea why Matthew begins his gospel with a genealogy of Jesus. I guess it has something to do with a person's roots.

We live in a world where we are taught to run, so thoughts about roots, which hold us to the ground, seem arcane and irrelevant. But such reflection can be meaningful, if done for the right reasons.

My eldest sister is the family archivist. She can not only identify every ancestral portrait but also tell you where the person lived and some interesting facts. I don't know what spurs her interest. Maybe it's because she is the oldest child—or maybe she has a strong need to feel connected to those who came before.

There was a time when I dismissed such things. The portraits were just paintings, and the stories were entertaining tales about people I'll never know. Now, I realize that even without knowing the people of my past, they're a part of my life. They're threads in a fabric intertwined with my own. Whether I knew them or not, they are the ground into which I am planted. Just like my roots sink deep beneath the surface, the influence of my ancestors lies beyond my sight or understanding.

Perhaps understanding who my people are is more valuable than I know.

Espresso Shots:

1. *How far back in your family tree can you climb?*

2. *Find someone on that tree that stands out and research them.*

3. *In what ways do you think your ancestors influence your life today?*

FILLING HOLES

A child went to the beach and began his favorite pastime, digging holes. He crouched beside the sea and dug like a dog and then knelt and scooped the sand with his hand until he felt the hole was deep and wide enough. Sitting beside his hole, he waited for a wave to make his project complete. Sometimes one came quickly; other times a wave only drew close enough to taunt the boy. Either way, the boy's happiness depended on the whims of the sea. One day, he dug deeper than usual and found the sand grew moist. Water became visible with each handful of sand, and before long he was sitting in a pool of water without any help from the sea.

Sand turned into books, digging into employment, but the game remained the same. As before, he worked hard to create a space but relied on the sea to complete his efforts. Only in time did he learn to dig deeper. When he did, he found water beneath the surface.

Espresso Shots:

1. *When have you dug holes and waited for the sea to fill them?*
2. *What kind of water are you searching for?*
3. *Have you ever dug deeper and found water beneath the surface?*

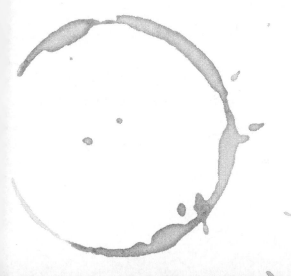

THE WHITES OF OUR EYES

"Don't shoot until you see the whites of their eyes," the American commander William Prescott shouted at Bunker Hill, reminding his troops to wait until the enemy was close enough to ensure a good chance of hitting their targets. This advice assumed the enemy would rise and climb the hill despite their fears. The soldiers would need to draw close and engage with the enemy, so close they could see the whites of their eyes.

Although the moment is tucked safely away in history, it can still speak to us today from a personal and spiritual perspective. It is easier to stay far apart than draw close. Staying hunkered down is safer than rising above our fears and climbing the hill that lies before us. Technology has increased our ability to stay far apart. We can now send an email, text, or tweet instead of looking someone in the eyes and saying what we want to say.

The same is true with causes and issues. We can watch or read the news and see need in the world, but we prefer the comfort of writing a check rather than serving meals at the soup kitchen, hammering for a Habitat of Humanity build, or demonstrating at a rally. To go into that neighborhood, sit in that meeting, or speak at that open forum is a big hill to climb.

Drawing close requires rising above our fears, making an effort, and seeing the whites of another's eyes. It's scary, but it's also where real life and true relationships are found.

Espresso Shots:

1. *Identify one way you use to distance yourself from others.*
2. *What fears cause you to hide and not see the whites of the eyes of a cause or a person?*
3. *Find one opportunity to make eye contact with someone you otherwise might ignore or avoid.*

TARNISHED SILVER

The silver pitcher sits majestically on the sideboard, at least it would if I would make an effort and polish it. Its captivating lines and electric shine lie shrouded under the tarnish that comes with neglect. Finding them is not a matter of making something new. It's about restoration, finding what's been there all along.

* * *

The group of men met in the chaplain's office each week. With faces that matched their wrinkled T-shirts, they spoke of lives of drugs and alcohol. Eager to change, they came seeking advice. "I want a new life," said one. "I want to be a new person," said another. In time, they learned the life of recovery was one of re-discovery, a journey of meeting one's self as if for the first time.

* * *

The banker stayed up late going over the numbers. He took some solace in the family's flush accounts, but he was empty. After years of ladder-climbing, his arms and legs were weary. *Look how far we've come,* he said to himself. He remembered how happy he and his wife had been when they lived in an apartment and ate takeout food while sitting on the floor. A smile appeared on his face for the first time in a while, and he grabbed his coat and went to find the nearest Chinese restaurant to pick up tonight's dinner.

Espresso Shots:

1. *In a world where we are taught to climb and march forward, have you lost touch with who you used to be?*

2. *Do you think the earlier self is still inside?*

3. *In what way could you remove the tarnish to reveal who you've always been?*

UNLIKELY PACKAGES

She wore Tory Burch sandals with newly painted toenails, but above her left ankle was a cumbersome black device wrapped around her leg. In an instant, I recognized the unsightly adornment as a court-appointed tracking device. I'd never seen one before, but the fancy footwear with dark anklet was too rich a contrast to ignore.

She did not try to hide the tracking device. She could have worn long pants and acted as if it wasn't there, but she left it out for all of us to see. She could have come and shared about the misery of life with such an overt restriction, but she spoke about the blessings of her life and how grateful she was to be able to come to a meeting.

Unlike this brave woman, I've spent my life trying to hide my imperfections. Insecure about the opinions of others, I've worn many costumes to hide the things of which I'm embarrassed. I have no court-appointed device, but my fears and insecurities hold me just as captive.

I have no idea what the topic of the meeting was that morning. Everything I learned was in an unlikely package, a woman with a tracking device on her leg, and that was plenty.

Espresso Shots:

1. *In what ways are you restricted or held captive by your fears and insecurities?*

2. *How often do they hold you back from going certain places or doing certain things?*

3. *Despite your limitations, can you find the freedom in not hiding your imperfections?*

NATURE'S RHYTHM

It had been a long year. There were many reasons to celebrate all that had happened at the school where I worked, but there were also significant challenges. I went to the beach for "a breather," as I called it, once the final faculty meetings were over. Just as the sun was coming up, I strolled along the shore, allowing the waves to wash over my feet.

I was thankful for a job that demanded my gifts and talents, yet I knew I was dangerously depleted. The countless fundraising events, faculty meetings, strategic planning sessions, and budget meetings had taken their toll on my family and me. I couldn't keep it up.

A wave washed up on the shore, and the sound the shells made as they shifted on the sand awakened me. I watched as the tide retreated to the sea. Up and back, the waves came as the sun broke over the horizon. Birds took flight, then settled to rest a few yards in front of me.

I was surrounded by nature's rhythm. Taking a deep breath and letting it out, I closed my eyes and allowed the morning to wrap me in its arms. Another breath, another wave, and a seagull laughed as if to say, "It's about time you caught on."

Espresso Shots:

1. *Have you ever felt as if you were overextended?*

2. *Did you realize that, like nature itself, there needs to be a rhythm, a give-and-take, to your life?*

3. *In what ways can you learn to adopt nature's rhythm of breathing in and out in your daily life?*

PRAYERS

Growing up in the Episcopal Church, I marinated in poetic language, which I adore to this day.

However, the eloquence of Thomas Cranmer and others made me think my prayers had to be equally impressive. Over time, I've learned God cares about clarity and sincerity more than beauty.

Here are some of my best prayers:

Hello? Where the heck (not the word I use) are you?

If you want people to follow you, why keep yourself such a secret?

I'm so sorry. I wouldn't blame you if you're done with me.

Help. I'm scared to death.

Why'd you make me this way? or Why didn't you make me that way?

I'm really down today.

Wow!

Now you're just showing off. You're outrageous.

I think I saw/heard you today. Thanks.

I love you.

Espresso Shots:

1. List five one-word (or really short) prayers.
2. When have you offered a prayer you felt came from a deep place?
3. How can your prayers grow in clarity, sincerity, and frequency?

DEATH AND LIFE

I heard a heartbreaking story last night. It came from a dear friend who's a nurse. When I asked about her work, she said it had been a tough week. For most of us, a hard week means missed deadlines, lost accounts, or difficult co-workers, but it was a matter of life and death for her. Of the many moments she described, it was the last story that stuck with me.

A woman suffering from COVID-19 had reached the point of surrender. She wasn't going to make it and asked my friend to help her FaceTime her family since they were not allowed to enter the hospital. Taking the woman in her arms, she lifted the phone and gave the woman the chance to say goodbye before she died moments later.

As painful as it was to hear, I was struck by the contrast between the work a nurse usually does and the work my friend ended up doing. As a nurse, she provides care for patients so they can get better, but in this case there was nothing she could do. Well, that's not exactly true. She did do something. She took the patient in her arms and lifted the phone. Usually, she works to help people live. In this case, she helped someone die.

The story broke my heart. It also filled it at the same time.

Espresso Shots:

1. *In what way have you served another person and made their life better?*

2. *Have you ever been unable to help or solve a problem?*

3. *If so, how did you offer your presence in the midst of the unsolvable problem?*

195

FREE TO BECOME REAL

I didn't know it at the time. I was just watching a Disney movie and enjoying the story of a puppet that became a real boy. Now I see *Pinocchio* as a story that speaks volumes about what it means to be free and what it takes to become real.

In the movie, Pinocchio is a wooden puppet made by Geppetto. The puppetmaker Geppetto prays that his puppet will become real, and it looks like his prayer comes true when Pinocchio's strings are removed and he can walk and talk—even though he's still made of wood. Pinocchio seeks fame and fortune, then a self-indulgent life on Pleasure Island, where he slowly turns into a donkey. It is only when Pinocchio thinks not of himself but of Geppetto that he finally becomes a real boy.

On this day, we remember and celebrate the gift of freedom. Freedom is more than just having strings removed and going wherever we want and doing whatever we please. We may seek fame, fortune, and pleasure, but they won't make us real. Only when we use our lives in service of someone else will we become the people and the country we were created to be.

Espresso Shots:

1. *In what ways are we blessed to live in a country without strings?*

2. *In what ways have we lived as if freedom was all about doing whatever we pleased?*

3. *What would it look like for us, and this country, to use our freedom to become real?*

MOATS

As a child, I spent most of my summer days on the beach with thirteen first cousins and a few other kids from our street. Two of the kids were particularly good at making sandcastles. They arrived with shovels, molds, and other tools and began working right away. I was younger, so I stood back far enough not to be in their way. One day, they invited me to help, which was like making the team, and they assigned me the role of "chief moat builder." My job was to dig a moat around their castle to protect it from oncoming waves. I took the work seriously and took a deep breath whenever a wave approached.

Building a sandcastle offers numerous life lessons. Until recently, I thought they were all to be found in the castle itself, but now I see the importance of being a moat builder too.

A moat is like a wall in that it's there to protect the castle. Unlike a wall, however, a moat channels the water rather than stands up to it. A wall takes the waves on directly, while a moat redirects the water around the castle.

When I look back on my work leading a school, I can see times when I was more like a wall than a moat. Parents came with a complaint, and I stood at my office door, ready to take them on. When I acted as a moat, I was able to use their love and concern for their children to help the school become a better place.

Walls are easier to make than moats, but moats are worth the extra effort.

Espresso Shots:

1. *Identify a time when you responded to a situation like a wall.*

2. *Identify a time when you responded like a moat.*

3. *In what way can you learn from the two approaches and apply them to your life—in work, marriage, friendships, political discussions, and parenting?*

SKIPPING STONES AND GOING DEEP

I attended a summer camp on Lake George in upstate New York. In the mornings, the water was often placid and perfect for skipping stones. My friends and I competed before breakfast to see who could send a rock out the farthest. We measured each throw by the number of times a rock skipped off the lake. Like machine-gun fire, the stones skipped along the surface until they slowed and plunged to the bottom.

Only recently have I recognized that I spent most of my life caught up in the same game. I sailed across life's surface like a rock before running out of speed and plunging to the bottom. It was all very exciting, until it wasn't.

I've come to appreciate what happens when one slows down. To plunge deep is not nearly as exciting as skipping across the surface, but there's wonder below the surface, as well. To slow down and go beneath the surface is to find another world. I wish I had learned that earlier. My life isn't as dramatic, but it's a whole lot deeper.

Espresso Shots:

1. *In what ways do you live your life skipping on the surface?*
2. *What frightens you about slowing down and sinking below?*
3. *How can you learn to live your life on a deeper level?*

FACES

"Can I see the rest of your face?" The four-year-old asked his new teacher. Because of the safety precautions surrounding COVID-19, the teacher had to meet her students wearing a mask. Undeterred, she crossed the room to stand at a safe distance before lowering her mask and revealing her smile.

How I wish we lived back in the time when we could see the rest of each other's faces. I get the whole mask thing, but, like the little boy, I miss smiles. I miss entire faces. I know it will be over one day, and masks will be things of the past, but hopefully we will never forget the important lessons we're learning through this pandemic. May we never take smiles for granted. May we never refuse a hug.

I'm seasoned enough to know that's unlikely. Like the promise made at a funeral of never taking a friend for granted, time makes us forget. I'm sure those who lived through the Depression vowed to never take their resources for granted, and the parents of Vietnam soldiers promised to hold their soldiers forever, but time has a way of weakening such promises.

Still, there's something to be said for missing things. Singer/songwriter Joni Mitchell once wrote the lyrics, "Don't it always seem to go that you don't know what you've got till it's gone." That's how it feels with smiles. I long to see the rest of everyone's face.

Espresso Shots:

1. *What has been the most disconcerting part of living through a pandemic?*

2. *What's lost by wearing masks?*

3. *What are you determined to never take for granted?*

LESSONS FROM THE BEACH: WHY I GO TO CHURCH

I watch as a brother and sister play with their boogie boards in the surf. The waves are almost nonexistent, but they're having a ball. Standing by is a woman who I think is their grandmother. She, too, enjoys watching the two play in the sea. Each time they come up on shore, she reaches for them, but they are too enamored to stop. She clearly adores the two children and longs to connect, but they're too caught up in their games to respond.

It's completely understandable, but I feel for the grandmother. By the looks of things, she's the one who made the trip possible. All she wants in return is a little connection or appreciation.

It made me think about how God must feel most of the time. Watching us, I'm sure God delights as we play in the sea. He's the one who's made the whole thing possible, and I think God reaches out in hopes of connecting with us. Like the grandmother, I suspect God longs to hug and kiss us, but, too often, we can't be bothered. Too much to do…so little time, we profess.

Like a grandparent, I'm sure God understands the way of youth despite the desire for connection. Lost in such thoughts, I watch as the boy runs up and nearly tackles his grandmother with a wet, sandy hug. She doesn't mind. She closes her eyes and smiles deeply. The boy smiles, too. Then, it's back to the sea.

Espresso Shots:

1. *Think of a time when you were caught up in the joy of living.*
2. *Do you ever stop and give thanks to God for such a moment?*
3. *What would it look like to express your gratitude?*

LESSONS FROM THE BEACH: WHY I'M A CHRISTIAN

The grandmother eventually returned to her seat while the brother and sister played their games in the surf. Each time they washed up on the shore, though, they looked over at their grandmother and parents. It was as if they were waiting for something. Then, it happened.

The dad rose from his seat, grabbed a boogie board, and walked toward the sea. The children squealed with delight, and the boy danced something like an Irish jig before falling back into the ocean. With their father beside them in the sea, the games took on new meaning. As independent as the children seemed, their father joining them made their day.

Independence is overrated. So often, we live our lives as if to say, "We've got this." We do it so often and have become so adept at it, we almost believe it. The fact is, deep down, we hope someone will join us, that we won't have to go it alone. We don't want to swim alone.

When we see God drawing close, when we feel God right beside us, it changes everything. Our lives take on new meaning, and we find ourselves squealing and dancing like children.

"I came that you should have life and have it more abundantly." Yahoo!!!

Espresso Shots:

1. Focus on a time when you have felt God draw near.
2. What did you know when you felt God's presence?
3. How would you change if you were able to feel God beside you all the time?

DIVING RIGHT IN

"If I don't have red, I use blue." —*Picasso*

He likes things just so. A creature of habit, with a meticulous eye for detail, his life is a thing of precision. His paints are arranged by color, canvases and brushes stand in descending order. Each day he arrives and spends the morning preparing for the day's work. After lunch, he returns to his studio and makes some final adjustments before sitting and waiting for inspiration to arrive. It never does.

If an artist waits for everything to be perfect, they will never begin. "Better to dive right in," an artist friend likes to say. She never waits because she knows the magic only happens when the brush is in her hand. I admire her artistic talent, but even more, I admire her ability to get to work without having everything exactly right. Too often, I arrange books before I write and fold the rags before I paint. It's a form of procrastination that can kill the best-intentioned artist.

It can hurt non-artists as well. Waiting for the precise moment to launch a new product can kill it. Waiting to have a child until you have the perfect house and the right amount of money can lead to never having children. Waiting until you have enough time and no distractions to begin your spiritual work can leave both your books and soul dusty.

Better to dive right in, or, as Picasso said, if you don't have red, use blue.

Espresso Shots:

1. *How does procrastination disguise itself as perfectionism in your life?*

2. *What would it take for you to dive right into some new venture?*

3. *How can you dive right into your spiritual practice?*

BURNING THE BOATS

In 1519, Captain Hernán Cortés began his great conquest of Veracruz. He reportedly gave an order to his men to burn the boats in which they arrived. That action has lived on as a reminder of fully committing to something.

I have always been afraid of burning the boats. I'm not sure exactly why, but partly it's because I want to keep my options open. What if this thing I'm doing doesn't work out?

When I think of Jesus calling the disciples, I wonder if following him felt like burning the boats. Did they walk away knowing they'd never make a living that way again or did they think they could return if following Jesus didn't work out?

I can't help but wonder what the world would look like if each of us burned the boats, spiritually. If we followed God utterly and completely, with no way to return to our old lives, what would our lives be like? In 12-step recovery circles, we are told that half-measures avail us of nothing, and yet half-measures are so often the way many of us approach our faith.

No wonder we get the results we do.

Espresso Shots:

1. *In what ways do you keep the boats on the shore in case you might need them, spiritually?*

2. *What would burning the boats look like for you, spiritually?*

3. *What's your greatest fear about fully committing your life to God?*

BEARING FRUIT

"Bear fruit worthy of repentance." —Matthew 3:8

Their daughter was put on the waiting list. It was only because there wasn't enough room in the class, but they were devastated. They felt it was the perfect school for their daughter. When a spot opened up just before school started, they screamed with delight and showed their gratitude in serving the school in countless ways.

Bear fruit worthy of repentance.

The student sat on the couch with both parents beside him, waiting to hear the verdict. He had been caught in a lie, and the school handbook said such an offense was grounds for dismissal. Never had he appreciated the school until he faced possible expulsion. When the headmaster said he was going to make an exception, the boy cried. More than that, he became one of the leaders of the school and spoke at graduation. "It was worth it," the headmaster said as he handed the boy his diploma.

Bear fruit worthy of repentance.

A lifelong churchgoer, she heard countless sermons on grace. In her mind, she believed God loved her no matter what, but her heart wasn't convinced. It wasn't until she messed up that all of that changed. In the quiet of her room, she heard and felt God's grace as never before. Despite the judgment she felt from others, she entered her life as if it were a daily second chance. No longer trying to earn God's love, she lived in response to already having it, and that made all the difference.

Bear fruit worthy of repentance.

Espresso Shots:

1. *Can you recall a time in which you were given a second chance?*
2. *If so, how did you live after it?*
3. *In what ways could your spiritual life become a response to grace, rather than an attempt to earn it?*

BAREFOOT LIVING

I have a friend who always posts pictures of her bare feet. Usually, they're lined up beside a friend or family member's feet. Often there's a beautiful sunrise or sunset behind them, and her feet are nestled in the sand or hanging above a mountain stream. Regardless of the particulars of the pictures, they remind me to live with bare feet, especially at this time of year.

When you take off your shoes, everything changes. Toes get wiggled, conversations become light, and life more joyful. I can still remember laughing when mud covered my feet and squeezed through my toes as a child. I remember how hard I tried not to laugh when a minister washed my feet during a worship service.

Imagine how a fancy cocktail party or business meeting would change if everyone was told to take off their shoes. Some would be reluctant, while others would excitedly kick them off. The conversations would be transformed, as would the people having them. It's hard to take yourself too seriously when you're barefoot.

Summer is the perfect time to take off our shoes and feel the earth beneath us. It's the time of year to wiggle our toes and feel joy down to the soles of our feet. My friend is quick to remind me that it's always barefoot time. I think she's right.

Espresso Shots:

1. Take off your shoes and describe a time when you had fun when your shoes were off.

2. What is it about bare feet that changes us?

3. How can you live a barefoot life—with or without your shoes on?

TASTING AIR

One of the things I love most about summer is the taste of the air. I can taste the air when I'm on the beach. I fill my lungs whenever I'm on a mountain peak. Tasting the air can also be a way to describe the fullness with which we live life in the summer.

A grandmother and grandchild play tag with the waves.

Parents enjoy a long candlelit dinner with their adult children and spouses.

A son encourages his father to try surfing.

A family hikes to a favorite campsite and cooks s' mores.

A campfire and a guitarist turn a starry night into a thing of magic.

A group of kids race through a sprinkler.

Children fill a jar with fireflies.

Summer is a time to taste the air. It's a time to breathe deeply and give thanks for the gift of life and for the others with whom we share it.

Espresso Shots:

1. *Make a list of ten times you tasted the summer air, literally and figuratively.*

2. *How can you taste the air today?*

3. *Who can you bring along?*

ROLLER COASTERS

We visited the Seaside Heights Amusement Park once a summer, and it was a big deal. Unlike the amusement park closer to home, Seaside Heights was bigger and more exciting. Of all the rides, the roller coaster thrilled me the most. I could have ridden it all day long—if my stomach and wallet allowed.

Located on the farthest corner of the pier, the roller coaster had the ocean on two sides. Once strapped in, we heard the clicking sound as the tracks lifted us to the summit. For a moment, we sat on top of the world, able to look out across the sea and down the shoreline. Then, everything changed. With a sudden turn, we plummeted toward the wooden pier, swerving to the left, right, then up and down and right again. I wasn't one of those riders who let go and held their arms in the air. I was a white-knuckler all the way. With eyes closed, I simply wanted to survive. The view at the top became a distant memory when twisting and turning. It wasn't until we were back on solid ground that I remembered the incredible view.

My life often feels like a roller-coaster ride. Sometimes it seems the horizon stretches forever, but these moments are hard to remember when I close my eyes through the twists and turns. A sweet job goes sour. A joyful marriage becomes a chore. A health scare leaves us frighened for the future. Such challenges make us lose sight of what filled our soul at the start of the ride.

But the ocean is still there. If we can open our eyes just a little and look beyond the twists and turns, if we can turn off the television and refrain from scrolling through the ups and downs of social media, we might catch a glimpse of the bigger world. With eyes open, we might see our family as if for the first time, approach work with renewed passion, and view the day as the gift it is. All those things have been there. The ride just caused us to forget.

Espresso Shots:

1. *Identify a time when the ride caused you to close your eyes.*
2. *What were you unable to see?*
3. *What can you do to keep your eyes open on the ride?*

CLOWNS

"Be a clown, be a clown. All the world loves a clown." —*Cole Porter*

I recently heard the story of Emmett Kelly, a name new to me but a story that was not. A gifted trapeze artist, Emmett came to Ringling Brothers and Barnum & Bailey Circus looking for a job. During his audition, as he flew in the air, it was clear Emmett was born to be a trapeze artist. Unfortunately, there were others who were more talented. Rather than give up, Emmett decided to become a clown. Today he is remembered as the most famous clown the circus has known.

While his story is an inspirational one about adaptability, it's also a convicting metaphor for those of us who have become clowns when we couldn't join the circus any other way.

When the boy couldn't read like the other students, he became the clown of the third-grade reading circle. When she didn't make the varsity team, she became the entertainer of the junior varsity team.

Unfortunately, we often hide our weaknesses with makeup, a red nose, and funny-looking shoes. It is only when we come to know God personally and find our true worth that we can take off the mask and be the people we were created to be.

Espresso Shots:

1. *When have you been embarrassed by your limitations or mistakes and become a clown?*
2. *Why was a clown such an effective disguise?*
3. *In what ways can you learn to take off the makeup and be your authentic self?*

ON THE ROCKS

"I like my Christianity on the rocks," said the family matriarch. "Like my bourbon, I want it chilled and slightly watered down."

It got the desired laughs from those gathered at the dining room table. They were like-minded family members. On her right was the son who complained that the prayers in church sounded like they came from some radical liberal group. On the left was the daughter who complained the sermons were too much about current events, and her husband at the far end hadn't been back to church since the minister said every family should tithe.

As easy as it would be to throw stones at such a gathering, I'm keenly aware of how I, too, pick and choose the religion I claim to follow. I believe we're called to serve the poor, but I do little more than nod my head when I hear such things. I give every year to the church and other organizations, but I'm not sure I give 10 percent of my income. I know that I'm supposed to love my enemies, yet I can hardly talk to people who interpret the gospel differently. Like the matriarch, I'm just as guilty of liking my gospel watered down.

The problem is, it's not "my gospel." It's not some new wardrobe accessory that comes in different sizes so I can try one on until I find the right fit. The gospel is the story of God, and any attempt to mold it to my desires or the whims of society is like pouring bourbon over ice to make it taste better.

I need to learn to drink mine straight up.

Espresso Shots:

1. *In what ways do you selectively follow the gospel?*

2. *What parts of your faith are hardest to follow, and what parts are the easiest?*

3. *What would be the implications of taking the gospel straight up?*

FLASHLIGHTS

The camper left the warmth and security of the campfire to walk toward her tent. Holding her flashlight tight, she shone its light ahead, revealing rocks, bushes, and trees as well as a portion of the path. While trying to focus on what she could see, her mind wandered to what might be out there, to her right or left or just beyond the light ahead. Such thoughts almost caused her to turn around, but she focused on what was before her and successfully made it to her tent.

I wish I was as disciplined. I, too, have a tent, a place I am headed, and I have been given a flashlight to help me get there. But too often, I try to see beyond the light I've been given and worry about what's beyond the range of my flashlight. Even though I can see all manner of rocks, bushes, and trees, as well as a portion of a path, I spend much of my time longing to see more than the light reveals. The uncertainty makes me want to quit and turn around.

Scripture tells us we should let God's grace be sufficient. In other words: let the light from the flashlight be enough for the journey. Use it to see your next step, but don't worry about things you cannot see or control ahead of you. Whatever your tent may be—a job, a relationship, a life's purpose, a spiritual destination—you've been given all the light you need to get there. By taking the next step, you move forward. The good news is that as you move forward, so does the light.

Espresso Shots:

1. *Do you live one step at a time, or try to look farther ahead than your flashlight allows?*
2. *What do you wish you could see that you cannot?*
3. *What advantage do you think there could be with a limited view?*

GOLF PROFESSIONALS

Golf professionals arrive days before a tournament. They get to know the course, learn the twists and turns of the fairways, and the ups and downs of the greens. With shots practiced and a strategy designed, they begin the tournament as prepared as possible. But the difference between weekend golfers and pros is that the professionals are ready for the unknown and unforeseen challenges. Shots will go awry, and greens will be misread.

Watching the tournament reminds me that while preparation is helpful, even essential, at some point, the pros still have to stand over the ball and hit it. No past shots, good or bad, seem to matter. They are focused on the shot at hand. They are fully present, ready to adapt their plan to whatever may or may not happen once the round has begun.

I'll never be a golf professional, but I can certainly learn from their example in the games I play. In my work, marriage, life as a parent, and as a person in recovery, I need to prepare and practice. It would serve me well to make a plan, but I also need to stand over the ball and hit it. Shots will go into the woods or trickle only a few yards; wind or storms will arrive suddenly. I need to respond like the golf professionals and focus on the shot at hand. I cannot dwell on the ones in the past nor anticipate the ones to come.

If I can learn to accept the things I cannot change and change the things I can, my golf game might improve. So might my life.

Espresso Shots:

1. *What kind of balance have you found between accepting the things you cannot change and changing the things you can?*
2. *When have you hit a shot in the woods, so to speak? How did you respond?*
3. *In what ways can you learn to focus only on the shot at hand?*

UNDER THE CLOUDS

I recently awakened to an interesting sermon. From the deck of a house high in the mountains, I could see the peaks of the surrounding mountains. They were basking in the morning light, but the valleys were stuffed with cotton-like clouds. Had I paid attention in science class, I might have been able to explain why such a thing happens, but, instead, I thought about the people in those valleys. For them, the morning was dark and cloudy. All they could see were the walls of the mountains and the clouds overhead. They couldn't see the bright morning and sunny peaks above the clouds. I wanted to shout below and tell them a beautiful day was coming, but they wouldn't have heard me.

In the next few hours, the sky above the valleys cleared, and the sun shone. It seemed an apt metaphor life. There are days when we are in the valley. The mountain walls close in, and the clouds descend. Darkness seems to take over, and it's hard to imagine clear skies and sunny peaks above the clouds. When I was in one of those valleys, someone came and assured me the clouds would not last, but I couldn't hear him.

My mountain morning helps me better understand the life of faith. Some might tell you it's about living life on a sun-drenched peak, but I think it's more about knowing the peaks are there even when you can't see them. Believing when it's sunny is much easier than believing when it's dark.

Faith is the assurance of things hoped for, the conviction of things not seen, as the book of Hebrews says. Looking out from above the clouds, I understood as if for the first time.

Espresso Shots:

1. *Think back on a time when you were under the clouds in a valley. Were you able to see beyond the clouds?*

2. *How does your faith help you when you're under the clouds?*

3. *How can you remind others that the sun will come back out?*

HEAD AND HEART

"My temptations have been my masters in divinity." —*Martin Luther*

At an early age, I learned to live in my head. It wasn't because I was particularly clever. It was because the head was easier to control than the heart. I've continued this practice throughout my life. In high school, I tried to figure out God. Later, I went to seminary, where I learned all kinds of things about God. In the end, I had a head full of knowledge and a heart longing for something more.

Looking around me, I can see I am not unique. Most people think more than they feel. Thinking is easier. Thinking about profits and losses at work is easier than exploring a company's purpose. Thinking about home logistics is easier for a couple than wrestling with love. Buying a book is easier than praying.

It takes effort and practice to move from head to heart. Like all things new, it's awkward and uncomfortable to explore your feelings. The uncertainty and lack of control when you go within may tempt you to run back to the mind, but don't.

God is more concerned with our hearts than our minds. We should be, too.

Espresso Shots:

1. *How often do you rely on your mind instead of your heart?*
2. *Why is the mind so much easier to use than the heart?*
3. *What would it take for you to rely more on your heart, spiritually, professionally, and relationally?*

LEARNING THROUGH OPPOSITES

There were certain characteristics the coach sought in his young football squad. He wanted them to be steady, quick, and confident. To that end, he created practices that were the complete opposite. Before the players arrived, he soaked the practice field, so it was all but impossible not to fall. He weighed down his players so they could hardly move during sprints, and when they scrimmaged, he called in the worst plays so his quarterback would learn to trust his instincts and call the right plays. No one understood the coaching method until the season began, and the team was steady, fast, and confident.

I've never coached football, but the illustration serves as an example of a spiritual truth: people grow particular strengths when presented with their opposites. One grows patient when put in exasperating situations. One grows more loving when presented with difficult people. One grows faithful when doubt abounds.

It's not some cruel joke or test on God's part. It's how we grow into the people we were created to be. Each time we fall, we grow steadier. When we are weighed down, we grow stronger. And each time we trust our instincts, we grow more confident.

I've sought a life devoid of conflict. I've always longed to be happy and content. Now I can see that there's no growth in such a life, even if it was possible to create. It is through the challenges that God pulls forth the spiritual gifts within us. I wish there were an easier way, but there's not.

Espresso Shots:

1. *In what ways do you try to avoid conflict and hardship at the expense of growth?*

2. *When have you seen how something difficult strengthened you in the end?*

3. *What spiritual gifts do you think God is trying to pull forth within you through a particular challenge?*

TRAIL MAGIC

On the Appalachian Trail, there's a thing called "Trail Magic." All along the 2,190-mile trail, people leave things for hikers. The magic could consist of an apple, a new pair of socks, a six-pack of beer, all gifts left along the way in hopes they will brighten the day of unknown travelers and encourage them on their journey. Although it's a hiking tradition, I believe trail magic should be a part of our daily lives, as well.

Imagine leaving trail magic in the supermarket parking lot, on the steps of the DMV, or outside the food pantry. It could be clothing, food or drink, or maybe a note or book. If we could follow the example of those who leave trail magic on the AT, our magic could brighten the days of fellow travelers and encourage them on their way.

There's no limit to our creative interpretation of this tradition. It could be purchasing a coffee for the car behind you in line or sending anonymous notes of encouragement for a minister or nonprofit volunteer. It could be a bouquet for a co-worker who's going through a rough patch or a gift certificate for a neighbor.

My hunch is this trail magic would encourage not only the sojourners who find the magic but also those who cared enough to leave it beside the trail.

Espresso Shots:

1. When have you come across trail magic in your travels?

2. When have you left some trail magic for others?

3. How could you incorporate trail magic into your spiritual practices?

LOST FRIENDS

"The thing I love most about our friendship," the high school classmate announced, "is that no matter how long it's been, it's as if we've never been apart."

"I know what you mean," replied the other. "But I fear we've played that card for too long."

The classmate was not saying that he no longer valued their friendship or that he wasn't glad when they saw one another, but he felt that they allowed too much time to pass between visits. Too much time and too many life events between visits put an unnecessary strain on their friendship. They needed to meet more often.

I feel the same way about my relationship with God. When I feel connected to God, when I feel God's presence beside me, life is as good as it gets. Unfortunately, I still allow long periods to pass before I reconnect with God.

Sometimes it feels like only an instant since the last visit, but usually it has been too long. Like the high school friends, the absence puts an unnecessary strain on the relationship.

Part of a spiritual life is getting to know God and becoming friends. Another aspect is not letting too much time pass between meetings so the friendship remains close and vibrant. It's not always easy to find the time, but the benefits are well worth it.

Espresso Shots:

1. *Do you have a friendship you value that has too much time between visits?*

2. *Do you have a friendship with God?*

3. *If so, what do you do to nurture that friendship? How often do you spend time together?*

HE LIVES IN YOU

I remember the first time I heard my mother referred to as a widow. My back stiffened, and I tried unsuccessfully to hide my discomfort. My father had only been dead for a few months, so I was still trying to adjust to life without him. Hearing my mother referred to as a widow only reminded me of the significant loss. The hardest part of accepting his death was thinking that all of him was suddenly gone. It was inconceivable that this larger-than-life figure was no longer with us.

Later that day, I heard my brother clear his throat in the next room. He sounded just like my father. A few days later, my sister looked at me with eyes that reminded me of my father's, and when I heard my other sister play the piano that my father had once played, I realized that he wasn't completely gone. There was part of him in each of his children, including me, which brought an incredible sense of comfort. He lived on in us.

I wonder if the same could be said of those of us who call ourselves Christians. Jesus died over two thousand years ago, but perhaps, in some way, he lives on in you and me. Can we hear his voice in something we say, see his eyes when we look at another? Yes, he died, but does he live on…in us?

Espresso Shots:

1. *When have you seen an aspect of a deceased person live on in another?*

2. *If you have lost one or more parents, can you see him or her living on in you?*

3. *How does God live on in you?*

Double Shot: *Listen to the song, "He Lives in You" from* The Lion King.

DEFINING MOMENTS

With seven seconds to go, the ball was snapped, caught, placed, kicked…and no good! The easy kick, which would have forced overtime and kept alive the dream of going to the Super Bowl, was missed. Now their season was over.

It was game six of the World Series. His team was one out away from winning when a hit came in his direction. It wasn't a difficult play and would have led to a long-desired World Series win, but the ball went through his leg. His team ended up losing the game and the World Series.

With seconds to go, and down by one point, the basketball player called for a time-out. Unfortunately, his team didn't have any time-outs left, so the clock continued, and the buzzer sounded. No last shot was taken. The game over.

As a person of faith, I have a soft spot for people with stories of near-misses. While I celebrate when my team wins, I also feel a deep ache for those whose mistakes cause a loss. Television audiences are indiscriminately passionate: they devour amazing plays and rail against heartbreaking blunders. Defining moments, as they are often called, can be for good or ill.

If you read the Bible, you'll find many people who dropped the ball or missed the kick. What stands out is that God seems to gravitate to such folk. Despite the worst mistakes, God calls these people, asks them to do things, and empowers them to live beyond their blunders.

Can you imagine a world where we did the same?

Espresso Shots:

1. *Think back on someone (it can be you) who made a colossal mistake.*

2. *Was the person ever known for something they did right?*

3. *Why do you think God has a heart for those who mess up?*

PRACTICE

A pianist plays his scales, a swimmer swims her laps, a doctor practices her procedures, and an athlete goes through his drills. Of course, we think. They practice to improve themselves. Yet, few of us see the value of practice when it comes to our spiritual lives. For many, we see our prayer life, worship, and service as something that should come naturally, but like everything we do, the spiritual life requires practice.

In 12-step recovery circles, we speak of "stumbling in the right direction." Such an outlook allows for imperfection, encourages practice, and inspires continuous effort. When it comes to my life of faith, I need those things, as well. There are certain tools I have to keep my faith alive, but I must use them. I must accept I am a beginner in many ways and won't get it right much of the time. Stumbling is part of the journey. The important thing is to head in the right direction, and, to do so, I need to practice regularly.

An artist speaks of his practice. A lawyer does the same. Perhaps we need to use the same language when we refer to our spiritual life. Spending time each morning praying, gathering regularly for worship, and serving others are part of one's spiritual work. All we need to do is practice.

Espresso Shots:

1. *How can you practice your faith?*
2. *What practices are a regular part of your spiritual life?*
3. *How often do you practice?*

CHANGING OUR POSE

If you were asked to stand in the position or pose of your faith, what would it look like? Would you have your hands up shielding your face from whatever may come your way because your faith is defensive? Would you stand with one foot extended, as if dipping your toe in the water, because your faith is timid? Would both hands be defiantly placed on either hip or across your chest, illustrating your "I'm in charge" faith? Or are your arms spread out and head tilted back, taking in the new day that's been given, trusting the world and the one who created it absolutely?

Such an exercise is helpful because we often think that we live our life of faith one way when, in fact, we live it another. Some claim they trust God completely but cling tightly to possessions, careers, and people. Some claim an openness to God's will but create rigid plans for their life.

What would it look like if we changed our pose? Could we open our hands and heart in a way that speaks to our trust in God? Could we greet others and encourage them in a visible way? Could we allow the joy we feel within to appear on our faces by smiling more?

We are told to love the Lord with our mind, body, and spirit. Many of us find one of those three easier than the others. Today is a day to focus on how our body reflects our faith.

Espresso Shots:

1. *Stand up and strike a pose that best describes your faith.*

2. *In what way could your faith transform the way you carry yourself physically?*

3. *Be deliberate in observing your body and try to change your pose or the look on your face when it does not reflect the faith within you.*

LIMITING BELIEFS

I once watched a fun horseback riding competition where the amateur riders had to ride to one end of the ring, dismount, put horse hobbles around their ankles, then run back. Everyone looked silly, and most participants fell flat on their faces into the dirt. I thought of this event when talking with a friend about how some of the thoughts we carry hold us back.

Sometimes our limiting beliefs are obvious; other times they're disguised. We sometimes give them voice; other times, we keep them hidden. They come in all shapes and sizes and cover all areas of our lives—money, looks, weight, athletic abilities, intellect, relationships, and even faith. We tell ourselves something, then live into whatever we've said. Tell yourself you'll always be fat, you'll never be as good as your (fill in the blank), you'll never amount to much, or you'll never find love, and, sure enough, the limiting belief becomes a reality.

Spiritual growth is hindered by limiting beliefs. Like hobbles, they hold us back and sometimes cause us to fall flat on our faces. Many of them have been with us since we were children, while others have arrived more recently. To challenge or remove them can be disconcerting and difficult, but the work is worth it.

In the end, we'll be able to run the race set before us with nothing holding us back.

Espresso Shots:

1. *What limiting beliefs do you tell yourself most often?*
2. *Where did they come from, and why do you think they hold such power over you?*
3. *What would it take to challenge or remove them?*

TEMPTATIONS

"I've never been tempted to be an opera singer," said the woman who couldn't carry a tune.

"I've never been tempted to run a marathon," said the heavy man with bad knees.

The examples could go on and on, but the fact is we're never tempted by the things that are beyond our grasp. It's the things that are possible that tempt us the most. That's why they are so tempting and why resisting them is so difficult.

Jesus went from his baptism into the desert where he was tempted in three specific ways, each of which was within his grasp as God's son. He resisted each temptation and, in doing so, became the Messiah he was meant to be.

I believe temptations that come our way serve the same purpose. As they dangle like apples on a tree, these temptations taunt us. We are tempted to do things that are within our grasp and tempted to be people we could easily be, but our true selves lie on the other side of such temptations.

As someone who has given in to temptations far too many times and with tragic consequences, I write not as a paragon of virtue but as a wounded traveler. I now see temptations as opportunities to grow stronger. Although I've never been one for push-ups, sit-ups, or weight training, they're the way to grow stronger. Temptations are equally unpleasant, but they serve the same purpose. While they offer me daily opportunities to be a person within my grasp, resisting them makes me into the person God has in mind.

Espresso Shots:

1. *In what ways are you tempted to do something within your grasp?*

2. *In what ways are you tempted to be someone you weren't created to be?*

3. *How can you see temptations as opportunities for growth?*

BODIES AND SOULS

I awakened with a pain in my right leg. It was particularly bad when I first got out of bed, but the pain continued throughout the day. I remembered something I'd done the day before that probably caused the injury and spent afternoon caring for my sore leg with stretches and ointment. In a few days, I was back to normal.

The body is good at letting us know when something is wrong. In fact, I think it's better at telling us than we are at listening. Our souls are equally communicative, but we are even worse at paying attention when they speakß. The soul's language is subtle, but its pains are just as real as those we feel in our bodies. Whether it's a childhood injury, a recent hurt, or something we chose to do or not do, our souls are affected by these actions.

As people trying to live spiritual lives, the health of our souls is paramount. We must learn how to listen to our souls when they try to tell us something. We must also learn ways to care for our souls when they suffer an injury.

Just as our bodies speak, so do our souls. We need to learn how to listen and how to respond on a daily basis.

Espresso Shots:

1. *Think back on a time when you injured your body and how you took care of it.*
2. *Have there been times when your soul was injured?*
3. *In what ways do you care for the health of your soul?*

SEA GLASS

She wanders down the shoreline searching for sea glass. Periodically, she looks up and adjusts the strap on her bathing suit. She used to wear a bikini, but those days are long gone. Her skin is weathered now, with the lines and folds of being broken in.

It's still early. Her children and their families are asleep. She and her ex-husband used to share this time to walk together. Now she sleeps and walks alone.

Last night, one of her daughters confessed her marriage was in trouble, and her son admitted his eldest child might need to go to rehab. There was a time when she longed for, even demanded, everyone be happy, but she gave up that pipe dream a few years ago. Now she tries to accept life for the struggle it sometimes is.

A blue piece of sea glass catches her eye, and she bends down to pick it up. It's still translucent with sharp edges, so she casts it back into the sea for more time. Farther down, she finds a green piece that's perfect. The tides have worn down its edges and softened its color.

As a child, she walked with her mother for hours, looking for sea glass and trying to convince her mother a piece was ready when it wasn't. "Give the sea time," her mother would repeat. "Give the sea time."

The woman eventually learned the sea takes a broken piece of glass and makes it a work of art. When pushed and pulled against the sand for years, edges soften and new shades of color appear. Kind of like me, she jokes to herself as she continues down the beach.

Espresso Shots:

1. *In what way are you like a piece of sea glass? Have you been broken? Have you been weathered by the tides?*

2. *Can you see how life has worn down your edges?*

3. *How is your life like a work of art?*

THE PULPIT AND THE SHADOWS

The moment was pregnant with meaning, but at the time I couldn't understand. I sat in a small city square while a Christian singing group prepared to perform in the modest amphitheater. Like me, other tourists also sat in chairs, waiting for the show, while over in the shade, some of the city's homeless population leaned on garbage bags filled with their possessions. Their arms were scarred and eyes empty.

Before singing, the leader spoke of the need for Christ and that an abundant life is waiting for us all. Having heard some talented street preachers, I was sorry he wasn't better. It was the contrast before us, the enthusiastic Christians and active addicts, that proved to be the sermon.

Telling others about Jesus is a fine thing to do, even brave sometimes, but I left the show wondering if telling is enough. Is standing at a microphone the best thing to do when poor and desperate people sit in the shadows? One claimed to have life, the other was all but lifeless. Rather than judge, I realized I've spent my life with both. I've dressed in fancy church clothes and proclaimed the gospel, and I've sat in the shadows trying to fill the emptiness with everything but God.

Fortunately, I found a way out of the darkness. Sitting there with my daughters, I prayed others would too.

Espresso Shots:

1. *In what ways are you in a position to deliver good news to the world?*

2. *In what ways have you lived in the shadows, unsuccessfully filling an emptiness within?*

3. *In what ways could you live your faith between the two?*

MOUNTAINS AND PLAINS

I love mountains. I always have. Each summer my parents used to take us to Jackson Hole, Wyoming, where the Grand Tetons shattered all my notions of what mountains looked like. There are no foothills, just massive mountains standing alone. Recently, the Sawtooth Mountains in Idaho caused my soul to gasp. Like the Tetons, they stand alone in majestic beauty and awesome power.

As impressive as the Tetons and Sawtooth mountains are, God, the supreme landscape architect, knows that creation cannot only be made up of majestic mountains. Plains and rolling hills are needed as well as rivers and lakes and places were land and sea meet. It is the combination and contrasts that shows us wonder and beauty.

Too often I forget the importance of the full landscape. As a painter, I need to be mindful of how the various images and colors work together. As a writer, I need to craft character and stories with a combination of highs and lows.

The same is true in relationships and careers. The glorious moments are to be treasured, but they only make sense when framed by the struggles and ordinary moments. This is also true of spiritual stories that shape our faith. Dramatic moments like falling off a horse on the road to Damascus or pledging life to God in a thunderstorm may have changed the spiritual world, but so have the simple ones, such as sharing meals, taking walks, and praying with one another. Together, these moments create a spiritual landscape that is rich and inspirational.

Espresso Shots:

1. *What is it about a dramatic landscape that makes it so captivating and inspirational?*

2. *Standing back, can you see how the landscape is a combination of elements that work together?*

3. *In what way can you incorporate the highs and lows, and everything in between, into your daily spiritual landscape?*

CHANGING THE GAME PLAN

He was one of the finest running backs in history until a tackle destroyed his right knee. Despite his best efforts and most optimistic thoughts, his football days were over. The darkness that descended upon him made him only see what had been lost and who he had been. Sitting on the sidelines reminded him how much he loved the game.

His wife suggested he change the game plan. He listened and became a coach and found he was quite good at it. In fact, when he retired years later and heard what players said at the dinner in his honor, he realized what a blessing his injury had been.

There's a dangerous view of the spiritual life that suggests one's connection with God will prevent bad things from happening. The Bible suggests nothing of the sort nor do the experiences of anyone I've known. The twists and turns and ups and downs are distributed among us, but what brings me to my knees in gratitude is how setbacks or failures can become blessings.

The student rejected from her first-choice ends up at the perfect school.

The doctor addicted to prescription medicine loses his license but opens a rehab facility for people in the medical field.

The widower finds a new love.

A minister loses his church but finds his true ministry.

I am not one who believes God brings about bad things to test or punish us. We are well-versed in bringing bad stuff upon ourselves, but what is remarkable is how God can take the worst that happens to us and transforms it. It's enough to make me a believer!

Espresso Shots:

1. *Look back at something that happened in your life that challenged you and your faith to the core.*

2. *How did that setback or failure change your life?*

3. *How can you more fully embrace the chances and changes of life, knowing God can work through all things to bring about good?*

SERVICE

"Non ut sibi ministretur sed ut ministret." —*The Taft School Motto*

There's a story in the gospels that I have always found strange. It describes a moment when Peter's mother is feeling ill and Jesus restores her to health. Her response is to get up from her bed and serve Jesus and Peter. Maybe it's because I grew up in a time of women's liberation, but I've always thought Peter and Jesus should have given Peter's mother the night off and served her.

On the other hand, the story is a powerful reminder of what it means to be people of faith. There was a time when I was extraordinarily unhealthy and needed God. In a real way, I was restored to health—maybe not as dramatically as Peter's mother but just as real. Like her, I needed to respond to my restored health—I still do. It is not enough to have received God's grace. I need to do something because of such a gift. We all do.

The question, then, is: what should we do? While the methods of answering are countless, the answer is the same: we are to serve others. Grace is a gift that is meant to be shared, but too often we keep it to ourselves. Instead, we need to rise up from our beds and serve others. Such service is our duty, but it comes not in an effort to earn God's grace but in response to it having been bestowed.

As my high school moto reminded us each time we walked under it, we are here not to be served, but to serve.

Espresso Shots:

1. Do you remember when you first felt the gift of God's grace?

2. If so, what was your response?

3. In what ways do you serve others because of the grace God gave to you?

FINDING YOUR KIND

My wife attended and later served as a counselor at a camp on the North Carolina coast. Although I did not know her at the time, I've learned what a profound impact the camp had on her soul. We recently attended what is called family camp, an effort to bring old campers back for a brief camp experience. I saw firsthand that my wife has an inner camper who needs to come out and play. At family camp, she no longer cared about her hair and makeup was a thing of the past.She bounced from activity to activity like a bubbly twelve-year old. Nowhere have I seen her happier, nowhere more at home. Surrounded by other returning campers, singing songs only they knew, I realized my wife was with "her kind."

The experience made me a little jealous until I spent a weekend in Vermont with childhood friends. The laughter and fun we shared reminded me that they were "my kind." I drove away hoping everyone has such a group. Maybe we find kindred spirits in a church, a school, or some other group, but I believe we all need to find our kind.

We'll know when we find them. We'll relax and be more authentic than usual. We won't care so much about appearances, and we'll laugh and sing in ways we've forgotten. So it is when you find your kind.

Espresso Shots:

1. Do you have a group who is "your kind?"

2. When you're together, how does it feel?

3. In what ways can you find your kind more often?

GETTING TO THE WAVES

The waves were good that day. They were curling and breaking fifty yards from shore, and it looked like a perfect afternoon for bodysurfing. To get to the waves, however, my pre-teen frame needed to forge its way through the surf and strong current. It'll be worth it, I told myself as I began, but more than a few times along the way I wondered if I had the strength to get out to where the waves were breaking.

I can see now how my struggle that day was a foreshadow of life. We aspire to countless waves of experiences: getting married, landing a great job, launching a start-up company, penning a novel, or crafting a piece of art. To reach these goals, we must journey through a tumultuous sea. We'll be tossed and twisted in every direction, and the struggles will cause us to question whether it'll be worth it in the end.

Some see the rough sea as a deterrent, placed between us and our goal as a way to test our resolve. Some have even given such resistance a horn, tail, and pitchfork! Others accept the journey as the price for having goals and dreams, just like the waves and surf are part of the same sea. Regardless of how you see it, to reach the waves—to have a successful marriage, a vibrant faith, a meaningful job, a thriving company— you must navigate the waters. The journey can be strenuous, which is why so many give up.

On that particular day, I made it beyond the surf to the waves. They were among the best I've ever ridden. They lifted me high and sent me soaring toward the shore. I would never have experienced the ride if I hadn't persevered through the rough seas. I need to remember that. Maybe we all do.

Espresso Shots:

1. *Think of something you have aspired to in the past.*

2. *What kind of surf did you navigate to get out to the waves? Did you want to turn back?*

3. *How can you apply what you've learned in the past to the waves calling to you now?*

PICKING UP STICKS

They just picked up some sticks. That's all.

When they heard the news of my father's death, my friends tried to figure out what they could do to reach out and say they cared. As twenty-year-olds, they weren't going to bake a casserole or compose a heartfelt note. Instead, they created their own language of empathy. They came over to our house before we returned from the hospital and picked up sticks in the backyard. With the funeral in a few days and the reception at our home, my friends figured they could at least make the backyard look good. I can't remember what the yard looked like when we arrived home, but I've never forgotten the friends who cared enough to come over and pick up sticks.

Opportunities abound to be present in the lives of others. Whether it's the death of a loved one, a struggling child, divorce, or job loss, people face countless challenges. Sometimes we don't know what to say or do, or we think whatever we do, we must act in some grand or significant way, so we put off doing anything. Waiting for the right time, right words, or right gestures, we wait too long and the moment is lost.

From now on, I want to be the kind of person who picks up sticks, picks up the phone, pulls someone aside and says something, even if the words aren't perfect. I don't want to miss the moment or speak in a language that is not my own. All it takes is a couple of sticks and a willingness to make a difference.

Who knows? Something simple may be remembered forever.

Espresso Shots:

1. *Think of a time when you went through something difficult and someone reached out and showed compassion and care.*

2. *What made their efforts or words particularly meaningful?*

3. *In what ways can you be a picker-upper of sticks?*

FROM THE HEART

He was a gifted orator. With meticulous preparation, he had slides and pictures to complement his talk. It was polished, and the transitions from one point to another were seamless. I left very impressed, but I cannot remember a thing he said.

She had been sober for a year and was giving her first AA talk. She was nervous and stumbled her way through her talk. She used no notes and had no slides. All she had was her story, and she told it with humility and sincerity, and I've never forgotten what she said.

We are surrounded by shiny people whose lives appear seamless, and yet it's the others who touch my heart. When I look at the gospel stories, it seems Jesus was frequently attracted to tattered souls and resilient spirits—the ragamuffins, as author Brennan Manning calls them.

It's one thing to have a bedraggled soul, and another to be willing to speak from it. So often, we hide our scars and speak as if we have it all together. It may lead to a wonderful performance, but that's all it is.

I want to spend more time with people who speak from their hearts. Being with them helps me follow their example.

Espresso Shots:

1. When have you heard someone speak from a place of deep authenticity?

2. How did it make you feel?

3. How could you learn to do the same?

CONNECTING THE DOTS

My sister and I used to play a game we called "Connecting the Dots." With several dots scrawled across a page, we took turns drawing lines from dot to dot. Each time a square between four dots was created, one of us put our initial in the square. The one with the most squares at the end won.

Although it has been years since I played the game, I often play connect the dots in my daily life. We all do. We connect dots while listening to the news, talking with a friend, hearing about a neighbor, or meeting with a therapist. Connecting dots is how we make sense of things.

The problem comes when we connect the wrong dots or connect them incorrectly. As satisfying as it might be to complete a square and put our initial in it, we sometimes draw the wrong conclusion. In our determination to make sense of a situation or a person, we connect dots that have no business being connected. Even a wrong conclusion gives a sense of closure.

In my spiritual life, I have often sought to connect the dots. In my determination to make sense of something or to figure God out, I connect dots that shouldn't be connected.

Slowly, I've learned to draw fewer lines between dots and wait for the dots to connect themselves. It's challenging work but a healthy reminder of my limited perspective—and who's really in charge.

Espresso Shots:

1. *In what ways do you connect dots?*

2. *Have you ever connected the wrong dots about someone else, a situation, or God?*

3. *How can you grow in your ability to let God connect the dots?*

RECEIVING

"It is more blessed to receive than to give." —*A friend*

I thought she was having a dyslexic moment. We're familiar with the quotation that it's better to give than receive and yet she said the opposite. Observing my discomfort over a celebration in my honor, she used the clever twist to teach me an important truth: we need to learn how to graciously receive the generosity of others.

I like to say it began on my tenth birthday when my parents had a band sing happy birthday, and I ran out of the restaurant in tears, but my discomfort with receiving began before that. It has continued ever since. I prefer giving attention and offering help to receiving them. On the surface, this can appear noble and generous, but the fact is it is just self-centeredness wearing a costume. Despite the giving, it's all about me.

When generosity flows in only one direction, a relationship can't grow. Receiving requires an uncomfortable amount of intimacy. One loses all sense of control. Learning to receive is vital to any relationship and challenges us on a personal level. It allows others the opportunity to express their love and concern for us, and our hearts grow in their ability to receive whenever we allow them to receive instead of always to give.

For many like me, it's uncomfortable, but all growth is.

Espresso Shots:

1. *How comfortable are you receiving?*
2. *Would you prefer to give or receive?*
3. *In what ways can you learn how to receive love as much as you give?*

CHANGING COLOR

I saw an advertisement for a mug that changes color when something hot is put in it. Watching the black mug transform into a red one was fascinating. I couldn't help but see the mug's transformation as a visible representation of what it's like to grow in faith.

Some people claim conversion is instantaneous: make the decision and say certain words and you are a new creation. That may be true for some, but not for me. I believe there's a moment at which you turn over your heart to God, but that is only the beginning of a lifelong transformation. Slowly, God works within us. Like the red on the coffee mug, our spiritual life begins to spread, changing colors over time.

I see such transformations daily in 12-step recovery circles, but I also see it in the faith community, as well:

A driven businessman slowly loses his sharp edges and becomes a kinder, more forgiving soul.

A woman loosens her tight grip on her political views and becomes more curious than certain.

A family begins volunteering each Wednesday at the local soup kitchen.

A Bible study needs to find more chairs for newcomers.

We live in an instant gratification world, so the timing of spiritual growth can seem strange and maybe even a little frustrating. I just have to remember the mug and realize that, with God in me, my color will slowly change.

Espresso Shots:

1. *Do you think spiritual transformation happens in a moment or over time?*
2. *In what ways have you "changed color" with God inside you?*
3. *How can you learn to accept God's timing and look for the transformation in you and others?*

CHURCHES AND SERMONS

When I was teaching, I gave the seniors two choices for their final project: build a model of a church or give a sermon. For both projects, I challenged the students to articulate their theology through either the structure they created or the sermon they delivered. I expected them to communicate their faith, and I was never disappointed.

The best churches are the ones that express what the people believe without saying a word. When the mass was said in Latin, which the common folk did not speak, church architecture took on greater importance. Through the shape of the building, the carvings, and the stained-glass windows, churches told the Christian story in such a way that everyone could understand.

A professor once gave our class sage preaching advice: make one point, touch my heart, and help people to know Jesus Christ better. The best sermons do just that. I love to hear sermons that are clear, offer a personal connection, and help me grow in my relationship with Christ. We all have a sermon in us, maybe more than one, and I wish we delivered them more often. But we have a chance every day, if we let our lives be our sermons, our expressions of faith.

Whether through the lives we have built or the things that we say, we are called to express what we believe. Today, look and see what theology you are bringing into the world.

Espresso Shots:

1. Visit, or think of, a church that spoke to you. What was its theology?

2. If you were to give a sermon, what would you say about God?

3. In the life you have built, and the words you say, what is your theology?

MEETING AGAIN FOR THE FIRST TIME

We went to school together for several years. We took the same classes and played on the same teams. When we met for lunch recently, we discussed some of the significant challenges we've faced since. As I left, I felt as if we met again for the first time.

I've known her since the morning she was born. I've watched as she has grown up. I've seen her interests in things come and go, and I've watched her navigate the difficult waters of life. On a long car ride, we turned off the radio and talked. She shared with me something that happened that had left her feeling hurt and alone. I shared with her moments from my life that had made me feel the same way. I may have known her all her life, I thought, but it was as if we were meeting each other for the first time.

She had gone to church all her life. She worked her way through Sunday school classes, was confirmed, and was adamant about having her wedding in the church where she had grown up. After all that, she thought she knew God. That is until she lost her child. No one could have prepared her for the darkness and heart-wrenching sadness that followed. She didn't have the strength to carry on, she didn't have the faith to make it through, and she didn't have anyone who knew what she was going through. That's when she turned to God and cried, screamed, begged, and cried some more. Although she had known God all her life, she felt like she had come to know him for the first time.

Espresso Shots:

1. *Think of a time when you and someone you've known meet again for the first time.*

2. *What made that happen?*

3. *In what way can we meet people again on a regular basis?*

RIDING WAVES

"No, not this one," I said to my son. "The right wave's coming."

Suddenly the familiar dark shadow on the ocean's surface grew until it became a big, perfect wave, and my son and I rode it all the way into shore.

I was fortunate enough to spend every summer of my youth at the beach. More than any other activity, riding waves was my favorite. I loved the excitement of seeing a wave coming, committing to it, and then feeling the moment when you've caught the wave and it pulls you toward the shore. Just writing about it gets my heart beating more quickly.

But I wasn't a natural body surfer. I've missed more waves than I've caught, been tossed countless times to the bottom, or "boiled" as we called it, and impatiently tried to ride waves that weren't right.

Like most memories, there's something to be learned from riding waves. When I think about my career, I can see the years of practice. I can remember the many missed attempts and the waves that threw me to the ocean floor. But the times when a wave carried me to the shore made all the practice—and falls—worthwhile. Even in the waiting and the missing, there's joy that needs to be savored.

Espresso Shots:

1. *Have you ever tried to catch a wave (job, relationship, etc.) that was not meant for you?*

2. *Did your early struggles make catching the right wave all the more meaningful?*

3. *Find an activity you love, particularly one you have not done in a long time, and do it before summer ends.*

TALL TREES

A friend of mine once said he grows taller by walking with trees. Such poetic words have stuck with me, and I think of him each time I find myself among tall trees. More than that, however, I use his words to remind me to dwell among the tall, walk with the fit, and run with those who run faster than I.

Who we surround ourselves with makes a difference. Others can inspire and challenge us to reach higher or they can encourage us to play it safe and do only that which comes easy. The choice about which crowd we put ourselves in is up to us.

A friend of mine significantly increased her running speed. When I asked her how, she said she did it by running with others who ran faster. A newcomer to the rooms of AA is told to hang out with the ones with a lot of sobriety, and couples with vibrant marriages are usually found in the company of other successful couples.

The spiritual journey is no different, and we do well to read and spend time with those who are farther along on the path. They'll call us to come and walk with them. We might even find ourselves in a grove of very tall trees!

Espresso Shots:

1. *Have you ever been in a group that has thwarted your growth?*

2. *Have you ever been surrounded by those who have caused you to grow taller?*

3. *How can you find tall trees to stand among, spiritually?*

CHOPPY WATERS

The summer after my father died, my mother rented a house on a New Hampshire lake. When I arrived, it was windy, the water choppy and gray. Only after the winds calmed and the lake settled was I able to see the rocks, sunken logs, and fish below the surface. Looking back, I see a valuable lesson the twenty-year-old at the time could not.

Long before that summer, I had formed habits of emotional protection. One I used often was to stay perpetually active. When I moved and rushed around like the wind, the waters of my life were choppy, and I could not (and often, didn't want to) see beneath the surface. Such frenetic activity made me appear exciting and confident, I thought, but the truth was that I was insecure and frightened. I didn't want the water to calm, forcing me to acknowledge and others to see the hurts and insecurities submerged like rocks beneath the surface. Better to keep the winds blowing, I thought often.

As I have matured, I'm slowly learning to allow the water to settle and am beginning to look beneath the surface. Old habits return like gusts of wind, but I keep trying to let the water settle. The key is to catch myself in the act of chasing the wind. When the breezes start and whitecaps appear, I remind myself of that lake in New Hampshire. I wait for the water to settle and trust there's nothing beneath the surface I can't handle, with God's help.

Espresso Shots:

1. *In what ways do you keep the waters choppy?*

2. *What lies beneath the surface that you're trying to avoid?*

3. *Try to catch yourself in the act. Pause and let the waters settle. Remind yourself: there's nothing beneath the surface you can't handle—with God's help.*

EXTREME MAKEOVER

I love to watch episodes of the TV show *Extreme Makeover.* The show restores old houses, then gives them to a deserving family. The show's success is due not only to the extreme nature of what they do to old places but also to the joy it gives to others.

I recently heard of one such house. Like the others, the starting point was a shack, but through creativity, money, and effort, the shack was transformed into a remarkable home. When a friend of mine drove by the home recently, she was shocked to see the lawn was overgrown, part of the siding had been removed, and three windows were broken.

"The neighborhood took it back," said the woman driving the car.

I felt for the family, as well as the volunteers who had worked to transform the place. It also made me think of my friends who've sought to turn their lives around, and the many "neighborhoods" that seek to take them back.

I believe we are all marvelously made, and yet we make choices and experience things that take us in unhealthy directions—physically, emotionally, and spiritually. The good news is we can turn our lives around. God is all about extreme makeovers, and yet the work can't stop with the grand return home. If we don't do ongoing maintenance, the grass will grow, the siding will fall, and the windows will break.

Through vigilance, we can keep the bleak neighborhoods from taking us back.

Espresso Shots:

1. *Can you recall an improvement you made that was lost by not maintaining it?*

2. *What are the tools you use to keep the neighborhood from taking you back?*

3. *How can you help others learn this important truth?*

PRODIGAL SON (PART I)

One of the great parables Jesus tells is called the Prodigal Son. In it, a father gives his younger son half of his property, but the younger son loses what he was given through a reckless lifestyle. He comes crawling home and is lovingly embraced by his father, but the older brother is slower to welcome his younger brother.

Despite the parable's title, the father is the star of the show. He gives freely to a younger son, even though society at the time did not require or expect such generosity—normally the oldest was the sole heir.

But the father couldn't help himself. It's just the kind of person he was. Not only was he exceedingly generous at the start, but he was generous in the end. In the first case, he was generous with property; in the end, he was generous with grace.

One of the reasons why Jesus tells this parable is to help people understand God. Jesus knows firsthand that God is generous beyond anyone's imagination—both with tangible gifts and more importantly, with grace.

Interestingly, it's the latter kind of generosity that often causes problems. When we see the wonders of creation and consider the blessings bestowed upon us, most everyone can agree that God is generous. It's when God forgives or loves those who mess up that people get upset.

"It's not fair," people cry.

Thanks be to God.

Espresso Shots:

1. *When have you experienced God's generosity of blessings?*

2. *When have you experienced God's generosity of forgiveness?*

3. *Do you get upset when others receive such generosity?*

PRODIGAL SON (Part II)

Most people who have heard the parable of the Prodigal Son identify with one of the brothers. For most of my life, I related to the younger son, the one who was given much and squandered it all. But the truth is, we all have a bit of both brothers in us.

The gateway to my faith was gratitude. As a child, I marveled at creation and saw how blessed I was on so many levels. My gratitude, however, morphed into entitlement, and I walked around the world with an inflated sense of self.

In time, I wasted what had been given to me, if not literally then certainly figuratively. I had been given all a person could possibly want, and yet it wasn't enough, and I lost it all. Like the younger son, I had to experience the pain of such loss before turning for home.

The world around me stood with crossed arms as if to say, "It serves you right," but God's arms were opened wide, as if to say, "Welcome home."

Espresso Shots:

1. *In what ways are you like the younger son?*
2. *How have you been blessed, and how have you squandered what has been given to you?*
3. *Did you return home, and, if so, did God welcome you home?*

PRODIGAL SON (Part III)

We focus on the younger son and the father in the parable of the Prodigal Son, but the older brother was equally lost. He never left home but was tormented by his resentment of his brother. His self-righteous indignation held his heart captive.

Fuming, he stormed away when he watched his father kill the fatted calf to celebrate his brother's return. But the father loved both of this sons and showed them with his words and deeds.

When grace is extended to us, we are big fans. When it is given to a "sinner" or someone who's done something we have not, we become the older brother and claim God's generosity is unfair. What's worse, we hold back God's grace, which isn't ours in the first place.

Both sons are lost and found again.

May that be true for each of us, as well.

Espresso Shots:

1. *In what way do you identify with the older brother?*
2. *Why do we struggle when grace is extended to someone we feel doesn't deserve it?*
3. *How does the attitude of the older brother show up in the way we respond to others?*

VALIDATION

"I'm an artist," she said with a quivering voice and a trace of question. All her life she thought of artists as the ones whose work hung on museum walls, bound and displayed in a bookstore, or played on the radio. She painted and wrote poems. She'd never had a show or published her poems. Yet, her mentor told her being an artist wasn't about shows or publishing. It was about making art, and she did that on a daily basis.

We live in a world that loves to quantify and measure people, places, and things. *It's not enough to be an athlete. Your value is found in seeing how you compete and place. It's not enough to be a minister. The quality of your ministry is based on the effectiveness of your preaching or the size of your congregation. It's not enough to be a mother. You need to display an overflowing calendar of events and playdates to prove your worth.*

To be an artist, father or mother, minister or church volunteer never seems to be enough, but it should be. If we could learn to be the people we claim to be and not worry so much about measuring or validating those claims, we'd probably paint better pictures, preach better sermons, and hold our children tighter.

Espresso Shots:

1. *In what ways do you try to prove your worth?*
2. *Why do you feel the need to measure and validate your worth?*
3. *How would it change things if you no longer had to validate your worth?*

NEW KNEES

A friend of mine just had knee surgery. He had suffered with chronic pain in his right knee for years, and the pain got so bad he finally had it replaced. The operation went well, the doctor said, but his knee was swollen and the pain severe. Just as the swelling began to go down and the pain diminished, my friend was told he needed to begin rehabilitation. After the first session, my friend almost fainted from the pain and was tempted to quit. The next session was only a little better, but eventually the rehab worked, and his new knee was as good as new.

In discussing some of the spiritual work I'd been doing, my friend drew upon his experience with his knee. He pointed out that he wasn't ready for the operation until the pain got bad enough. He described his apprehension when he saw his swollen knee bandaged in the hospital.

"Then there was the rehab," he said, shaking his head. "That was the most painful part, but I wouldn't have this healthy knee now if I didn't go through all that pain."

Listening to him, I understood why so few are willing to do the painful work that is often a part of spiritual growth. The pain they carry is nothing compared to the pain of doing the work, or so they think.

Things always feel worse before they feel better, but it's working through the pain that leads to new life.

Espresso Shots:

1. *What inner pain are you enduring right now?*
2. *What would it take to address the cause of that pain?*
3. *What would your life be like if that pain was gone, and what would you be willing to endure to get there?*

Double Shot: *Take the first step toward spiritual health today.*

ONE VOTE

After two years of work, the search committee at the church made its recommendation for the new senior minister. After looking across the country, reading through more than 150 resumes, and conducting many interviews, the committee felt they had found the perfect candidate, one with local roots, academic prowess, and preaching talent. The candidate was a woman, the first in the parish's history. Her name was put forward and the congregation voted. It was 841 in favor, 1 opposed. Despite the overwhelming support for the new minister, I found myself only thinking of the one vote.

Who cast the one vote? Was the person's opposition based upon the candidate being a woman? Why did that person not like the selection?

Rather than travel down the path of what-ifs and whys, I realized the more relevant issue was the fact that I was focused on the one opposing vote instead of the 841 in favor. I'm like the student who receives a 99 percent on a test and obsesses over the one incorrect answer or the politician who is elected but can't stop thinking about the people who voted for his opponent.

All-or-nothing thinking can ruin a wonderful achievement.

Espresso Shots:

1. *When have you obsessed on the one vote (or minority opinion) and not the 841 in your life?*

2. *How can you shift your perspective and focus on the good and not the bad?*

3. *How can you learn to accept people with different opinions?*

MOUNTAIN STORMS

In the mountains, storms come frequently. Because of the ridges, they often stay hidden until they suddenly appear and envelop the area with wind, rain, and sometimes lightning and thunder. The storms are dramatic, much like the terrain they drench. When they pass, clouds and mist remain in the valleys and slowly meander away.

After a recent storm, I watched this familiar ritual and thought about how the storms I've known in my life do much the same thing. Many seem to have come out of nowhere. They've brought rain and wind—and occasionally more than that. Some have been mild, more like inconveniences, but the ones I remember most are the dramatic ones that caused the earth to shake. In each case, the storms passed, but clouds and mist remained. Water dripped from the leaves, water flowed into the valleys, and I had to sit and wait for the remaining clouds to disappear. The process never happened as quickly as I would have liked. Valleys are such safe harbors for clouds.

Watching the weather and trying to understand what it has to teach me about living does not explain away the reality of storms. It does not make the thunder and lightning any less frightening nor the persistent clouds any less frustrating. But it does help me embrace the reality of storms and the need for patience and trust that not only will the storms pass but the other clouds as well.

Espresso Shots:

1. *Think back on a storm in your life (past or present).*
2. *Did it come out of nowhere? Was it a gentle storm or a torrential storm?*
3. *What did it feel like during the storm?*

HARDENED HEARTS

In the biblical story of the exodus, there's a detail that seems absurd. A plague descends, Pharaoh agrees the Hebrew people can leave Egypt, then his heart hardens, and he refuses to let them go. As a child, I thought the story sounded silly. Pharaoh seems extraordinarily fickle, his heart a revolving door between soft and hard. It wasn't until I grew older that I realized how much I have in common with the Egyptian leader's heart.

A close friend died, and his closest friends gathered outside the church, vowing to never take our friendships for granted. I haven't been in touch with one of them for several years.

The doctor said I needed to pay closer attention to my diet and exercise. I joined a gym and stocked up on fruit and vegetables but was back to my usual routine within a few weeks.

The news showed a despicable act of racial violence. A group at church met to discuss a fitting response. Not much has happened since.

Like the time I began falling asleep at the wheel only to startle when my tires hit the ribbed edge of the highway, we are given moments that awaken us. They are often shocking and cause us to sit up and take notice, but we soon fall back asleep. Like Pharaoh, our hearts harden, and we forget.

Today, and every day, God calls us to soften our hearts and awaken to the present.

"Oh, that today you would harken to his voice." (Psalm 95:7)

Espresso Shots:

1. *What are examples in your life when you have fallen asleep?*
2. *When has your heart been hardened?*
3. *How can you learn to stay awake and keep your heart soft?*

TEDDY BEARS

The car was silent as they drove toward the school. It was her first day, and, while she was eager to go to school like her older siblings, now that the moment had come, she wasn't so sure. Clutching her teddy bear with both hands, she tried to be brave. As they turned into the drive, her grip tightened. Her mother tried to lighten the moment, but nothing helped. The door opened, and a smiling teacher offered her daughter a hand. With great reluctance, she let go of her teddy bear and climbed out of the car.

Letting go was hard. Walking away with empty hands was scary. The stuffed animal had always provided a sense of comfort. It made the happy times happier, the adventures more adventurous, and the nights less dark. But she did it, and now she was walking into the entrance of her new school.

The mother got out of the car and went to the backseat where she took the bear and buckled it into her child's seat. As tears flowed, she thought of the day her daughter was born, the wonderful days since, and how she didn't want them to end. Like her daughter, she didn't want to let go.

Espresso Shots:

1. Think of a time when it was particularly hard to let go of something or someone.

2. What was it that made you cling so tight, and what happened when you finally let go?

3. To what are you clinging now, and how can you release your grip, trusting that there's new life ahead?

WEBS

It was a bright August morning, and the minister looked forward to worship. It had been months since his congregation was able to worship together, but today they were meeting for an outdoor service. He was excited to see familiar faces in person and not on his computer screen. They had done their best to stay connected through the pandemic, but there's nothing like being together, he said to himself.

He made his Sunday morning pilgrimage across the church grounds to ring the bell. Even the birds were singing songs of praise. His heart was full. His daughter had just given birth to his second grandchild the day before, a girl named after his grandmother. He wished his mother had hung on a little longer so she could have met the newest member of the family. He would be gathering withing his siblings in a few weeks to spread her ashes.

A ray of light shone through the branches as he rang the church bell. The light flitted upon a large, intricate spider web beside the cemetery entrance. Glistening with dew, its extensive symmetry was impossible to ignore. Each strand connected to another, round and round, a comprehensive whole.

On his way back to the church, he realized he'd already seen this morning's sermon.

Espresso Shots:

1. *When was the last time you saw a sermon?*
2. *When was the last time you were aware of your life's web and its connected parts?*
3. *In what ways does your heart take comfort that "to everything there is a season?"*

STREAM CLEARING (Part I)

A dramatic storm caused sticks, leaves, and other debris to clog the stream. Some of the dams released themselves under the water pressure from upstream. Others needed help to move the debris.

Their marriage was the envy of many until the phone rang with the news of a tragic accident involving their three-year-old daughter. Bewildered and numb, they clung to each other in a way they never had before, but the pain eventually wedged itself between them. First it was less and less eye contact, then conversations only about the weather and logistical concerns. In time, they became two separate people living in the same house.

A dramatic storm caused sticks, leaves, and other debris to clog the stream. Some of the dams released themselves under the water pressure from upstream. Others needed help to move the debris.

Espresso Shots

1. *What sticks and leaves are clogging the stream of relationships within your family?*
2. *How have you let the storm reshape your interactions?*
3. *What help do you need to clear the debris?*

STREAM CLEARING (Part II)

A dramatic storm caused sticks, leaves, and other debris to clog the stream. Some of the dams released themselves under the water pressure from upstream. Others needed help to move the debris.

She thought the trauma of her youth would go away in time. After all, it happened through no fault of her own, and yet she somehow felt responsible for what occurred. Each time she remembered, she pushed the memories down, out of sight, but they always found a way to resurface. When she was old enough to date, the memories pulled up a chair at the table and lay between them in bed. She took out her pain on countless men. "Hurt people, hurt people," her therapist said, and, slowly, they began to look at her wounds.

A dramatic storm caused sticks, leaves, and other debris to clog the stream. Some of the dams released themselves under the water pressure from upstream. Others needed help to move the debris.

Espresso Shots:

1. What experiences from your past haunt you today?
2. What steps can you take to start addressing that pain?
3. How can you help others clear their debris?

STREAM CLEARING (Part III)

A dramatic storm caused sticks, leaves, and other debris to clog the stream. Some of the dams released themselves under the water pressure from upstream. Others needed help to move the debris.

He couldn't tell you when drinking became a problem, but he thinks it was some time during high school. Back then, he didn't even like the way alcohol tasted, but he loved the way it made him feel. It calmed his anxiety and silenced his blabbering mind. Eventually, it got in the way. He thought only about his next drink. Those around him hoped he'd learn to manage his drinking; others figured he was weak and morally depraved. "Drinking isn't your problem," a wise friend pointed out. "It's just a symptom of something else. Until you remove the things getting in the way inside, your spirit will never flow freely."

A dramatic storm caused sticks, leaves, and other debris to clog the stream. Some of the dams released themselves under the water pressure from upstream. Others needed help to move the debris.

Espresso Shots:

1. *Do you use alcohol or some other substance to numb your pain or transform your reality?*

2. *Take an honest assessment of your "crutch"—whether it's alcohol, drugs, food, work. How is this addiction impacting your life and your relationships with others and with God?*

3. *What can you do today to start removing the debris?*

SCREWING IN LIGHT BULBS

"We are the light bulbs, Richard, and our job is just to stay screwed in!"

—*Archbishop Desmond Tutu (to author Richard Rohr)*

As another school year was about to begin, I was excited to have a new lamp for my writing table. I climbed underneath to plug it in, but it didn't work. I checked the plug then remembered certain outlets in the house are activated by switches. I tried them all, but none turned on the lamp. It was then I saw that the light bulb wasn't screwed in all the way. With a simple twist, there was light, and it was good!

Maybe it was because school was about to begin or because this was the table at which I do much of my spiritual writing, but I couldn't help but see a lesson in my fumbling.

This is the time when teachers, students, and many others are preparing for a new year. We move from the carefree thoughts of summer to a more focused fall. It's time to get back into a routine, and one of the most important things we can do is keep the light bulbs screwed in. There are many ways to do so, like beginning the day with reflection or ending it with a walk. Whatever works, this is the time to make sure the connection is there, and the light is burning bright.

Espresso Shots:

1. *When have you felt disconnected from God?*
2. *What did you do to screw in the light bulb?*
3. *As we begin another season, what specific thing(s) can you do to stay connected?*

PAUL

I was a trembling ninth-grader, desperate to seem confident and secure, as my parents drove away from the boarding school. Climbing the three flights of stairs to my room, all I could hear was the echo of my steps. I made no eye contact with strangers I passed. I felt utterly lost and alone. As I made my way down the shiny linoleum hallway to unpack my room, a boy with curly hair and a soccer ball under his arm came up to me with an outstretched hand: "Hi, I'm Paul. A bunch of us are going outside to play soccer. Want to join us?"

It's been forty-six years since that moment, but each September, I remember Paul with profound gratitude. I think about all the students arriving at schools for the first time and pray they come across a Paul, someone who reaches out their hand and asks them to join in.

Of course, such a prayer is not limited to students arriving at school. It's for anyone who feels alone. We pass "new students" all the time. May we be the ones who break the silence, reach out a hand, and ask someone to join.

Espresso Shots:

1. *Recall a time when you were desperately alone.*
2. *Recall a time when someone broke the silence and included you.*
3. *In what way could you be that person, be that Paul, to someone else?*

BARNACLES

I grew up going to a small town on the Jersey shore. The beaches weren't as crowded, and I wandered along the ocean's edge for hours. Often, my walks were along a series of jetties. Built to protect the shoreline and the beachfront homes, they began on the beach with wooden pilings and walls embedded in the sand and led to massive boulders stacked upon one another in the ocean. Waves crashed on the rocks and provided constant entertainment.

I liked to sit on the pilings and watch the sea and rocks meet. No matter how picturesque the wave, the rocks always brought its dance to a dramatic end. On the rocks were white barnacles. Tiny in comparison to their hosts, these barnacles could be fierce: I had scars on my hands and feet to remind me not to take them lightly. I have no idea what role barnacles play in nature's drama, but they appear without invitation on anything that remains in the water for a significant period of time. I doubt they have a brain, but I marvel at how smart they are. They cling to the rocks knowing they'll keep them safe. No matter how tumultuous the sea, they'll be all right as long as they hold onto the rocks.

Only after some awful storms in my life have I remembered what barnacles seem to naturally know—it's important to find a rock and cling to it. These days, I hold on tight to God, my rock. More storms will come, but I, like the barnacles, have a rock to protect me.

Espresso Shots:

1. *Recall a storm you experienced.*
2. *Were you washed away, or did you cling to a rock?*
3. *In what way could you find such a rock, or cling more tightly?*

FIXING THE TRUCK

"Our philosophy is grounded in the history of the school," said the headmaster of a rural school to the assembled parents. "If the truck breaks down, learn how to fix it."

I've spent most of my life in schools, many of which have glorious visions and elaborate mission statements, but something about the simplicity of this school's philosophy reawakened my passion for education. Schools have become as glossy as their brochures. They come wired with every form of technology, dripping with endless educational theory, strategic plans, and pristine facilities. All of this helps educate children, I'm sure, but I wonder if the tree of knowledge hasn't become overgrown. The educational "toys" seem to be the tail wagging the dog. Finding the truck has become as challenging as learning to fix it.

Such overgrowth is not unique to schools. You can find it in corporations and churches, as well as marriages and friendships. You can also find it in one's spiritual life. An earnest desire to know and be known by God can become overtaken with books you need to read, creeds you must recite, and practices you must demonstrate.

One of the most important things about learning is keeping it simple, even if that means rolling up your sleeves and learning to fix a truck.

Espresso Shots:

1. *What is at the heart of your desire for a spiritual life?*
2. *In what way does your spiritual life become cluttered?*
3. *What needs fixing in your spiritual truck?*

SPIRITUAL PRACTICE I: SITTING STILL

I need to sit still each morning. I need this time to allow my heart and mind to awaken. I'm not a contemplative in the traditional sense of the word. I can't sit on the floor with my legs crossed and hope to get up again. Instead, I find a comfortable chair and sit still. I don't read, write, or even pray (in the traditional sense). I simply let my heart and mind wander. They need time for their morning stretches, and when I give it to them, I am astounded by what they come up with.

They begin by chattering about calls I need to make and emails I need to send, but eventually, the chatter quiets. My heart and mind are able to turn their attention to the people dear to me or others going through difficult times. I picture their faces and lift them as if to place them on a mental altar. Then, like a child scampering around a playground when she first arrives, I begin to imagine things I could do—writing, painting, volunteering.

When sitting still goes well, my spiritual and creative batteries are charged, and I'm eager to get up and get going.

Espresso Shots:

1. *Do you make time to sit still?*
2. *What do your heart and mind say when you give them a chance to speak freely?*
3. *How can you make sitting still each day a part of your spiritual practice?*

SPIRITUAL PRACTICE II: LET YOUR HEART DOODLE

I've always been a doodler. I filled the margins with scribbles in class and doodled while in business meetings. Those looking on thought I was bored or not paying attention, but it was the opposite. Doodling with a pen is the best way for me to listen.

Picking up a pen is still the most effective spiritual tool I have to help me listen. For some, a keyboard works, but I'm old-school and still need a pen. When I hold the pen in my hand and begin doodling words, it's as if I'm connecting directly to the right side of my brain. I'm composing new words and thoughts by letting my soul breathe through the ink and paper. I doodle-write about anything that comes to mind. I tell the inner editor and critic to take a break and leave me alone during this time. Spelling and grammar don't count. Moving the pen across the page does.

At first, my handwriting is neat, and my thoughts are logical, but as I keep going, both become unharnessed. This is when I start saying what's really on my mind and in my heart. It's the time the best ideas arrive. I express gratitude, admit fears, confess mistakes, and ask for help. Knowing I'll throw the pages away when I'm finished, I'm completely honest. In the end, I have stretched my soul and can breathe more easily.

Espresso Shots:

1. Go to a store and buy a pen and pad of paper or a journal that speaks to you.
2. Spend some time doodling, with words or images.
3. Let your mind and heart speak freely.

SPIRITUAL PRACTICE III: GO FLY A KITE

I learned this spiritual practice from *The Artist's Way,* a book for renewal by Julia Cameron. She recommends people take their inner child on a date each week. In an effort to put air in our spiritual and creative tires, she commends that we schedule an hour each week for something fun. It can be listening to a favorite album from start to finish, going to a concert, watching a favorite movie, going to a museum, building a dam in a stream, constructing a fort, making a favorite childhood meal, or countless other things. The important thing is to do something that feeds your soul. It's not an "I should" kind of thing but an "I get to."

At first, there will be resistance. The adult within you will protest that it's silly or you can't afford the time, but the child inside will plead, *please, please, please.* This time is not frivolous. It's an opportunity for your soul to come and play, and when it does, your heart and mind will say things they usually keep to themselves.

Espresso Shots:

1. *What was something you loved to do as a child that you haven't in years?*

2. *Schedule a time to do that thing.*

3. *What else would you like to do if you allowed the child within you to come out and play?*

SPIRITUAL PRACTICE IV: THESE BOOTS WERE MADE FOR WALKING

I live in a neighborhood of walkers. Some begin before the sun rises, but many walk in the early morning or late afternoon. Regardless of the timing, walking is one of the best spiritual tools I know. Like other tools, it takes a few minutes for my mind and heart to find their stride. Logistical thoughts dominate the conversation until enough time has passed. I can set my watch to it. Once I've walked for twenty minutes, it's like a switch has turned on (or off, you might say). No longer am I recounting my to-do-list or the day's events. Instead, my thoughts become more random, and my concerns more esoteric. It's as if I go from reading a financial report to a children's book, from black and white to color. The repetitive nature of walking knocks on our soul's door. Monks have known this for years.

I do better on a trail than on a sidewalk, among trees instead of houses, but any walk will do. I sometimes listen to music, but most often, I try to walk without it. I never talk on the phone. It's exercise but not the kind that makes a person flail his or her arms up and down to maximize the effort. It's spiritual exercise, a time to connect to yourself, the world in which you live, and the one who created it.

Espresso Shots:

1. *Go for a walk.*

2. *Notice where your heart and soul take you once you've walked for twenty minutes.*

3. *Incorporate walking into your spiritual practices for a month and see if it helps you connect with yourself, the world, and the creator.*

STICKS

It only takes a stick to make her wag her tail. The shape, size, or type of wood matters not. Just put a stick in her mouth or, better yet, give it toss and she'll wag her tail for the rest of the day. How I wish I could be more like my dog.

There was a time, I suppose, when I was as easily pleased, but those days seem long past. Each year of life brought a revised list of things that make me happy. The list didn't necessarily grow longer, but it certainly grew more expensive. Somewhere around high school, I experienced the fickle nature of happiness brought about by possessions. The passionate "I've just got to have it" turned to "What's next?" in record time. Radios turned to stereos, stereos to televisions, televisions to cars, cars to houses. The snowball of my incessant wants rolled quickly down the hill.

No wonder Jesus spoke about this. Don't be anxious, he said. Consider the lilies of the field. For too long, I dismissed such words but now hear them with renewed appreciation. Exhausted from the material race, I stand catching my breath, able to hear what I couldn't before.

Watching my dog with a stick reminds me that I'm the one who's made life so complicated. It's time to stop clinging to stuff and open my hands.

Espresso Shots:

1. *What was something you "had to have" when you were young?*
2. *Do you still find happiness in acquiring things?*
3. *How can you learn to find happiness by opening your hands and letting go?*

SECRETS

"We are only as sick as the secrets we hold." —*AA adage*

I didn't like it when I first heard it, but I knew it was true. If I had any hope of getting well, I needed to address the many secrets I held. I mistakenly hoped all I needed to do to get better was to stop drinking, but there's a lot more to recovery than abstinence. Once you stop drinking and the perpetual fog lifts, you must then deal with what you see. For most of us, it's the secrets we've clung to, the relationships we've shattered, and the reputations we've decimated.

Regardless of whether a person has a problem with alcohol or some other addiction, the danger of secrets is universal. Whether big or small, the secrets we hold eat away at our souls.

We may believe we can move on, that whatever happened is in the past, but the fact is the secrets hold us captive until we let them go. That's why confession has always been essential in the church and why a person in recovery takes a fifth step, which is to admit to God, yourself, and another human being the exact nature of our wrongs. To move forward spiritually, we need to clear the path of the debris. It is not easy, which is why so few are willing to do the work. Once you begin, it's as if one secret leads to another.

It can be overwhelming, but the view at the other end of the climb is marvelous.

Espresso Shots:

1. *List every secret to which you cling.*
2. *In what way are your secrets holding you back from living a full life?*
3. *How can you begin to let go of your secrets so they will let go of you?*

9/11

It was a bright, cool Tuesday morning. I thought a colleague was joking when she walked into my office and told me a plane had just flown into the World Trade Center. When I looked at her face, I realized the truth. The rest of the day was a blur. I was running a school and needed to make countless decisions, but when I got home that night, I watched the news until dawn.

The days following the attacks felt surreal. Life seemed to hush. No planes flew. People allowed others to go ahead of them in line. Church pews were full, and Democrats and Republicans stood side by side on the capitol steps singing, "God Bless America."

What happened?

People eventually returned to their original pace, car horns began to blow, and politicians became polarized again. It's as if 9/11 never happened, and that's almost the worst tragedy of all.

I remember leaving a friend's funeral years ago with a new resolve to live a meaningful life. Because of the loss, I was determined to make every moment count and take no one for granted. As you might guess, it didn't last.

Anniversaries serve many purposes, but my prayer is that this one will always remind us how we responded in the days after the tragedy—as individuals and as a country. Perhaps we will honor those who died by caring about others and loving our country as one.

Espresso Shots:

1. *Where were you when you heard about the 9/11 attacks?*
2. *What are your most vivid memories of that day and the days that followed?*
3. *How can you keep alive the spirit we shared after the attacks?*

EXPOSED ROOTS

A dramatic storm blew through the night before my hike, and I was surprised by the damage along the trail. Leaves and limbs were strewn all over, but the enormous tree lying on its side caught my attention the most. It fell to the left, exposing a network of roots. They looked like the fingers of Snow White's wicked stepmother pointing in every direction.

I passed the fallen tree with reverence. What a sound it must have made. What fierce wind it must have been to fell such a tree.

I thought about the tree and its roots for the rest of my hike. I thought about the storms I've faced and my friends who have faced violent winds as well. In each case, I'm happy the storms did not knock us over, but they did expose our roots. It's what storms do.

Espresso Shots:

1. *Read Matthew 13.*

2. *Has a storm ever revealed your roots? Did you have deeper roots than you thought? Were the roots shallow?*

3. *How can you strengthen your roots before the storms arrive?*

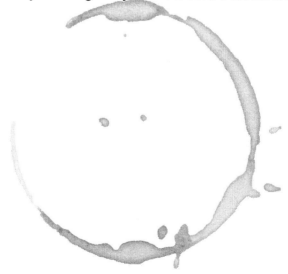

MORNING COMMUTE

For a time, I was a commuter. I tried many things to fill the time, but daydreaming was what I used most often. I spent so much time thinking about being somewhere else, I was never fully present where I was. I now realize what a dangerous pastime that can be.

One of the gifts of being creative is you have an imagination. That gift, like many others, can work for good or ill. I was born a dreamer, and that has always allowed me to imagine things that have served me well in my work. The danger of dreaming is that it can transport you from the present and lead to escapism or avoidance, which are just other words for a disconnected life.

In 12-step recovery circles, they refer to a "geographical cure." It means thinking you can leave where you are and head to a better place. In most cases, you think a geographic cure will enable you to leave worries or troubles behind, but as anyone in recovery circles will tell you, you take you wherever you go!

I'm embarrassed to admit how often I've used my faith as a trip away from reality, but I've learned that faith is more about becoming present than leaving. Some become present through prayer and meditation. Some focus by taking deep breaths, others by repeating phrases or actions. The methods for becoming present vary, but the need to be present is the same.

With each morning commute, I became more distant from my life. Now I'm slowly learning to focus on where I am so that I can be the person I was created to be.

Espresso Shots:

1. In what ways do you commute from your life? (Physically, emotionally, and/or spiritually)

2. What is gained by such geographical cures? What are you leaving? What are you looking for?

3. What would it look like to become fully present in the life you have and the person you are?

THE WOMEN WITH THE CANES

I decided to join the 1,600 other folks riding in the local fundraiser for multiple sclerosis called "The Tour to Tanglewood." The 50-mile bike ride aimed to raise money for and awareness about the awful disease. As I lined up behind the other riders, all I thought about was handling the physical challenge ahead of me. I hadn't trained much and was ten years older than the last time I rode in the fundraiser.

The day was bright, clear, and cool enough, and I felt good as we made our way out of the park. However, within a few miles, I was already thinking about how much farther I had to go. I tried to cycle as far as I could without taking a break, but the "walls" kept coming. Hills and wind made me wonder why I hadn't just written a check. The final twenty miles were excruciating, but I made it.

I dragged my fifty-three-year-old body over to where the other riders were gathered and looked forward to sharing my woes. It was then I came across three African American women standing together talking, each with a cane. It didn't take me long to realize they suffered from MS. They were the reason for the event. They were the reason we rode.

My weary legs became insignificant, my moaning an embarrassment. The day wasn't about the riders. It was about the women with the canes.

Espresso Shots:

1. *When have you participated in a fundraiser for a worthy cause?*

2. *Did you wish you had simply written a check rather than participate fully?*

3. *When have you thought it was all about you only to realize there are others less fortunate?*

SOOOOO MUCH!

"How much does Mommy love you? Sooooo much!" she says as she stretches her arms as wide as possible. Her words always make her son giggle no matter how many times she says them.

A stained-glass window in the front of the school chapel depicts Jesus as a child with his arms spread wide. I couldn't help but imagine him saying what mothers and fathers have said through the ages: "How much does God love you? Sooooo much!"

I know such a thought is beneath the dignity of any reputable theologian, but it shouldn't be. Regardless of how many sermons are delivered, books written, or classes taken, maybe this is all we really need to know. When we're overwhelmed with a mistake, when our careers are falling apart, when our families don't look or act like the dream we envisioned, and when our bank account is full but our hearts are empty, we need to remember those open arms and that God loves us.

Sooooo much!

Espresso Shots:

1. *Have you ever felt God loves you sooooo much?*

2. *What gets in the way of your feeling that?*

3. *How could remembering God's love change how you live?*

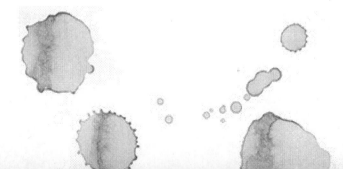

WAKE-UP CALLS

I've always had a thing for John the Baptist. The fact that he wore a hair shirt and ate locusts certainly caught my attention as a young boy, but the way he awakened people has made the lasting impression. Like the chef who clanks pots together to get her staff's attention, the teacher who claps his hands, or the protester who holds a megaphone, John the Baptist has a way of waking people up that I admire.

As a teacher, my first classroom had a blackboard, and whenever I taught about John or any of the prophets from the Old Testament, I would reach up and drag my fingernails down the board. Recalling the sound still gives me chills, and the effect on my students was dramatic. I got their attention, just like the ones about whom I was going to teach.

Waking up is perhaps the most important spiritual discipline. It's important because falling to sleep, or getting stuck in mindless living, is such a common occurrence. God has always sent people or events to awaken us. Like my nails on the board, what awakens us is not always pleasant to hear or go through, but some of us are sound sleepers. It takes a great deal to wake us up!

John and the other waker-uppers were not universally loved, but they were not brought into the world to be popular. Not all the events in our lives are pleasant, yet each, in its own way, awakens us, and for that, we should be grateful.

Espresso Shots:

1. *Think back on a person or event that awakened you.*
2. *In what way had you fallen asleep?*
3. *How did your waking up change the way you proceeded in life?*

PARK DAY

Today was Park Day, a semi-annual day when folks in our community gather to work in our local park. Each time we gather, I am amazed by how much has grown since the last work day. Small trees seem to have taken root out of nowhere, vines that were cut away strangle trees and bushes with renewed vigor, and the bamboo grove we decimated last time has grown back and then some. "It's always like this," a neighbor assured me. "It grows back, and then we come and clear it away."

I got out my clippers and began to clear the small patch in front of our house. As I started ripping the vines away from the bushes and picking up the countless sticks that had fallen since our last park day, I thought about how similar it was to the spiritual life.

Like the park, my soul gets overgrown. Vines and branches come out of nowhere and try to overtake the trees and bushes. I need to remember the wise words of my neighbor: "It grows back, and then we come and clear it away."

The weeds can be stubborn, but determination can win the day if I remain vigilant. Part of my spiritual work is clearing away the weeds.

Yes, the spiritual life is about growth, but weeding is what makes the growth possible.

Espresso Shots:

1. *How much of your spiritual work is spent weeding?*
2. *What are the vines or branches that most hinder your growth?*
3. *How can you make weeding a part of your soul's growth?*

ROCKS

"Why on earth are we gathered here?" asked the disgruntled resident of the New Jersey seaside community. "If you ask me, the whole idea of putting rocks in front of the dunes is as foolish as it is expensive. After all, the ocean's never come close to our houses before."

Others shared this opinion, and the debate lasted for weeks. Many felt the cost was higher than the risk, but the prevailing opinion was to fortify the shore. Each time the opponents to the idea had the chance, they ridiculed the town leadership. Looking to the sea, they pointed out how far the waves were from the houses.

Those who were for and opposed to the rocks died over time. Sand covered the rocks, and everyone in the town forgot they were there—until Superstorm Sandy arrived. With winds and raging seas unlike any they'd ever known, Sandy pummeled the Jersey shore. When the residents of that one seaside community came to inspect the damage after the storm, they realized they had fared better than many towns. The rocks, hidden for years by sand and sea, had protected the beach and their town.

The storms will come. When the skies are sunny, it's hard to believe we need to do the work of putting rocks in front of our houses. It was true for this one community, and it is true for those who seek to live spiritual lives. Adopting daily practices and addressing behaviors that are not in keeping with our faith are some of the ways we shore up our spiritual houses. Some may scoff at our efforts, but, in the end, such rocks provide protection from life's storms.

Espresso Shots:

1. *What do you do about your faith when skies are sunny?*
2. *What storms have you endured?*
3. *Did you run to faith, or was it already there, under the sand, when the storms came?*

BALANCING THE BOOKS

He was as meticulous as Bob Cratchit when it came to keeping his ledger. Each day he closed the books with all accounts reconciled. Taking a deep breath, he closed the book with a deep sense of satisfaction. He put on his coat and hat, wrapped his scarf around his neck, and walked home.

If only we could learn to be equally meticulous about the ledgers of our lives. In 12-step recovery circles, we're told to take a "daily inventory." The idea behind such advice is to stay on top of our lives, see where we have done well and where we have not. Each day we are to assess our behaviors, thoughts, and actions and to reconcile our accounts. We are to admit our wrongs and make amends as quickly as possible.

The church has long known the wisdom of reconciling our spiritual accounts. In each worship service, there's a time to reflect and confess those things we have done and left undone. There are also seasons designed for looking at our accounts with increased vigor and candor. Such daily and seasonal work is essential to one's spiritual well-being. Not only does it keep little things small, as people like to say these days, but also it allows us to realign our lives on a regular basis.

When reconciling accounts becomes part of our spiritual practice, we're able to close the books, take a deep breath, and head home restored.

Espresso Shots:

1. *How often do you take the time to reconcile your spiritual books?*

2. *Where are your accounts unbalanced today?*

3. *How can you make daily reflection a part of your spiritual practice?*

THE GOSPEL ACCORDING TO TREES (PART I)

The big tree outside my office window was a gift. It provided shade in the hot summer months and bright colors in the fall. I stared out at the tree when on a phone call or searching for words to write, and that's when I noticed its leaves didn't look quite right. I don't know much about trees, but I do know that you can gauge the health of a tree by its leaves. When they are healthy, so is the tree, but when they become withered or sparse, the tree is not well.

It didn't happen all at once, but slowly the outward and visible parts of my life, like leaves on a tree, started to change. Hardly noticeable at first, the leaves eventually began to show something was wrong. I lost interest in things that used to captivate me, and fear constricted my heart. I became increasingly self-absorbed. The changes were noticeable only to those who knew me well. They heard the difference in my words and saw it in my actions. I was not healthy, and, at the risk of sounding melodramatic, if I didn't change, I'd die, if only spiritually.

The fact is, the signs were there. The leaves were showing the change. They always do. The relapse of a recovering alcoholic begins long before he or she picks up a drink. The loss of a job starts months before a worker is called into the boss's office. A marriage is in need of attention long before the couple agrees to see a counselor.

It's all about the leaves.

Espresso Shots:

1. *When have you seen leaves indicating a change in health in yourself and in others?*
2. *What did you tell yourself that allowed you to ignore the leaves?*
3. *Looking back, what could you have done differently?*

THE GOSPEL ACCORDING TO TREES (Part II)

The tree was unhealthy. Anyone looking at its leaves could tell, but the solution was not in the leaves but the roots. It's a common mistake among amateur tree enthusiasts. Focusing on the unhealthy leaves ignores the real problem and real solution: the roots.

This is also a common mistake among people like you and me. We see the outward signs in our life or the life of someone we care about, and they become our focus. *She's drinking too much. They never seem to be together anymore. All he does is work.*

The problem lies deeper than the external signs. Any recovering alcoholic will tell you alcohol is but a symptom. So is losing interest in a spouse or becoming obsessed with our work or our children. Such outward and visible signs are important, but they point to a need to address issues beneath the surface.

"What's really going on?" my therapist asks whenever I come in distraught over something. She knows it's never about the leaves but rather the roots. Ask anyone who has ever been through a spiritual, moral, relational, or professional trauma: the signs were there long before the crisis arrived. The real issue and the lasting solution lies not in the outward appearance but beneath the surface, at the roots.

Trees have been trying to teach us this for ages. Perhaps it's time we pay attention not only to the leaves but also the roots.

Espresso Shots:

1. *When have you mistakenly focused on the leaf and not the root?*
2. *Identify one leaf, an outward and visible sign of something wrong, and see if you can trace it to something beneath the surface?*
3. *In what ways can you learn to use the leaves to point you to the deeper issues of your life?*

SMELLS LIKE CHRISTMAS

"It smells like Christmas," the woman hiker said as she and her companion made their way through the thick cluster of pines just below and out of sight from where I was resting. It had been a challenging four-mile hike up the mountain, and the squeak in her voice made me smile. It was late September, but her comment prompted me to think about Christmas. After they passed, I wandered over to the pine trees and took a deep breath before beginning my descent.

I felt a bond with the other hikers. We were glad to be alive and spending the morning in such a way. In other words, there were good tidings on the mountain that day. There was also great joy as we watched a hawk, with its enormous wings, glide below as if on snow. The leaves on the top of the mountain were changing color and clung, like ornaments, while others twirled like candy canes in the mountain breeze. I passed a father and daughter hiking. She was excited to be spending time alone with her father and scurried down the trail as if heading to open a gift. Farther down the trail, a college-aged couple walked hand-in-hand, as if walking through a silent night, while a mother and father chased after their two young children who were running toward the stream like it was a stocking full of treats. The dark green rhododendron looked like holly, and people greeted each other, not thinking about what they did for a living or where they grew up or went to school.

I realized as I got into my car, the woman had been right; it smelled like Christmas.

Espresso Shots:

1. *Take a walk or hike and try to use all of your senses.*

2. *Which sense speaks to you most easily?*

3. *In what way can you use your senses more to enter the present more fully?*

FIELD STONES

Stone walls are as synonymous with New England as lobster, autumn leaves, and endless conversations about the weather. The stone walls were built as farmers cleared their fields. Whenever they came across a rock, they'd dig it up and place it off to the side with the other rocks until they could figure out what to do with them. Eventually, they were placed along the edges of the property to delineate where one field ended and another began.

A writing teacher once spoke of "field stones," which made me think of the New England tradition. He'd learned the concept from another writer. A field stone is something you come across and save, knowing it will come in handy in a future essay or story. It could be an overheard phrase in a coffee shop, an event you witness, or anything that causes you to pause and take notice. Whatever the field stone, it sits off to the side until it can be used.

The idea of field stones can also apply to one's spiritual journey. We hear and see things that cause us to take notice. What if we saw these field stones as a spiritual practice? We could gather them as they come along and place them off to the side until we know what to do with them. In time, we could use the stones to give definition to our lives.

Espresso Shots:

1. *What's one thing you've heard or seen that could be a spiritual field stone?*

2. *How could you take such moments and put them aside for safekeeping?*

3. *How could you put a field stone to use?*

MINISTERS (Part I)

They announced the name of our new minister at church this afternoon. It was the culmination of a two-year search that involved many parish meetings and countless hours of work by the search committee. They combed through resumes, held initial interviews, and met with finalists before reaching a decision. They read candidates' writings, heard their sermons, and talked to people who knew them well. In the end, they found someone, which is a miracle in and of itself.

My experience is that there are as many opinions about what makes a good minister as there are parishioners. Some people carry wounds from their childhood that shape the kind of minister they'd like, and some want to find someone like the minister they had growing up. Some want a minister with an engaging personality, while others want a contemplative soul. Many expect a minister to be a strong pastor with a sweet bedside manner as well as a savvy administrator capable of making tough decisions.

Given that most parishes want someone who can walk on water while delivering the sermon on the mount, turn water into wine while feeding five thousand, it's a wonder congregations find anyone to call as their minister.

It's a good thing Jesus never had to live up to such expectations. Oh wait, yes, he did.

That's why they killed him.

Espresso Shots:

1. *What would you look for in a minister for your congregation?*
2. *In what ways are our expectations too high?*
3. *What's the most important thing you want in a minister?*

MINISTERS (Part II)

Jesus never had a chance. The time in which he came was religiously and politically charged. News of a messiah caused a landslide of expectations. Some wanted a prominent leader who could hold his own among the politicians of his day. Some wanted a person who could go toe-to-toe with the religious leaders. Others wanted to be delivered from Roman occupation, while others sought spiritual deliverance. Everyone had an idea what the messiah would be like, and Jesus was going to let them all down in one way or another. It's a good thing he didn't care.

To the people who had much, he said, give it all away.

To those who held important positions, he questioned their authority.

To those who sought prominence, he offered a towel and bowl of water.

To those who wanted to be first, he saved a place in the back of the line.

To those who liked the way things were, he turned the tables over.

To those who wanted a revolution, he told them to pay Caesar what was due to Caesar.

To those who wanted a crown, he offered a cross.

Jesus didn't stand a chance of ever being able to fulfill everyone's expectations. Instead of being the messiah we wanted, however, Jesus was the messiah we needed, and that is enough to get down on our knees in deep gratitude.

Espresso Shots:

1. *What expectations or desires do you have about Jesus?*
2. *In what ways does he meet those expectations, and in what ways does he not?*
3. *How is the messiah you want different from the messiah you need?*

MINISTERS (PART III)

When Jesus began his public ministry, he walked along the shore and called some fishermen to come and follow him. He walked by the tax collector's office and asked him to join his disciples too. One was passionate and a bit headstrong, another full of doubt.

They were quite a collection of followers. Those looking on dismissed Jesus because of his followers and the company he kept.

I grew up surrounded by giants of the faith. Prominent leaders and amazing preachers, they were an inspiration to my young eyes. Never did I think they made mistakes or lost their tempers. They always seemed armed with the right answers, and I never heard any echo of doubt in what they said.

It was an inspirational collage but a dangerous one as well. As I built the many pedestals on which I would place them, I lost sight of the first ministers.

Jesus had a large number of followers of all shapes and sizes and genders. They were a diverse collection of souls who had one thing in common: they needed Jesus.

Like the people back then, we have particular expectations when it comes to modern-day disciples. They need to hold certain beliefs, look a certain way, and worship a certain way. Jesus didn't have such expectations. He only sought one thing. Did they need Jesus?

Espresso Shots:

1. *How do you think today's disciples should look and act?*

2. *What makes you qualified to be a follower?*

3. *In what ways can we learn from Jesus about what it takes to be a disciple?*

HEART GRAFFITI

Leaves blanketed the university walkway on our tour, making me notice the changing seasons. The sounds and smell of fall summoned me back to the days when I was in college, running late to class or sitting on the quad with friends. Just as such memories are enjoyable, they also bring regret and a desire to have done things differently. Partying less and learning more, entertaining less and listening more, regurgitating less and thinking more.

The one subject I wish I had majored in was "me," but not in a self-absorbed way (I had that covered). I wish I had spent more time in the search for my true self. Getting beyond, or beneath, the veneer, learning to embrace my weaknesses as well as my strengths, would have proven an education worth having. Instead of figuring out who I was going to be, I wish I had discovered who I was. Rather than looking to the hills beyond, I wish I had focused on the present.

Turning the corner on our tour, I noticed graffiti on a wall. Someone wrote, "I love me" in chalk. I was happy to see they'd learned a life-changing lesson on their way to class. I hope others would learn it as well.

Espresso Shots:

1. _How well do you know your true self?_

2. _What would it take to shift your focus from what you do to who you are?_

3. _Write a letter to yourself, inviting your true self to come out of hiding._

READING CIRCLES

Just thinking about it causes me to sweat and squirm. Once a week, in Mrs. Dennison's third-grade class, we were called to sit in reading circles. While others worked independently, those of us who were summoned approached with book in hand to read aloud. Mrs. Dennison always went first, then we took turns, starting on her left, each student reading a paragraph. I always sat far enough from her so I could count the paragraphs in advance and begin practicing.

No matter how hard I tried, I always messed up. Sometimes it was only a slight stumble, but other times the gaffe was big enough to cause the others to roll their eyes or laugh. Their laughter only made things worse, and, like a rolling snowball, mistakes piled up.

I try hard not to think about reading circle, but an experience recently reminded me of those days. I was in a circle of recovering alcoholics and addicts, taking turns reading from what is called "The Big Book." Like my third-grade reading circle, we went around the room, and everyone read a paragraph. Even though I'm an adult, I still found myself counting paragraphs to prepare.

Some read with ease, others struggled, but what stood out was that no one laughed when someone struggled. We all carry enough shame. There's no need to add to it. Getting and staying sober is hard enough.

I don't remember anything I read, but I'll never forget the lesson.

Espresso Shots:

1. *Think back on a time when you were embarrassed about doing something badly.*

2. *What did it feel like to hear people laugh or see them whisper about you?*

3. *Does the fear of messing up prevent you from doing something?*

FULLY ALIVE

"Go do . . . the Voo Doo . . . that you do!"
—*Hedley Lamarr (in the film,* Blazing Saddles)

I have spent most of my life in schools, not only as a student but also as a teacher and administrator. For me, schools are churches in which I feel comfortable.

Traditional churches have always made me feel uncomfortable. Growing up, churches were formal places where people walked gingerly down halls, speaking in hushed tones. There were so many rules about how to behave that I found it hard to be me. Schools had playing fields as well as classes. We were encouraged to run, jump, and shout, all in the name of becoming whoever we were created to be. No wonder schools have been my church!

When I had the opportunity to lead a school, I knew very little about budgets, governance, or the latest pedagogical thinking. What I knew was that school was here to help us grow into the people we were created to be. Whether as teachers or students, each day, we had the chance to reach and try something we'd never tried before and to discover something within us that we didn't know existed. Because I always worked at church schools, our daily lives were framed in the belief that God made us, and we owed it to God to be all that God had in mind.

The days I remember most fondly are when I looked out my window and saw children playing with all their hearts or when I peeked in a classroom, and I saw a teacher teaching with particular passion.

Saint Irenaeus said, "The glory of God is a human being fully alive!" Whether it's in a school, church, or neighborhood, becoming fully alive is what I believe God desires most.

Espresso Shots:

1. *Think back on a time in your life when you were fully alive.*
2. *What was happening, and what did that moment bring out in you?*
3. *How can you recapture that moment today?*

I'M SICK, TOO

I remember the day that a friend I hired messed up, and we were meeting in my office to discuss the mistake. Having met each other in the rooms of AA, I felt I was doing him a favor by employing him, but I had my doubts as I drove to my office for the confrontation. We sat facing each other, and I went through what occurred. I can't remember what had happened. All I remember was his response: "I'm sorry. I'm sick, too." Like an elixir, his response transformed the tense encounter. No longer were we two individuals addressing a mistake. We were two wounded souls doing the best we could.

Since that morning in my office, I've tried to imagine a world where we all admit we're sick, too. How it would change the world!

Couples could love more freely, politicians could lead more authentically, and clergy could pray more sincerely if we all admitted our humanity to one another. We might discover we have more in common than we realized. Beneath the surface, we all have fears and insecurities, wounds, and mistakes. To hide them is to live a charade. To own them or acknowledge that we're sick, too, transforms the moment and can transform the world.

Espresso Shots:

1. *How hard do you try to appear like you have it all together?*
2. *Have you ever admitted to anyone that you're sick, too?*
3. *How would it transform your work and relationships to admit your fears and insecurities, wounds, and mistakes?*

MAKING HOME

I'm embarrassed to admit it, but when I went to the carport to get my hiking boots, I found a bird's nest in each of them. My left boot even had an unhatched egg. I knew it had been a while since I last went for a hike, but the nests rubbed my inactivity in my face.

I love both the mountains and the sea, but ever since my father died when I was a college freshman, I've considered the mountains my soul's home. I was lost after his death, and it wasn't until I made it to the mountains that I began to feel found. The dramatic contours of the land with its peaks and valleys spoke to my soul in a language it understood. I could see God's fingerprints in the earth's clay, and his name etched in the granite cliffs. Even when I was by myself, I didn't feel alone. Streams sang and birds danced. It was as if I was being invited to join in. Even unpredictable New England weather was a part of the mountain liturgy. No organ or choir could compete when thunder and lightning joined forces among the mountains.

Putting on my boots, I gave thanks for finding a home. Just like the birds used my boots to make a home, it was now my turn.

Espresso Shots:

1. *Where do you feel most at home?*

2. *What is it about that place that makes you feel like God is speaking to your soul?*

3. *Do you make an effort to get there regularly? If so, how do you do it? If not, why not?*

A MATTER OF CHOICE

"Is the glass half empty, or half full?" This was probably the first philosophical question I was asked in school. Of course, this question is about much more than a glass of water. "It's all in the way you look at it," the teacher cautioned, "and how we look at it is a matter of choice."

Seeing things from a new perspective is why I'm drawn to art. Regardless of the medium, a painting, poem, song, or story can challenge me to see things in a new way. It's not always comfortable, which is why so many people prefer to see things as they always have. Growth is hard, uncomfortable work, but life on the other side of growth is the reward for the effort.

I spend my mornings with folks trying to see things from a new perspective. "My old thinking is what got me here," says the man sitting across from me. "It's time I tried doing things another way." Those in the circle nod their heads, as do I, knowing it's one thing to want to see things from a new perspective, and another to actually do so. Like the teacher long ago pointed out, it's a matter of choice.

Espresso Shots:

1. When was the last time something, or someone, challenged your perspective?

2. Are you attracted to, or repelled by, new ways of seeing or thinking?

3. In what way could you challenge your perspective on an issue, person, or event?

STORIES

Caldwell Owens was a storyteller. Folks would gather on his cabin porch, coffee in hand, each morning to listen to his newest tale.

"Once upon a time…" was all it took to quiet the crowd, and then with castles and knights, farmers and land, friends and family members, he wove the fabric of his lightly veiled commentary on life. Never without a story, he entertained people continuously.

One day, a young child began to fidget after one of Caldwell's stories.

"Excuse me, Mr. Owens, sir," the child said with hand raised, "but would you tell us one of your stories?"

"That's what I'm doing," replied Owens.

"No, I mean one from your life. You know, one about you as a boy, or something that really happened to you."

For the first time in ages, there was silence on Caldwell Owen's porch. With a face changing shape and color, Caldwell searched for something to say. "My story isn't interesting," he said, to which the boy lifted his head as if to say that's not good enough. "These stories are better," Caldwell added.

"But they're not real," said the boy.

Owens sighed and looked at the boy and said: "I'm afraid they're the only ones I know."

Espresso Shots:

1. *Are you someone who tells stories to entertain others?*
2. *Do you ever share stories from your life?*
3. *How do you use entertaining stories, humor, or other devices to keep people from knowing the real you?*

THE RED CAR PHENOMENON

I was recently introduced to the red car phenomenon, which goes something like this: you purchase a red car and suddenly notice red cars everywhere. Before you purchased the car, you paid no attention to the countless red cars on the road, but once you own one, your sensitivity to red cars is heightened, and you notice them wherever you are.

The phenomenon applies to things other than red cars. You hear of a new band, then hear their music three times later in the week; you learn about a soldier in the Civil War and hear his name in a conversation soon after; or you come across the work of an artist you've never known only to see an article about that artist in a local magazine.

It also applies to the spiritual life. You read a passage from scripture and then see how it applies to something that happens later that day, or a sermon on Sunday speaks directly to something that happens on Thursday.

It's all a matter of focus, and focus is what a spiritual life is all about. You're awake and paying attention. You hear or notice something and then see an amazing chain of connections. God's showing off, I often say when it happens, but the fact is God isn't doing anything unusual. I'm just paying attention.

Espresso Shots:

1. *Have you ever experienced the red car phenomenon?*

2. *In what ways is it like your spiritual life?*

3. *How can you learn to pay closer attention to the world around you on a regular basis?*

ALWAYS LEARNING

"I'm seventy years old!" the senior member of AA declared. "I'm done learning."

I understood what he meant. In a program that demands daily effort, it would be easy, or at least tempting, to throw up our hands and give up, but there's also a sadness to his decision. While he may never take a drink again, his unwillingness to learn marks the end of his program. By quitting, the demands stop but so do the rewards.

Such a truth is not limited to people in recovery. No matter what we are doing, there's always an opportunity to learn, but it can become exhausting.

"I don't need to write a sermon," the preacher decides. "I can use one from a few years back."

"I'll go to the conference," says the attorney, "but I don't plan on attending any of the seminars."

"I paint landscapes," says the painter. "Abstracts are not my thing."

"I'm a Republican. I don't give a damn what the liberals think."

"I provide for my children, but I'm not going to some parenting class."

The examples are endless. But there's "a more excellent way." It requires the humility to admit we don't know it all and that there's more to learn. No matter the length of our days, or depth of our wisdom, there's always more to learn and more to unlearn. Yes, it takes work. Yes, it will be frustrating. But, in the end, we'll find new life, a new us, and regardless of our age, that's something to be celebrated.

Espresso Shots:

1. When have you been tempted to stop learning?
2. What has prompted your resistance?
3. Find one thing and learn all about it.

CLIMBING WALLS

"What are we doing this for?" I thought to myself as we entered the climbing facility. I grew increasingly nervous as I put my legs through the stirrups of the harness. Wearing climbing shoes that made bowling shoes look like high-fashion, I abandoned all thoughts of appearance and kept my focus on the climb.

I was determined to participate and go as high as I could. My comfort with heights has decreased as my years have increased, but I climbed anyway.

My hand reached for the first hold, while a foot found its place. Then, step by step, I began to climb. Focusing only on the next step, I did my best not to look down or up. I thought of quitting often, but, much to my surprise, I made it to the top. The unexpected achievement left me pleased all day.

Success has numerous definitions. Some participants really struggled while others made it look like physical poetry. As inspirational as the climbers were, I was equally moved by those offering support. It was like watching the kingdom of God from a climbing wall.

If we could only stop measuring success and offer support for everyone doing the best they can, life would be a wonderful climb. If we could allow ourselves to be vulnerable, we might reach heights otherwise thought out of reach. Whether climbing effortlessly or struggling to get the harness on, our willingness to climb and share that experience with others could change us and the world.

Legs will shake and hands will sweat, but there's a hold within our grasp. We might need someone to help us find it or encouraging words to carry on, but if we're open to the experience, everyone can play a part in our common climb.

Espresso Shots:

1. *When have you tried to climb alone?*
2. *When have you relied on someone else's help or encouragement to climb?*
3. *In what way could you take a risk or offer encouragement today?*

WHEEE!

I arrived at the closed café looking for a table at which to write my morning pages. My heart was full of worries, and writing always made me feel better. My doctor was supposed to call today with the results of my blood work, my child called asking for more money, and this morning's news was so depressing I had to put the paper down.

It was a crisp fall New England morning, and I sat and watched a stream by the café before picking up the pen. An unassuming stream, it seemed indifferent to my attention. Still, I'm sure artists had sat on its banks before, trying to capture its tranquility. Beneath the surface, rocks rested where they had for years. Content to let the water flow over, they provided a bed for the stream. A leaf glided on the surface, twisting and turning like a dancer as it followed the water's lead. Downstream, small rapids waited, and the leaf lifted its edges as if to say, "Wheee" as it flowed over the edge. Just enjoying the ride, I thought to myself.

I wished in that moment to be like the stream, indifferent to the opinions of others and content with providing a channel for life to flow. I would love to be like the leaf, floating on life's surface, spinning and riding down the rapids with my arms held high, shouting, "Wheee!"

That would be a change.

Espresso Shots:

1. *When was the last time you were overwhelmed with life's demands?*

2. *In what way do you long for the peace and serenity found when sitting beside a stream?*

3. *What would it take for you to be more like the leaf?*

READING ALONG

I have a friend who refuses to write in any book he reads. He considers books pieces of art that should remain untouched. He also thinks writing in a book decreases its value. He would have been horrified to see the book of the man sitting beside me at a 12-step recovery meeting. The book had originally belonged to his brother who had since died, and it was filled with underlined passages and scribbled notes.

"I feel like my brother's reading along with me," he said when I asked about the book. "It's like he's saying, 'Pay attention to this,' or 'Boy, is this true.'"

I knew exactly what he meant. The purpose of all books, and all art and theology for that matter, is to create a connection. It may be to stir, inspire, comfort, or entertain, but a book only comes alive when it's read. Looking over at my friend's marked-up book, I could see how books can take on new life when they're not only read but also marked up with the thoughts and reactions of others.

To read along with others is to see things in a new way and to feel as if we're not alone. After all, wasn't that why the book was written in the first place?

Espresso Shots:

1. *What do you think is the purpose of writing a book?*
2. *Do you underline passages or write in the margins of books?*
3. *In what way could marking up a book be seen as enlarging the conversation?*

Double Shot:

Write in the margins of this book. Doodle, draw, underline, and highlight. Make these words come alive.

HURRICANES

When you live in North Carolina, hurricanes are a part of life. I don't panic and stock up on milk and bread for weeks at a time, but the storms certainly draw my attention. Part of me likes the drama, and, like a snow day, they interrupt regular routines. Life becomes refreshingly basic.

Such storms also make me feel small, and that's a good thing too. Each gust of wind reminds me of nature's might and my smallness. In a world where we can get caught up with all we have to do and where we sometimes get too full of ourselves, storms bring us to a humble appreciation for things far greater than ourselves.

Hurricanes also teach us a lesson that all storms eventually end. Regardless of size or power, every storm moves on, sometimes quickly, sometimes slowly. The dark nights give way to the dawn.

Storms will sweep in and force us to shift our perspectives and priorities to a most basic level. They remind us that we are in charge of almost nothing but that grace—and a new day—awaits us on the other side.

Espresso Shots:

1. *Think of a storm you were caught in.*
2. *How did it change your perspective and interrupt your routines?*
3. *In what ways were you changed when it passed?*

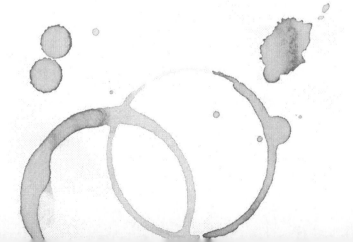

LEAVES

There are no white picket fences in my neighborhood, but it's pretty neat and tidy anyway. You can learn a lot about a family by the way they tend to their yard, particularly in the fall. Take, for example, the way people deal with leaves. There are those who hire others to remove their leaves. They care not where the leaves go, just that they go away. It's as if they want to pretend the leaves don't exist.

Others rake or blow their leaves into piles on the curb and wait for the city to take them away. For these neighbors, leaves are part of having a lawn; they are tolerated until they're removed. Then life goes on as before.

Then there are the mulchers, people who don't see leaves as debris to be whisked away or nuisances to be tolerated but as potential food for their lawns. They grind the leaves into little pieces and scatter them over the lawn. Their approach is the messiest, but it's also the healthiest.

Whether we have lawns or not, we approach our lives in similar ways. Some of us try to deny parts of ourselves. We have those parts whisked away as if they never existed. Others accept their shortcomings but take them to the curb to be removed. But mulchers not only accept the leaves but also use them as food for growth. They look at the leaves of their lives and transform them into nutrition for their soul. It's messy work, but it's also the healthiest way to live.

Espresso Shots:

1. *When have you tried to deny or hide a shortcoming?*

2. *When have you acknowledged a shortcoming but worked to remove it?*

3. *When did you not only accept a shortcoming but also use it to grow spiritually?*

OUT OF THE CLOSET

I received the call the day before leaving for a new job in England. My best friend from college called to tell me he was gay. I was shocked, but, looking back, I shouldn't have been. Still, on my flight across the ocean, I thought about our friendship and my friend. I thought about what it must have been like for him to have lived in the closet for all these years—and what a relief it must have been to come out.

Living in a closet is not unique to sexual orientation. Closets come in all shapes and sizes. So do the reasons to hide in them. Everyone finds refuge in a closet at some point.

I grew up with a room that had a big closet. I used to bring my stuffed animals in there with me, along with a blanket and a flashlight. It was cozy and safe. Over time, however, cozy became cramped, and safe became lonely. I remember how good it felt to breathe the fresh air when I opened the door. I'm sure my friend felt that way after he came out of his closet.

Closets provide refuge. In them, we can hide part or all of us because, for whatever reason, we feel something about us is wrong or needs hiding. Fearing we're not good enough, we retreat to a place where no one will see, judge, or laugh at us. Just writing that makes me sad.

I marvel at my friend's courage even after all these years. I give thanks for the way he expanded my heart and empowered me to see in a new way. I believe we've all been given the gift of life, and God wants us to live life fully, with all that we are, with all that we have. That's what abundant life is all about, and on this, my friend's birthday, I write to invite us all to open the closet doors and breathe the fresh air waiting for us all.

Espresso Shots:

1. *What parts of your life do you hide from others? From yourself?*

2. *Why do you think those parts need to be hidden?*

3. *What would it take to bring them out of the closet, and what would such a full or abundant life look and feel like?*

OPEN THE CHECKBOOK

This is the time when churches and other nonprofits begin their efforts to raise money for the upcoming year. Where we go to church, it's a month-long effort culminating with a service where every member is asked to bring forth an envelope with their pledge. It's deliberate and dramatic.

It's a fiscal moment of truth that always reminds me of something a consultant said when she came to help a church define its mission. "Don't show me your brochure," she said. "Show me your finances. That'll tell me what your mission is."

Ouch.

The consultant was right. Opening our checkbooks and looking at where the money is really going says more about our heart than anything we may claim.

• There are those who cling to their resources with clinched fists. Gifts are minimal and given more out of a desire to be listed with other donors than to support the organization.

• There are those who give out of habit or discipline, but they always play it safe. Knowing that others will carry the financial load, they give just enough.

• There are those who try to give enough to be uncomfortable. For them, charitable donations are opportunities for growth, and they give just beyond what is comfortable so that they, and their relationship to God, can grow.

• Then there are those who give freely. For them, all that they have belongs to God and they see themselves as channels of generosity.

It's tempting to think or say we're one kind of giver, but it's only when we open our checkbooks that we will really know.

Espresso Shots:

1. *Do you consider yourself generous?*
2. *Open your checkbook and look at where your money has gone over the last year. What does it say about your priorities?*
3. *What is your view of, or relationship with, money?*

MANNA

There's a story about God feeding the Hebrew people manna when they were in the wilderness. Each day it arrived like a gift and it fed the people, but it never lasted for more than a day. The people, fearful that they would have no food the next day, tried to store up the manna, but it went rotten. Slowly, they learned to accept the day's gift and to trust there would be more given tomorrow.

As a creative, I've had to learn the same lesson. I have been given countless ideas over the years. I've seen each as a gift, but in my fear that the supply was limited, I've gathered the ideas and stored them away. Over time, the ideas I clung to spoiled. Slowly, I learned to take what was given and do with them what I could and trust that more ideas would come. This is yet another way in which creativity has become an act of faith for me.

Whether you consider yourself creative or not, the lesson of the manna applies to all aspects of living a spiritual life. We are given many gifts, and we sometimes want to cling to them because we doubt there will be others. With our hands full, we are unable to receive the new gifts that arrive—and the ones we cling to suffocate because we hold on too tight.

There is great freedom feeding our souls with the food given each day and trusting there will be more tomorrow.

Espresso Shots:

1. When have you clung to a gift, fearing there would be no others in the future?

2. How can you shift your perspective and trust manna will always be given?

3. In what ways can you learn to trust God more?

THE DOGWOOD TREE

There once was a tree that sought to be like the others. As she grew, she looked over at the older trees and marveled at the way their leaves turned color each fall. One had bright yellow leaves, the other orange, and the third deep red.

"We're maple trees," they informed her with great pride, and she hoped she was, too.

She loved being surrounded by such color but was jealous as well. She had no color of her own, and her jealousy turned to sadness as time passed. Then one spring, something wonderful happened. While the maple trees were bringing forth green leaves, she blossomed like a flower. She stood like a bouquet of white among the other trees. Now it's their time to be jealous, she thought.

Finally, she had color of her own. She realized she was a dogwood, not a maple, and shook her branches, sending her colorful blossoms into the air.

Espresso Shots:

1. *When have you wanted to be like the other trees surrounding you?*

2. *When have you feared you had no color of your own and were not as good as others?*

3. *Have you ever discovered your unique colors and let them fly?*

REUSING TRASH

There are people down the street from where we live who reuse their trash. Unlike the rest of the neighborhood, they bring trash to the curb only every other week. When I asked them about it, they said they do their best to put their trash to new use. In exceedingly creative ways, they take what the rest of us throw away and find new purposes for it. Each time I pass their house and see an empty spot on garbage day, I remember how they transform their trash. Although I doubt I'll ever learn to be as creative with the things in my garbage cans as they are, I hope I'll learn how to reuse the trash from my life.

For a long time, all I wanted to do was throw my trash away. Mistakes, embarrassing moments, and unsuccessful ideas could not be taken to the curb fast enough. Slowly I've begun to see the value in such things and am trying to learn how to reuse my trash. Each mistake can make me wiser, each embarrassment more compassionate, and each unsuccessful idea more determined. It takes work to find new uses for my trash, and I'm still tempted to throw the worst of it away, but my neighbors taught me the value of reusing my trash.

Espresso Shots:

1. *What are things from your past you consider trash?*
2. *In what ways could you learn to reuse them and not be so quick to throw them away?*
3. *Find one piece of trash and transform it into something useful.*

BEST FRIENDS (Part I)

He was my best friend, when I was still young enough to consider such things. We played in the park every day after school, slept over at each other's house on the weekends, and talked about things only best friends could discuss. We stood up for each other when the other was not around, and we were able to laugh at our mistakes and quirks without fear of being judged.

As time passed, we went away to school and lost touch with one another.

The memory of having a best friend remained, however, and it still lingers deep within my soul. I suppose the longing for a best friend is one of the reasons I consider myself a religious person. God is the one I turn to when I need to talk about things I don't feel comfortable talking about with anyone else. God is the one I need to spend time with on a regular basis. I need to stand up for God when people are questioning him, and I need to know God's the one who will always stand up for me. God knows about all my mistakes and quirks and loves me still.

There have been times when I have moved away from our friendship. There have also been times I have felt God has been distant. The longing for my best friend always brings me back, though, and that is what the spiritual life is all about.

Espresso Shots:

1. *How would you describe your friendship with God?*
2. *In what ways could you deepen your relationship with God?*
3. *How could an intimate relationship with God empower you to be more fully yourself?*

BEST FRIENDS (Part II)

"If God is for us, who is against us?" —*Romans 8:31*

I missed an easy shot on the tennis court and exclaimed something particularly unkind. My partner looked over and said he was glad he wasn't the one who missed the shot. "I'd hate to hear what you'd say to me."

The fact is I would never say such a thing to him or anyone else. This recognition caused me to wonder why I was willing to say such things to myself. I saved my most severe criticisms and harshest rebukes for myself, and it wasn't until that moment that I saw it clearly. I never saw my behavior as unkind because I wasn't directing it to anyone else.

A friend suggested I try to become my own best friend. "Do unto yourself as you would do unto others," he said in what sounded like a twisted biblical phrase. I suddenly felt convicted. I was meaner to myself than I would ever dream of being to someone else. His advice invited me to try something new. Whether as an athlete, a husband, a father, writer, or painter, I'm often quick to criticize myself rather than encourage, to see what is wrong and not what's right.

If God is for us, who can be against us? That goes for how we view ourselves as well. If God is for us, then how dare we say things and look at ourselves with such a critical heart.

Espresso Shots:

1. *Do you often criticize or find fault in yourself?*
2. *How could you be kinder and more encouraging to yourself?*
3. *What would it look like if you became your own best friend?*

TAKING A CLOSER LOOK

He was a giant of finance, but he was short in physical stature. A tax collector with great wealth, Zacchaeus longed for something more than material things. That's why his ears perked up when he heard Jesus was coming to town. He'd heard about this teacher, but he wanted to see him for himself. Leaving his office, Zacchaeus joined the others, but because he was short, he couldn't see over the crowd, so he climbed a tree to get a better look at Jesus. The rest is history. Salvation came to Zacchaeus's house that day.

There are many reasons to admire Zacchaeus. While his business acumen and obvious success may be commendable, what I admire most is his desire to take a closer look. He must have looked ridiculous climbing a tree in first-century attire, but he didn't care. He wanted to see Jesus for himself.

Many of us grew up going to church, at least from time to time, and we heard about this Jesus— what he did, what he taught, and what happened to him— but most of us never climbed the tree to get close and see him for ourselves. The question for us today is: do we care enough to climb a tree? Are we willing to risk embarrassment to see God up close and personal?

Espresso Shots:

1. *Do you have a longing for something more?*
2. *Have you ever departed from your routine to go searching?*
3. *Are you willing to do what's necessary to see Jesus for yourself?*

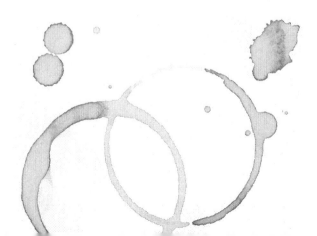

BOTH/AND

"I never liked that Mary," my mother said, slightly joking. "She should have gotten off the floor and helped Martha in the kitchen."

Every time I hear the biblical story of Martha and Mary, I think about what my mother said and feel like I have to pick sides. Am I with Martha or Mary?

In the Gospel of Luke, Jesus goes to the house of Martha and Mary. While sitting there, Martha scurries off to the kitchen to prepare food for their special guest, while Mary, who wants to hear everything he has to say, sits at Jesus' feet.

People, ever since, have divided the two sisters. You are either a Martha or a Mary. You're busy working in the kitchen, or you're sitting at the master's feet.

Despite Jesus commending Mary for her devotion, the spiritual life is about reconciling the two. It's not an either/or thing but a both/and. Sitting at Jesus' feet is where it begins. To draw close to God and hear what God has to say is the bedrock of the spiritual life, but such contemplation must lead a person into the kitchen. It's not enough to simply contemplate. One must take the fruits of contemplation and put them into action in a meaningful way.

It's not a choice about which path to follow. It's about following both.

Espresso Shots:

1. *Which of the two characters do you identify with most, and why?*

2. *How can you grow more contemplative?*

3. *How can you grow more active in living out your faith?*

Double shot: *How can you avoid picking sides and reconcile the two?*

DENYING

It was the most public denial in history. In fact, there were three denials, and they've been talked about for more than 2,000 years. After Jesus' arrest, the disciples scattered for fear they'd be next. Drawing his cloak over his head, Peter tried to hide, but someone recognized him. Three times, Peter was confronted, and each time, he denied knowing Jesus. It must have been hard to hear the cock crow over Peter's weeping as he wrestled with how he had betrayed and denied the man he vowed to serve for the rest of his life.

The stones in my hand grow heavy as I read the description of Peter's denial. As hard as it is to understand how someone like Peter could deny Jesus, it's equally upsetting to see how often I deny him as well. My denials aren't written about and read in church every year, but they're just as real. I deny Christ each time I choose the easy wrong over the more difficult right. I deny him each time I downplay my faith. I deny him when I play it safe, shroud my face, and listen to my fear. Perhaps you know what I mean.

Peter's story, however, did not end in denial. Far from it. He grew to lead the church and eventually die for the one he denied. God empowered the denier to a courageous life of faith. It happened for Peter, and it can happen for us, too.

Espresso Shots:

1. *In what ways do you deny your faith?*

2. *What fear lies beneath those denials?*

3. *In what ways could you follow Peter to a courageous life of faith?*

MOVING THE FRAMES

I have a mischievous side. I try to keep it under control, but sometimes I just can't help myself. So it was the night a friend hosted a dinner party at her house. She's the most organized person I've ever met, and she likes her office, home, and life a certain way. Wandering her house, I marveled at how perfect everything was.

One table had a number of well-polished silver picture frames perfectly arranged. Reaching over, I moved one of the frames. It gave me such satisfaction, I continued around her entire house. I slightly moved other frames and a statue and even changed the order of the books stacked in descending sizes. The next morning, I got a call. She knew it was me, and she wanted me to know everything was back in place.

Jesus had a mischievous side as well, particularly when it came to the religious leaders in his day. They, like my friend, liked things a certain way. With his new, radical doctrine, Jesus moved the neatly arranged thoughts and practices of his time. You say we're created in God's image, that means everyone. You say we should love our neighbors as ourselves, how about *that* neighbor? You say to honor the sabbath, but the sabbath was made for you, not the other way around.

Jesus moved the neatly arranged frames. He still does.

Espresso Shots:

1. *In what ways do you like your faith to be neat and tidy?*
2. *When has God moved the frames?*
3. *How can you learn to embrace a mischievous God?*

FINGERS

It was one thing to hear that the chapel at my seminary burned and another to drive onto campus and see the charred shell. The smell of smoke and fire permeated the grounds; without the stained-glass windows to fill the arches of the Gothic building, it seemed as empty as my heart.

The chapel and required worship were the two main reasons I chose this seminary. Chapel provided the spiritual rhythm I craved and worship offered the liturgical education I needed. Above the large window behind the altar were inscribed the words, "Go ye into all the world and preach the Gospel," and now it was all gone. It felt like my faith had burned to the ground along with the chapel.

As I walked closer, kicking some of the debris with my foot, I thought about the Hebrew people when they lost the Promised Land, the Israelites when they lost their temple, and the disciples after Jesus was gone. I thought about the giants of my faith who led me toward the church but who were now gone.

I realized how often loss is a part of spiritual journeys.

Rather than blame or question God, I sat beside the destroyed chapel and listened to the breeze. A sudden gust blew a cloud of ash in my direction causing me to shield my eyes. "Ashes to ashes, dust to dust," I whispered as I stood up. I realized God was not the chapel. God was not the temple or the Promised Land or an inspirational person in my life. Each was a finger pointing to God. Too often, I focused on the finger and not the one to whom they were pointing.

Looking up into the sky where the chapel once stood, I realized this important, yet painful, lesson.

Espresso Shots:

1. *Name some of the significant losses in your spiritual journey.*

2. *Have you made something the object of your focus and not God?*

3. *How can you learn to see beyond the fingers to where they are pointing?*

CARVING PUMPKINS

"It's never too late to have a happy childhood." —Novelist Tom Robbins

As we assembled in the common room of the residential rehab facility, one of the residents in his late thirties looked at the table of pumpkins and said, "I've never carved a pumpkin before." "Neither have I," replied another. I was shocked. I couldn't imagine carving my first pumpkin so late in life. I thought carving pumpkins was an essential part of childhood. As we carved, they told me about all the things in their lives that took away such activities and deprived them of what we might call a normal childhood.

When we shared our carved pumpkins, the spirit in the room was joyful, almost giddy. Like children playing in a sandbox, we were celebrating our funny-looking creations. More than the pumpkins, however, we were enjoying life beside one another.

Most of our lives are spent growing up. Our progress is measured in a variety of ways but sitting with the residents that afternoon made me wonder if something gets lost in all of our growing up. It happens in all aspects of our lives, including spirituality. Somewhere along the way, we surrender the wonder of faith for logic and replace magic with practicality. Yes, it's written that we should put away childish things but we should celebrate our childlike hearts—the ones that trust God without question, that marvel at a centipede, and sing and laugh without reservation.

After all, it's never too late to have a happy childhood.

Espresso Shots:

1. *In what ways has your spiritual life become too grown up?*
2. *What was your faith like when you had a childlike heart?*
3. *What would it look like to discover (or rediscover) your childlike heart?*

ISN'T THAT JOSEPH'S SON?

The monumental sermons and spectacular miracles get the headlines in the gospels, but I'm drawn to the ordinary moments, those times when Jesus is doing the everyday, mundane actions. One of my favorites is when Jesus returns to his hometown and the people ask if he is Joseph's son. The Gospel of Matthew shares their wondering. "Is not this the carpenter's son? Is not his mother called Mary? And are not his brothers James and Joseph and Simon and Judas?" Their interest was not only in identifying the grown man but also in keeping him as the boy they knew.

People have always worked hard to make sense of their lives. We construct boxes and put people, places, and events in partitions that make sense. *She's a nurse, and he's a grocer; she's a gossip, and he's a living saint.* Such boxes help us bring order and understanding to our lives. The problem comes when someone leaves the box. When they do something unexpected or become someone new, our boxes collapse.

We make a box for God, too. God is this way, we say, and God thinks this. Such a box gives us comfort, but God doesn't go for boxes. In fact, God is all about bursting out of our boxes and empowering others to do the same.

Keeping Jesus in the box as Joseph's son gave people comfort, but Jesus was more than that. Staying in the boxes people have made for us might give them comfort, but we're made for more than that too.

Espresso Shots:

1. *Who are some of the people we have put in a box?*

2. *When has someone burst out of their box?*

3. *How can we get God and others out of the boxes we have made?*

CANDLELIGHT

I began the morning in a favorite chair with a cup of coffee, hoping to center myself before a busy day. Unfortunately, my mind was distracted by questions. What am I supposed to do with my life? Do I have a purpose? Why is it so hard to figure out what it is? God, can you send me a sign—or at least some hints? A blast of a trumpet or a chorus of angels would do.

After several minutes of such thoughts, I looked over and stared at the candle burning beside me. As the flame danced with the breeze, I wondered about candles. Who invented the first candle? Who invented the wick? Who thought to dip the wick in wax so the flame would burn slowly?

Watching the flame dance, I began to think about the light we are called to bring into the world. It is a light that moves with a breeze (the Spirit) we cannot see. The wick is surrounded by wax to keep it from burning too quickly. The wax may melt and change shape, but in time, it will cool so that it can help bring light into the world time and again. I don't have all the answers, but when I let the light of Christ burn within me, I can see the path and be bold to take the next step.

Espresso Shots:

1. *Do you believe you have a light to shine into the world?*

2. *How are you like the candle wax?*

3. *Do you need a wick to help you slow down?*

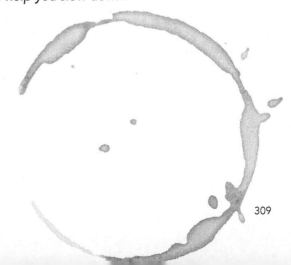

TOUCHING WOUNDS

Huddled with the other disciples after the crucifixion, Thomas couldn't believe what he was hearing. "Jesus is risen," some were saying, but he wouldn't believe it unless he put his fingers into Jesus' wounds. Later, when Jesus appeared to Thomas and put his wounds out for him to touch, Thomas replied, "My Lord, and my God." By touching his wounds, Thomas came to know the risen Lord.

I think of Thomas often when I am gathered in a circle with other wounded people. We share our experience, strength, and hope with one another through our words, but the fact is we touch each other's wounds and, by doing so, come to know one another.

Whenever wounds are touched, people are known. It happens in marriages, friendships, and any other time people are willing to show their wounds and someone else is willing to touch them gently. It could be a wound from childhood or a recent injury. It could be something easily noticed by all or something the person carries within. Wounds come in all shapes and sizes, but they are wounds nevertheless. It is a sacred act whenever someone is willing to show a wound, just as sacred as reaching out and touching a wound. Thomas led the way, and many others have followed. Each time it happens, God is present. Like Thomas, may we recognize the holiness of the moment, saying, "My Lord, and my God."

Espresso Shots:

1. *Have you ever shared a wound with someone?*
2. *Has someone ever shared a wound with you?*
3. *In what ways was God known in the moment?*

WOULD YOU CARE TO DANCE?

When I was young, I went to dancing school. It was an awkward time each Tuesday afternoon, but my friends and I endured it together. The most uncomfortable part wasn't the dancing but walking over to a girl and asking her to dance. Remembering those afternoons all these years later still makes my palms sweat. Who should I ask? How should I ask? What if she refuses?

I'm not sure God gets nervous, but I do think God is continuously asking us to dance. He gets up, comes to each of us, and extends his hand as if to invite us onto the dance floor. Each sunrise or sunset is a request. Each inspirational song, passage in a book, or poem is a request. Each inner stirring to do or say something to someone in need is a request. I even think each hardship is a request.

Although the requests come in countless ways, the question is: will we extend our hand and accept God's invitation to dance? When I see children painting rainbows and colorful landscapes, I see that as a yes. When I see people serving meals at the local soup kitchen, I see a yes. When I see someone transforming into a new creation before my eyes, I know they've said yes.

This morning, I awaken and sit eagerly in my chair, hoping God will draw near and ask me to dance. More than that, I hope I say yes.

Espresso Shots:

1. *When do you feel God has asked you to dance?*

2. *When have you said yes?*

3. *How can you learn to dance more often?*

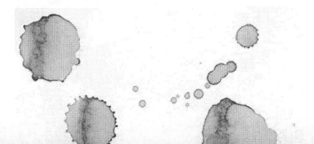

CURIOSITY

"Judge not, lest ye be judged." The words are familiar. Jesus said them to help us understand how damaging, unhealthy, and ultimately futile judging someone else can be. He was talking about judging others, but I've come to see how damaging, unhealthy, and ultimately futile it is to judge ourselves.

When it comes to self-judgement, I hold a doctorate. It's something I've practiced all my life.

Recently, I was shown the damage my relentless judging can cause. Like a piling being pounded into the ground, my judgment pounded spikes into my soul. What was it that caused me to do what I did or say what I said? What is the fear or hurt lying beneath the surface? What was the basic need I was trying to meet in the wrong way?

Cynics might say looking at one's behavior in such a way is only disguised self-justification, but I think asking these questions is self-compassion. We were marvelously created, but over time things happened, and fears emerged, which caused us to alter our behavior. We compensate in a variety of ways in an effort to survive or get our most basic needs met, and that can lead to some bad decisions.

Rather than bring out the hammers to pound once again, perhaps we should bring out our magnifying glass and look closer.

Espresso Shots:

1. _How often and harshly do you judge yourself?_

2. _Have you ever looked beneath the surface at why you might have done what you did?_

3. _How can asking these questions be a helpful tool in your self-examination?_

DUETS

Giacomo Puccini, the composer of *Madame Butterfly*, claimed the opera was given to him. His role was to write it down, like dictation.

Such stories of creativity inspire me—and make me a little jealous—but they also remind me there's a bountiful, inspirational spirit surrounding us all. Our job is to listen and write them down, not with a pen, but with our lives.

As a person who lives a creative life, I know firsthand when I'm making something and when something is being made through me. The first is efficient, the second magical. The first depletes, the second fills. The first is work, the second play.

The same is true with our lives. Economic needs and societal expectations often lead us to create a life through hard work and stubborn determination. On the surface, such lives look successful, but those living them feel depleted. There are some who feel they have a calling, which is why they refer to their work as a vocation and not a profession. These folks often look like they are playing instead of working.

Hard work is involved with either approach to life, but one is a solo act, the other a duet.

Espresso Shots:

1.   When have you felt as if life was something you were making, and when was it being made through you?

2.   Is your work more profession than vocation?

3.   In what way could you make your life a duet with God?

POLITE SOCIETY

They were usually the first to put up a political sign. This year was different. Although their political views had not changed, their willingness to publicize them had. I learned an important lesson from my neighbors: what we don't admit says as much as what we do.

Early on, I was taught there are three things not to talk about in polite society: politics, religion, and money. They are sensitive topics and can lead to disagreements, arguments, and hurt feelings. But as an adult, I recognize that each of these areas is an integral part of our lives. They reveal much about who we are, what we believe, and how we live our day-to-day lives.

While I'm all for polite society, I wonder if not talking about such things is a way to keep from admitting things of which we are not proud. Maybe we don't make much money, or maybe we make a ton. Not talking about money allows us the freedom to hide our embarrassment or greed. Maybe we prefer not to talk about religion because we're embarrassed by how little we worship or how inconsistent our lives are with the faith we profess. And maybe by not talking about politics we can avoid admitting views that may not reflect well on us.

Jesus spoke about keeping secrets. Whether we're proud or ashamed of our secrets, God knows them all. It doesn't change a thing if we cling to our bank statements, duck in the back pew, or pull the voting booth curtain tight. God already knows.

I should take a look at why I'm trying to hide those things. It's certainly not because of polite society.

Espresso Shots:

1. *What parts of your life are you reluctant to talk about?*
2. *Is your reticence due to a desire not to offend others or to admit things you're embarrassed about?*
3. *What do your secrets say about you?*

OCTOBER 31, 1517

More than five hundred years ago, on the eve of All Saints' Day, a monk named Martin Luther walked quietly up the steps to the doors of the Wittenberg Cathedral in Germany where he posted a list of ways in which he felt the church needed to reform. He loved the church but felt it had become distracted from the gospel and become engaged in practices that contradicted scripture. He believed grace is a gift, not an achievement, something that is given, not earned. With what became known at the Ninety-Five Theses, Luther wanted to awaken the church and bring about change within it. But the church didn't want to listen and banished Luther, which led to the Protestant (Protestors') Reformation.

I've always been fascinated with Luther. I love his far-from-saintly life, his struggle to live a holy life while remaining aware of his humanity, and his willingness to climb the stairs that night. The Good News was too good to keep to himself, even if it meant getting into trouble.

I'm no Luther, but I have found myself in a similar, but not nearly as important, struggle with the church. Like him, I loved the church, but after undergoing a self-created crisis, I came to understand the enormity of God's grace. It's available to us all and is not as conditional as so many churches suggest.

"We're all fallen," they say. "Just don't be too fallen." After a life of trying to earn God's love, I crashed and stood in the shards of my achievements. Like Luther, my struggle helped me find the love for which I'd been looking. It was waiting patiently on the other side of all my striving.

On this day, and many others, I celebrate Luther's discovery—and mine. Like him, may I carry the Good News to church doors and everywhere I go.

Espresso Shots:

1. *Have you ever tried to earn God's love?*
2. *Have you ever come to know God's unconditional grace personally?*
3. *If you climbed church steps and posted something on the door, what would it say?*

ALL SAINTS

I was asked to officiate at the wedding of a former student. For safety precautions stemming from the pandemic, the wedding was held outside on a dock on the edge of a beautiful lake. As we began to take our places, neighbors and friends of the couple got into their small electric boats and surrounded the dock. When I asked if those witnessing the marriage would support the couple in their married life, those on the dock and in the boats responded with a resounding "We will!" It was a glimpse of heaven.

In our day-to-day lives, we are those gathered on the dock. We go about our business as if we are the only ones around. Occasionally, we experience moments when we sense that others looking on. Although we cannot see them, the space between us becomes thin, as the Irish mystics call it, and we become aware of the great cloud of witnesses surrounding us.

Those moments are to be treasured and celebrated—on All Saints Day and every day.

Espresso Shots:

1. *Do you believe there are those who surround us, even though we cannot see them?*

2. *If you were to hear their chorus of "We will!", whose voice would you most like to hear?*

3. *What's your experience of thin places?*

UNINVITED GUESTS

The uninvited guests
knocked on my door.
I pulled the blinds,
Turned off the lights,
Pretending I wasn't home.
They knew better.

Fear and anger stood hand in hand,
Waiting for me to answer.
Shame and grief stood close by.
They had all night,
And all day,
No matter how long I paced within.

"Go away," I shouted. "I have no time, no space for you!"
Silence was their reply.
"We've met before," I offered. "It ended badly."
Silence, still.

I walked to the door,
Turned its many locks,
Pausing at the last.

"If you must!" I sighed,
And opened the door.
To an empty porch.
Leaves danced in a swirling breeze, laughing.

Espresso Shots:

1. *In what ways do you avoid unpleasant feelings?*
2. *What locks do you use to keep them from getting inside?*
3. *Have you ever faced them, only to have them disappear or diminish in size?*

LUMP IN MY THROAT

It never gets old. My love for this country was cemented from years of living abroad, and I feel the love most acutely on the day we vote. My wife and I walk to the polls each year, as if on a pilgrimage. We arrive early but don't vote often, as the saying goes. Standing in line, we greet the other voters and talk about anything but the recipient of our vote.

Everyone gathered is tired, not because of the early hour but from the grueling months leading to election day. Unpleasant debates, scathing advertisements, and countless speeches have worn us all out.

At 6:30 a.m. sharp, a woman appears and announces: "This polling site is now open. You may now vote."

Electricity shoots through my body and washes away my fatigue. My lost spirit returns as I am ushered to my station. The volunteer leaves, and I feel a wonderful lump in my throat. No matter how fed up, exhausted, or bitter I have been feeling, standing there, performing my sacred duty, I stand tall and hope the lump in my throat will never disappear.

Espresso Shots:

1. *Vote.*
2. *Thank the volunteers at the polling site.*
3. *Reflect on a tangible way to keep the lump in your throat.*

TEAMMATES

I didn't like him. I helped him move into his room but only because I had to. When I arrived at soccer tryouts, he was there. When they split us into positions, he and I were in the same group. He was a goalie, and I was a deep sweeper, which meant we would be playing next to each other all season. Neither of us thought that was going to work.

That is, until the games began. Instantly, our focus was on the opposing team and what we needed to do to play well. The two of us looked downfield, beyond each other, and that changed everything. We became quite a team, and he became one of the closest friends I've ever known.

I am reminded of this lesson as I look out at a divided country. Our motto— *Out of many, one*—seems to be a forgotten dream. Regardless on which side of the political spectrum you fall, we're only focused on what divides us. We've forgotten how to look down the field at the issues that should unite us, and I fear it's ripping us apart.

I am reminded of and give thanks for my high school friend. I hope our nation will find its way beyond our differences and back to the game. I hope we'll find a way to become a team again.

Espresso Shots:

1. *When have differences divided you from friends?*
2. *Has there been a time when looking downfield brought you together?*
3. *In what way can you work to become a teammate with others who differ from you?*

EMPTY MICROPHONES

The concert had just begun when Bruce Springsteen announced it was time for "roll call," the time he goes around the stage and introduces the members of the E Street Band. I listened and wondered what he'd do when he reached stage right, the place where Clarence Clemons used to stand. It was the first Springsteen concert I'd attended since the famed saxophone player died. Springsteen paused after introducing everyone, then asked, "Is there someone missing?" Everyone cheered. He repeated the question while a spotlight fell on the microphone off to the side. "If you're here, and we're here … He's here!" Springsteen said, and the place went wild.

It was a fitting tribute to Clemons but was also a vivid reminder of how a presence can remain long after a person leaves. I couldn't help but think of those I've lost, the empty microphones, in my life. Over time I've forgotten them and ceased to turn on the spotlight.

My list is long. Perhaps yours is, too. Time puts distance between us and our losses, but remembering those we have lost is important.

I don't know how this whole life and death thing works, but I've always wondered about the connection between those we have lost and those who remain. I can only hope that if you're here, and I'm here… then they're here.

Espresso Shots:

1. *Picture yourself on stage with an empty microphone beside you. Who used to stand there?*

2. *What do you miss most about that person?*

3. *In what way can you recognize the loss and give thanks for their life?*

Double Shot:

Listen to the song, "Tenth Avenue Freezeout." Pay attention to the moment when "the big man (Clemons) joined the band."

NASTY MEDICINE

The medicine tasted nasty. Neither my sister nor I could swallow what our mother was holding before us in a spoon without scrunching our faces and making some audible show of disgust. Even when the pharmacy flavored it with cherry, the medicine was still disgusting. I guess the makers of the medicine were more concerned with the benefits than the taste. Turns out God is too.

My life has involved a lot of medicine, and like the stuff in my mother's spoon, most of it has tasted awful. Apologizing can have a bitter taste, changing my behavior was painful, and refraining from saying something hurtful made me gag. All of it tasted bad, but each spoonful provided medicine I needed to feel better.

I'm sure the Hebrew people didn't like their forty years in the wilderness and Jacob probably resented his limp, but this tough medicine helped them become the people and the nation they were created to be. No one enjoys going to counseling or making amends, but such medicine can restore our health and make us into the people we were created to be.

Mary Poppins told us it only takes a spoonful of sugar to help the medicine go down, but with some of the medicine we're given, not even sugar can help. We just need to scrunch our faces and groan. In the end, we'll get better.

Espresso Shots:

1. *What has been some of the hardest medicine you've had to swallow?*

2. *In what way did it restore your health?*

3. *How can you learn to see medicine as a good thing even when it tastes awful?*

GOD DON'T MAKE JUNK

It was the second week of rehab, a week known for being particularly hard, and after a rough session with my counselor, he said words that have stayed with me ever since: "God Don't Make Junk." Like a needle popping a balloon of self-pity, my thoughts swirled around the room.

Growing up, I wanted to be like anybody but me. I wanted to play sports like this classmate, read like that one, be popular like this one, and smart like that one. I tried to make up for my perceived shortcomings, but this behavior led to costumes and masks. Only now can I see that God gave me all the gifts I needed. They weren't the same gifts as others. They were mine. I just needed to use them.

It's not surprising that when I wrote a Christmas children's book, I told of a star that only had four points instead of five. Sad, she went to the star maker who assured her she was marvelously made and told her to go shine above a small town called Bethlehem. Because she didn't look like the other stars, the wisemen spotted her and found the child in a manger below.

She used her gifts to bring people to Christ because, after all, God don't make junk.

Espresso Shots:

1. *What were the gifts you envied most as a child?*
2. *Did you ever come to see that you had all the gifts you could need?*
3. *How do you use your gifts and for what purpose?*

GOD DON'T MAKE JUNK: WILLIE

His name was Willie. I never knew his last name. His job was to open the car doors for the elementary school children, and he did so in such a way that each child felt they were special. In the food chain of school employees, I doubt Willie was very high, and yet he was my favorite person on campus.

Too often we measure a person by the position they hold. Willie was the first person to show me that it's not the job you do but the way you do it that matters. Unfortunately, I did not follow his example. When it was my turn to work in schools, I was determined to climb as high as I could. In my relentless quest, I became a person I wish I hadn't. I should have been like Willie.

When I was in third grade, my parents allowed me to get a dog. It was the happiest day of my life, and I held my puppy tight as we drove to school the next day. I wanted the man who opened the car door to meet my dog, Willie, named after the kindest person I had ever known.

Espresso Shots:

1. *Who was an unlikely person who made a big impression on you?*
2. *Do you focus more on what you do than who you are?*
3. *How can a Willie in your life remind you that God don't make junk?*

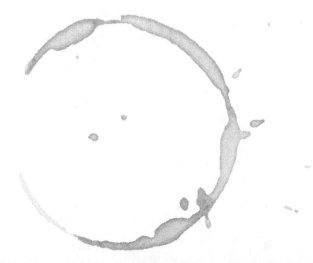

GOD DON'T MAKE JUNK: SALLY

We were in high school together. We were good friends but nothing more. In fact, Sally was everyone's good friend. No classmate had a more pervasive presence in our class. I'm sure she had many gifts, but the one I remember most vividly is her smile. It was the biggest smile I'd ever known, and it was available in an instant, any time you needed it. She brought it to the student whose parents were divorcing, to the student in the midst of disciplinary action, and to our entire class when we lost a beloved friend.

I always thought God-given gifts had to be big, but Sally taught me some of our greatest gifts can be small and simple. Everyone has the ability to smile, and smiles come in all shapes and sizes. Some people smile often, others not so much. Sally used hers a lot. I mean a *lot*, and her use of such a gift changed the lives of many people, including mine.

Espresso Shots:

1. *What gift do you have that you often overlook or discount because it seems insignificant?*

2. *What simple gift do you bring to your world, like Sally brought a smile?*

3. *How can you use your simple, take-for-granted gifts more often?*

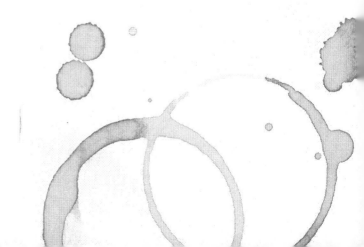

GOD DON'T MAKE JUNK: JOHN

He always thought he was meant to be a minister. He can still remember the moment on a mission trip when he felt the call to serve God, but when he graduated from college, he was set on becoming a lawyer. It wasn't because of a deep love of the law so much as he had the intellect for such a career and wanted to earn enough money to support a family.

He graduated from law school and found a position at a prominent firm in Boston. He became a partner in record time but never felt he was using his gifts in ways that mattered. He lost his job many years later because of alcoholism. In the silence of his apartment, he heard echoes of the call he heard on the mission trip. Instead of going to seminary or serving a church, he offered aid to other alcoholics who were in need of legal assistance. With the help of others in the AA program, he created a resource center for people in recovery that has now been replicated in more than a hundred cities.

Espresso Shots:

1. *What do you feel are your greatest gifts?*
2. *Are you using them in a way that matters to you and others?*
3. *Do you feel called to the work you're doing or do you feel you should be doing something else?*

GOD DON'T MAKE JUNK: JANICE

She needed to find a job after her husband died, but after years of being a stay-at-home mom, she felt she had little to offer the world. All she knew how to do was care for children and make quilts, a hobby handed down from her mother. For some reason, she spotted an advertisement on the bulletin board at church: Hospice Activity Director Needed, experience preferred, but not required. During her interview, they discussed the mission of hospice and how they were looking for someone to care for the patients and teach them something new. Janice was hired.

It turned out she was a natural caregiver. With no one left at home, she sat with the patients long after others left work. If she had learned anything as a mother, it was how to listen and that was all the patients wanted. She also started a quilting class that became wildly popular. She invited the patients to bring in old T-shirts and taught them how to turn them into quilts. From the notes she received from the families of patients who had died, she learned the quilts had become sacred keepsakes.

When she eventually retired, the banquet hall was packed and hanging all around the room were the quilts she'd help the patients make.

Espresso Shots:

1. Have you ever felt you had little to offer the world?
2. Have you ever discovered you had the right gifts at the right time?
3. When you retire, who will be in the room, and what will be hanging on the walls?

THE CROWD

He played to the crowd. Desperate to keep the peace, the *Pax Romana*, he didn't listen to the voice inside but rather the voices outside. His gut told him Jesus had done nothing wrong, but the crowd cried, "Crucify!" Pilate listened to the crowd.

Crowds are safe. Crowds are loud. Crowds are convincing. Even if the crowd is wrong, standing together makes it seem right. Pilate hardly stood a chance. No wonder he went along with the crowd.

When it comes to listening to the crowd, I make Pilate look like an amateur. Many of us do. In a desperate need to be accepted, we go against the voice within and listen to the crowd. Sometimes the crowd cheers, but, most of the time, the crowd just moves on. Crowds are fickle.

When it comes to living a spiritual life, it rarely helps to listen to the crowd. The crowd will try to convince you to go this way when your faith tells you to go that way. The crowd will welcome you with open arms as long as you learn its cheer, but your faith may teach you a different refrain.

Listening to the crowd is easier than listening to the voice within, but the voice within comes from the one who created us in the first place. The voice within is singular, consistent, and far from fickle. The trick is learning to listen to it.

Espresso Shots:

1. *When have you listened to the crowd over the voice within?*
2. *When have you listened to the voice within and not to the crowd?*
3. *In what ways can you develop your ability to hear, and your willingness to listen to, God's voice?*

SCAR TISSUE

A friend of mine has had so many knee operations the doctor should just put in a zipper.

I hate it for him, particularly when he's in pain. Recently, his knee tightened up, and the doctor had to go back in and remove the scar tissue that had formed and constricted movement in his knee.

Emotional injuries form scar tissue, too. No one lives without incurring some kind of injury but keeping the scar tissue from causing additional pain is a lifelong endeavor.

When a boy who was always made to feel inadequate by his parents becomes a relentless father, that's scar tissue. When a woman suffers emotional or physical abuse and becomes incapable of letting men close, that's scar tissue. When a mother loses a child and never returns to church, that's scar tissue.

Hurt people hurt people is an adage used in 12-step recovery circles and aptly describes the effects of scar tissue. Like my friend's most recent visit to the doctor, the only way to remove scar tissue is to open the area back up and remove it. Emotional scar tissue is not as obvious or easy as physical, so the excavation can take a long time, but we all have it. The sooner we admit that and decide to do something about it, the sooner we'll be able to walk freely again.

Espresso Shots:

1. What's an injury you've suffered around which scar tissue has formed?

2. How has the scar tissue affected the way you live your life?

3. What would it look like to remove that scar tissue?

PSSST!

Pssst, went my sister when she wanted to get my attention. *Pssst*, went my mother when she wanted me to come closer so she could show me something. Pssst seems to be a universal language to which we all respond.

When it comes to hearing God's voice, I'm afraid all I ever get is pssst. I'm always jealous when people say God spoke to them. I wonder how it is that God spoke to them and he doesn't speak to me? Is there something wrong with my hearing? Is it because I've done too many things wrong? I've prayed to hear God's voice, and yet all I get is a pssst.

In a dark moment when I questioned whether I was called to school ministry, a young student surprised me with a small clay angel and a note saying, "Thank you for all you do for us."

Pssst!

Worried about my children and how to be present in their lives even though we live apart, I go to an AA meeting where the topic is relationships with our children.

Pssst!

Feeling alone, I sit on the deck and watch the sun set. A gust of wind travels through the valley and reaches my face, making me feel as if God is listening.

Pssst!

All I've ever heard from God is pssst, but that's something for which to be profoundly grateful.

Espresso Shots:

1. *In what ways has God spoken to you?*
2. *Have you had experiences that sounded like God saying, "Pssst"?*
3. *Keep track of when you hear a pssst over the next few days. How often do you hear it? What is God saying?*

THE WOOD GATHERER

There once was a man who liked to collect wood. Like a squirrel gathering nuts, the man picked up pieces whenever he found them and slowly collected a large pile. He was careful to store and protect the wood from the weather. His hobby turned into a habit, then an obsession. Despite the many fireplaces in his home, he never burned the wood. "You never know when the furnace might go out," he explained to his wife and children. "That's when we'll need this wood to keep us warm." In time, the wood began to rot. Piece after piece surrendered to weather and bugs, leaving the man with a pile of rotten wood, a cold house, and a bewildered family.

This tale reminds me of the story Jesus told about the people given talents. Each did something different with the talents given to them. One person buried his talents so they would be safe, and Jesus chided the man for not using what had been given to him.

Again and again, Jesus' stories speak powerfully to the various gifts we have been given. No matter how ordinary we might feel, we each have more than enough gifts to make a difference in the world. Unfortunately, we underuse our gifts, bury them, or store them away for a rainy day. As a result, our gifts collect dust or, even worse, rot away.

It's time to uncover our gifts, lift them out from under the ground, and use them to make a difference in the world. We might even warm the house and dazzle the family!

Espresso Shots:

1. *List your gifts, and not only the big ones! Gifts come in all shapes and sizes.*

2. *How many of those gifts are you using fully?*

3. *In what ways can you use your gifts more?*

IF ONLY

I once read a story about a spiritual apprentice who came to his mentor, claiming a desire to know God. Smiling, the mentor rose from where he was sitting and led the novice to a water trough. Reaching up, he pushed the boy's head under water and held it there until the boy's arms were flailing. As the boy gasped to catch his breath, the mentor handed him a towel and said, "When you want God as much as you just wanted air, come back and see me."

Although not as dramatic, there's a moment in Jesus' life that taught me the importance of desire. A woman suffering from an illness makes the effort to go find Jesus. She must navigate the large crowd, who all want to get close to Jesus. Still, she pushes and shoves her way toward Jesus, saying "If only I can touch the hem of his garment, I'll be made well."

If only. Those two small words make all the difference.

Many of us claim to want to know God, but we're not gasping for God like the boy gasped for air. Many of us want to draw closer to God, but pushing through a crowd often demands too much effort.

When we're brought to our knees and utter the words, *if only,* we'll be ready. So will God.

Espresso Shots:

1. *Have you ever claimed to want to know God but not done much about it?*

2. *Have you ever been gasping for God?*

3. *In what ways have you reached for the hem of God's garment?*

BREAKING

There once was a potter who made sheets of clay and then glazed them in bright colors. When they were ready, she smashed them into pieces with a hammer. Looking down at the countless shards, she sighed, "Let the work begin." Using the broken pieces, she created world-famous mosaics.

I think of her each time I think of the way God works with us. I don't believe God does the smashing. We, and life itself, are good enough at the smashing. What God does is take our broken pieces and make works of art.

I saw a wonderful mosaic the other day in hospital scrubs. She and her husband went through an awful divorce, which led her to nursing school. She discovered she was a natural at working in health care and is now one of the most popular nurses at the hospital.

I saw a mosaic the other day having ice cream with his children. He made a public spectacle of himself a few years back and all but lost his family. Now he's sober and making time to know his children and let them know him.

I also saw a mosaic in a minister who was once a powerful politician. He was caught doing illegal things and sent to prison. While incarcerated, the work began and now he's free and serving as a prison chaplain.

I wish there were other ways to make works of art, but I guess I just need to be grateful for the way God works with our broken pieces.

Espresso Shots:

1. *When have you, or some part of you, been smashed to pieces?*

2. *In what ways did God take your broken pieces and make them into art?*

3. *How can you bring that art into the world?*

WHEN FEAR SPEAKS

When fear speaks,
   A student thinks he's stupid because he gave the wrong answer.

When fear speaks,
   A boy doesn't call the girl he met last night.

When fear speaks,
   A girl doesn't pick up the phone when it rings.

When fear speaks,
   A wife hears that her husband no longer loves her because he wants
   to go out with his friends.

When fear speaks,
   A business owner thinks he's a failure because his company had to close.

When fear speaks,
   A player passes the ball rather than takes the shot.

When fear speaks,
   A person stays in a stagnant career rather than try something new.

When fear speaks,
   A writer puts the draft in a drawer, or even worse, in the trash.

When fear speaks,
   A person takes her life rather than be a burden to others.

How about we stop letting fear speak so much?

Espresso Shots:

1. *In what ways does fear speak to you?*
2. *How does what fear says change the way you live your life?*
3. *What would your life look like, and your heart feal like, if fear didn't speak (or you learned not to listen)?*

WHO DO YOU SAY THAT I AM?

It has been said that a camel is a horse designed by a committee. Having seen a building designed by a committee, a strategic plan meant to make everyone happy, and a co-authored novel, I understand this humorous comment.

While I believe in giving everyone a voice, at some point, someone needs to take all the opinions and shape them into a comprehensive whole.

God so loved the world that he sent not a committee. I can only imagine what Jesus would have looked like, what he would have taught or done, had it been left up to the likes of you and me. Even still, people throughout the ages have looked at Christ and come up with their ideas of who he was, what he meant, and what he accomplished. Sometimes, the opinions and insights of others have been helpful. Other times, the opinions have been confusing.

Jesus asked his disciples who people thought he was. They told him some of what they had heard. Then, Jesus turned to the disciples and asked, "Who do you say that I am?" I can only imagine the way the disciples cleared their throats, looked down, and shuffled their sandals in the dirt.

I recently purchased a Bible with no footnotes or commentary of any kind. The publisher intentionally left such biblical hallmarks out because he wanted to let readers meet Jesus and the other characters without any filters. The result has been like meeting Jesus as if for the first time.

Espresso Shots:

1. *How much of your opinion of God has come from others?*
2. *Who do you think you would find if you stripped away all that you have learned about God?*
3. *Write a paragraph that describes who you say God is.*

RED AND BLACK PENCILS

Red—The teacher assumed her position at the desk with a regal sense of power. With the stack of essays before her, she reached for her sacred red pencil and began her professional rite. Crossing out the extraneous clauses, circling misspelled words, she did her best to identify all that was wrong.

Black—The writer closed his office door and began a new novel. Although he had a clear vision of the plot and characters, it was his job to allow the story to come however it wanted. He picked up his pencil and began to write.

Red—The boss sat at his desk and waited for his employee to arrive. It was time for annual reviews, and he had a long list of improvements his workers needed to make. Productivity was his concern, not morale. It was the same every year.

Black—Hers was a spontaneous family. Unlike the neighbors who ate at seven every night, dinner was served whenever it was ready. Conversations at the table were unpredictable and lively. Their parents sat at each end of the table allowing the children to discuss whatever was on their minds, and sometimes they stayed in their seats long after the dishes were done.

Red—"That was a wonderful sermon," the parishioner offered as she greeted her minister at the door. He thanked her and then pointed out the sermon's shortcomings. Better to point out the mistakes before they do, he told himself.

Black—The team gathered in the conference room to problem solve. Their boss had presented a challenge, and it was up to them to come up with a solution. "Nothing is off the table," he said—and truly meant it. "Let the ideas flow freely. I'm sure you'll come up with something."

Espresso Shots:

1. *Do you live in a red or black pencil world?*
2. *Do you find it easier to see mistakes or possibilities?*
3. *How could you hold a black pencil more than a red one?*

MILITARY MARCH OR SACRED DANCE?

Our church has an outreach ministry at Thanksgiving called Hands Across the City. It provides meals for more than 300 families. It sounds straightforward, but the effort is complicated. Addresses are incorrect, people don't follow up on their commitments, and we step on each other's feet trying to do the work of the church. I struggle between wanting everything to be neat and tidy and celebrating the messiness of ministry. In that way, Thanksgiving brings to bear the spiritual struggle I have throughout the year.

I often want my life of faith to be neat and tidy. I want to know what to believe and then to march with spiritual precision toward the life God intends. The problem is, my life of faith is nothing like that. It's full of doubts and questions, and I stumble more than I march. It's messy, but maybe that is the way it should be.

I come to God with weaknesses as well as talents. My faith is an awkward balance of the two. Too often, I reach out my arms to dance with God and try to lead. Twirling and stepping on toes, the dance is far from perfect. It's messy, but somewhere in the mess is an encounter with grace and authentic life.

Our work each Thanksgiving is a messy dance, but God wouldn't have it (or us) any other way.

Espresso Shots:

1. *When have you wanted your life and your faith to be neat and tidy?*

2. *When have you been able to see God in the mess of real life and real ministry?*

3. *When you dance with God, do you try to lead? Have you ever tried to let God lead? Really?*

THE KIDS' TABLE

I never liked sitting at the kids' table.

With a large crowd each year at Thanksgiving, there was never enough room at the big table. The youngest were assigned to the kids' table, off to the side or, even worse, in the kitchen. I looked longingly at the big table and wondered what it was like to sit there. At the kid's table, we talked about the latest TV shows and who had a boyfriend or girlfriend, but I wondered what they talked about at the big table.

In time, I graduated from the kids' table. I sat in a seat wedged between a beloved aunt and an unfamiliar guest who could have used a breath mint. The food was the same, but the conversation about politics and neighborhood scandals was as dry as the turkey.

Each year I got a better seat, and now I'm surrounded by the other kids with whom I sat long ago. We're the old people now, and all I can think about are the people no longer sitting at the Thanksgiving table. "*To everything there is a season,*" someone quoted, when I pointed out the change. She might as well have said, "*ashes to ashes, dust to dust.*" I want everyone to come back. I want Thanksgiving to be the way it used to be. I want to go back to sitting at the kids' table.

Espresso Shots:

1. *What were your Thanksgivings like as a child?*
2. *How have they changed over the years?*
3. *Who do you wish was sitting at the table this year?*

THE WOODSHOP

There are many moments in Jesus' life not recorded in the gospels. I wish we could pull up a chair and hear some of these conversations. Listening to Jesus and the disciples talk by a fire after the crowd was gone would be fascinating. Listening to what people were saying during the Last Supper, especially while Jesus was breaking the bread and serving the wine, would be incredible.

But one of the places I would most like to eavesdrop is Joseph's woodshop. We know very little about Jesus' childhood, but the things he learned from Joseph when they were working together must have proven invaluable years later. Joseph must have shown Jesus about how to read the grain, smooth edges, and work around knots and other imperfections.

Jesus didn't have much time to learn from Joseph, but I have no doubt the time he had with his earthly father helped shape his life and work as an adult.

Espresso Shots:

1. *In what ways have you been a piece of wood in God's hands?*

2. *How has God smoothed your edges and worked around your knots and other imperfections?*

3. *What other moments in Jesus' life would you like to witness?*

WE GATHER TOGETHER

*We gather together...*as we have year after year with gratitude for all that's been given to us—our health, families, friends, and food enough for all. We gather together to give you thanks.

*We gather together...*with children whose feet now touch the floor, whose bibs have given way to napkins, sippy cups to glasses of wine. No longer squirming to play outside, they sit content and speak about life. For who they were, and who they now are, we gather together to give you thanks.

*We gather together...*with an empty chair at the table. Without that laugh and those stories, the emptiness at the table matches the emptiness in our hearts. Still, we reach across the void to the hand that completes the circle. For those who were once with us, and who, by some wonderous and mysterious way, are with us still, we gather together to give you thanks.

*We gather together...*fully aware we're not a Norman Rockwell painting. There are challenges at work, struggles in relationships, disagreements within families, and distance from friends, even those sitting beside us at the table. For these challenges and others, we gather together to give you thanks.

*We gather together...*while the world spins in uncontrollable directions. Wars tire us, terrorists frighten us, and illnesses scare us, and yet we feel better holding the hands of those we love. For the gift of life, for the gift of these lives, we gather together to give you thanks.

*We gather together...*and maybe it's that simple fact that leaves us feeling most grateful of all. To be given the gift of not walking through life alone, to have others we can love and by whom we can be loved, is perhaps the greatest gift of all. For that, we gather together to give you thanks.

Espresso Shots:

1. *Be fully present in the moments of Thanksgiving.*
2. *If you cannot gather in person, how can you still experience gathering?*
3. *Offer your praise to God.*

THANKSGIVING CHECKLIST

Sit quietly before the day begins. The time will do more than extra sleep.

Go in and lie on your child's bed with your coffee in the morning and talk about whatever. (It may be the only time you get to talk all day.)

Limit your expectations (better yet, don't have any).

Don't even think about wearing a tie.

Have authentic conversations (golf scores, promotions, and past vacations don't count).

If someone puts nuts in the beans, say, "MMMMM," and eat around them.

When Aunt Eunice brings her favorite dish of parsnip cranberry sauce, receive it like the gift it is and tell her you were hoping she wouldn't forget.

Put on the Macy's Thanksgiving Day Parade and don't pay attention to the lip-syncing.

Take a deep breath and think about the people who have lost loved ones this year.

Call someone and tell them you're thankful for them.

Make the day your church service.

Say something nice to as many people as you can.

Take a long walk and count your blessings.

Play a game with the kids.

Look around the room and talk to the person who seems least comfortable.

Ask more questions than you answer, and listen more than you talk.

Don't drink too much. (If you are in recovery, don't drink at all.)

When Uncle Bob whips out his ukulele, when Tommy wants to show his newest magic trick, and when Alice cuts in line to be sure she gets the best dessert, give thanks.

Say grace.

Espresso Shot: *Enjoy the day and its preparations.*

THANK YOU NOTES

For her birthday, I found the perfect gift. Once it was wrapped, it was hard for me not to give it to her early. I made it, though, and proudly handed her the package and waited to see if she liked it as much as I. She seemed pleased with the present, but she moved on to the other gifts soon after opening mine. She thanked me, but I had hoped for a bigger reaction. It wasn't until a week later that I received a handwritten note with a drawing of what I had given her. The note and drawing were all I needed. It was as if the gift was now complete.

I didn't buy the present so she would write the note, but the note made me feel like the gift was appreciated. When she moved on to the other gifts, I thought the one I bought would be forgotten. It wasn't, and that made the gift all I hoped it would be.

I think God knew exactly how I felt. The gifts given to each of us are as plentiful as they are perfect. Just for us, I think God watches as we unwrap the gifts he has so carefully planned and hopes we'll like them. Sometimes we get distracted and move on to the rest of the packages, but when we stop and give thanks, it changes everything.

Saying thanks completes the gift. The love that offered the gift is met with the love of the one who received it.

Espresso Shots:

1. Have you ever been excited by a gift you bought or made for someone else?

2. Do you remember a time when a gift was appreciated—and when one was not?

3. In what way can you express your gratitude to God for all the gifts you've been given?

HOW AM I DOING?

"Hey, Mom, look!" said the boy as he carefully walked across a fallen tree. Suddenly, he tottered and fell into the brook below.

"Hey, guys, look, I'm walking on water," said Peter as he made his way toward Jesus, only to plunge into the sea.

The author Julia Cameron, one of my most valuable mentors, warns against what she calls the, "How Am I Doing Syndrome." It's a pervasive danger not only for the creative people for whom she writes but for all of us. It can derail anyone professionally, relationally, and spiritually. Just when we begin to walk on water, we realize what's happening and plunge into the sea.

Just ask the band that gets into the zone, as they refer to it, and are creating amazing music. The minute they think about how the music will be received, what doors the new album will open, the inspiration floats away.

Just ask the nonprofit that's having a huge impact in its community. Located in rent-free space in the basement of a church, it's singularly focused on the people it feels called to serve, but when an article about it appears in a local paper, and donations allow them to rent fancier space, the magic disappears.

Just ask the minister whose vibrant ministry disappeared the moment it became all about him and not God and the people he was called to serve.

The minute we look down at our own feet, the water below awaits.

Espresso Shots:

1. *When have you lived an inspired life?*
2. *Did you suddenly look at your own feet and wonder how you were doing?*
3. *What happened then?*

CARRYING THE LOAD

One of my favorite pictures of my son is from a camping trip. He's carrying two backpacks, with one pack strapped on his back and a second one draped over his shoulder. He's hunched over, but a small boy with no pack is walking beside him with a smile. My son looks tired and filthy, but when I heard the story of why he was carrying two packs, I thought he looked wonderful.

They were completing a particularly grueling hike. Everyone was eager to reach camp, but one hiker couldn't carry his pack any longer. He tried as hard as he could but simply didn't have the strength. That's when my son said he'd carry it and the picture was taken.

The picture reminds me what a special boy my son is, but it also reminds me of when I once fell to the ground and couldn't walk another step. Like the young boy, my load was too heavy and despite my efforts, I could no longer go on. That's when I finally met God.

All the theories and dreams about God gave way to the reality. He reached for my pack and said, "Here, let me carry that for you."

Perhaps you've had such a moment. If not, maybe you will. I celebrate today that in my weakness I came to know God's strength. In my dropping, I saw God's picking up. And in my brokenness, I found God's strength.

Espresso Shots:

1. Have you ever reached a point where you could no longer carry on?
2. Did God come and carry your load?
3. How is God's strength known through our weakness?

GETTING IT DONE

Each Christmas, I drove one of my parents' cars to a centrally located parking spot, had breakfast in a favorite diner while writing out as much of a Christmas list as I could, then did all my Christmas shopping in one day. It drove my mother crazy because she usually began her Christmas shopping in July. I liked my tradition because it was a challenge to meet, a race to win. All I had to do was keep going and get it done.

I don't think I could do that now if I tried. I wouldn't want to if I could. I love the Christmas season and sometimes go looking for gifts even when I have no one in particular in mind, just to be out in the frenzy of the season. I love the music, decorations, and people watching. Despite the occasional sigh or rolled eyes by those who feel burdened by the season, I'm fed by the joy and love of the season. "Who else but God can create traffic jams two thousand years after the fact?" my father used to ask.

To race through the season just to get through it, to shop just to get it done, removes all the meaning. Although I'm militant about not starting the season early, I'm equally adamant about not rushing through it once it begins.

Espresso Shots:

1. *How do you make your way through the Christmas season? Do you walk or run?*

2. *How can you resist the temptation to simply get it done?*

3. *How can you enter the Christmas season more fully this year?*

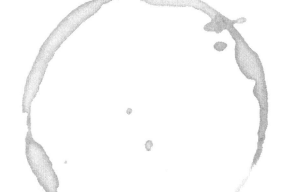

TO ALL PEOPLE

"For behold, I bring you good tidings of great joy, which shall be to all people."

Mangers come in all shapes and sizes. They're found in unlikely places, still.

On a bleak November morning in 1932, a bewildered soul, with shaky hands and bloodshot eyes, sat at his kitchen table waiting for his childhood friend. They were regular drinking buddies, or so the man thought. When he opened the door and greeted his friend, he could see his friend was different. He was sober, he explained as he politely refused the invitation for a morning nip. He spoke about the presence of God he had found and the transformative power of that presence. No longer struggling in the dark, longing for something to fill the emptiness within, God came early that year for him. God became personal.

Years later, the man across the table described his impressions:

"That floored me. It began to look as though religious people were right after all. Here was something at work in a human heart that had done the impossible. My ideas about miracles were drastically revised right then. Never mind the musty past; here sat a miracle directly across the kitchen table. He shouted great tidings" (*The Big Book*, page 11).

From that kitchen table, a movement began for all people, or at least for those who need it. The two gathered like wisemen with gifts, one bringing deep hunger, the other great tidings. As happened 2,000 years ago (and just the other day, and, most likely, later today and tomorrow), a presence came and changed the world, yet again.

Mangers come in all shapes and sizes. They're found in unlikely places, still.

Espresso Shots:
1. *When have you seen God in an unexpected place?*
2. *Have you ever noticed God working in and through someone else?*
3. *Has anyone ever said they've seen God working through you?*

ROOM CLEANING

"I don't want to," my daughter whined after we asked her to clean up her room. Her godparents were coming for a visit, and we wanted things to look nice. "But they'll love me with or without a messy room," she pleaded.

I assured her that was true, but she still needed to clean her messy room. "Think of it as a way of loving them," I explained. "It'll show them you cared enough about their visit to clean your room." She begrudgingly obliged.

I thought about our conversation as I drove to school where I was delivering the homily in chapel. It was the first week of Advent, and I wanted to talk about the season of preparation before Christmas. Despite my earlier intentions, my daughter gave me that morning's message.

Advent is a time to prepare, to clean things up in anticipation of Christmas. We sometimes whine about needing to do such spiritual work, particularly when we'd rather sing carols, eat sweets, or go shopping. We anticipate God's arrival, and we should do what we can to show that we care, with giving special attention to prayer, worship, and reading the Bible.

It isn't so that God will love us more. It's because we love God enough to do the work.

Espresso Shots:

1. *In what way does your room need straightening up?*

2. *Do you do the work so that God will like you more?*

3. *In what ways can you help make your Advent season be about you loving God more?*

DIMMING THE LIGHTS

I was fortunate to go to the Metropolitan Opera in New York City as a child. Although I've never been one to fully appreciate opera, there was nothing like the moment when the performance was about to begin. The lights didn't just dim; the crystal chandeliers literally rose three or four stories to the roof of the hall. Despite my parents' best efforts to convert me into an opera lover, the moment when the lights went up was, by far, the most exciting moment of every performance.

To this day, when the lights dim or a conductor lifts their hands to signal the start of the music, my heart fills with childlike enthusiasm. It doesn't matter whether I've seen the show before. Each beginning feels like the first time. The audience quiets as we wait for the show to begin. We put aside thoughts and concerns, and we enter the moment fully.

Advent is the moment when the lights dim for Christians. The audience quiets, candles are lit, and the music begins. We draw close and listen as the drama unfolds. Cares are put aside, so we can enter the story fully. It's as if our teacher has opened a book and said, "Once upon a time."

Regardless of how many times we've heard the story of Christ's birth, it fills our souls with child-like enthusiasm. Each time Gabriel shows up with God's annunciation, we listen in with the frightened young woman. When the angels say, "For behold…" to the shepherds keeping watch over their flocks by night, it's as if they're speaking to us, as well.

The magic of Advent awaits. May we dim the lights and hear the ageless song of angels.

Espresso Shots:

1. *What stirred your heart the most at this time of year when you were young?*

2. *How can you recapture your childlike enthusiasm?*

3. *In what ways can you dim the lights and put your cares aside and enter into the story as if for the first time?*

GETTING STOKED

Sitting before a fire reconnects me to the whatever lies within and beyond. Dancing flames lure my soul from daily concerns to eternal hopes. The crackling sounds and smoky smells add to the domestic liturgy and create a time as sacred as any worship.

Diminishing flames and smoldering wood cause me to rise and tend the fire. I reach for a tool, move the logs, and wait for the flames to reclaim their earlier glory. All the fire needed was attention, a bit of rearranging and more air. It needed to be stoked.

That's good advice for those of us seeking stronger spiritual lives. We're drawn to the fire within, the flame not of our making. Its flames dance and move us from the mundane to the sacred, from daily concerns to life dreams.

Keeping a vibrant fire, however, requires attention. There are many tools that we can use to tend the fire: prayer and meditation, reading scripture or some other spiritual book, or speaking authentically with a friend. Each, in their own way, can rearrange the logs of our lives, just as walking, listening to music, or attending worship or a support group can provide much needed air.

Sometimes our attention is piqued and our lives rearranged, through no doing of our own. A loved one becomes ill, jobs are lost, marriages crumble. Such struggles challenge us at our core, but these moments can also become the very things that cause our internal flames to burn stronger.

Select your tool—or a couple—and take care of the fire. 'Tis the season to get stoked.

Espresso Shots:

1. _What stokes your spiritual flames?_
2. _How often do you use tools to tend the fire?_
3. _In what ways will you deliberately stoke your flame this Advent?_

CROSSING THE ROOM

"Prepare for Christ's birth?" The child asked, somewhat confused. "Didn't Jesus already come?"

It was an honest moment that slightly rattled the Sunday school teacher. Trying to explain the expectation of Advent while acknowledging Christ's ongoing presence in the world, he told the class the following story:

Not long ago, I went to a Christmas party. All my neighbors were there, those I knew well and others I didn't. It was the first party of the Christmas season and we were all excited and dressed in our holiday best. I started to head toward the guests I knew but decided to talk to others I hadn't met yet.

I met a man named Jack who lived down the street from me. We always waved whenever we passed each other but never spoke. After we greeted each other at the party, Jack told me about the day he and his wife bought the house. He's still there, even though she died ten years ago. He spoke of his service in World War II as well as how the neighborhood had changed over the years. I shared things about my life, and soon we realized we'd talked through the entire party. I left the party feeling as if I had a new friend. We'd seen each other many times, but we now knew each other, all because I crossed the room.

"I think that's what Advent is like," the teacher explained. "Jesus is always in the room with us, but we're often distracted by other guests or drawn to the ones we know well. Advent is about crossing the room and making the effort to talk with Christ. If we do that, we'll come to know him and be known by him as if for the first time."

Espresso Shots:

1. *How could you cross the room and come to know Jesus better?*
2. *What part of you could you share with him?*
3. *As you watch and wait this season, make a plan to talk with a neighbor or casual friend.*

REVOLVING DOORS

I don't remember the first time I saw a revolving door. I'm sure it was on a visit to New York City, but the Christmas movie, *Elf*, reminded me how funny they must seem on the first encounter, more like an amusement park ride than an entrance to a department store.

Buddy the Elf is fascinated by the revolving door and keeps going round and round until he's so dizzy that he can hardly walk. I can relate.

In my life of sobriety, I get caught between my old and new life. I try to go to the same places and hang out with the same people while also trying to practice the principles of AA in all my affairs. I've met people who inspire me and point me in a wonderful new direction, and I cling to old habits and familiar paths. Trying to live in both worlds can make me feel dizzy and sick.

Even possessions can become revolving doors. I cling to things from my past even though they no longer speak to me. My tastes have changed, but I try to make room for the old and the new. The result is a cluttered home that leaves me dizzy.

The answer, of course, is to leave the revolving door. That's easier said than done, at least for me. Getting out of a revolving door can be frightening. Entering something new is just as frightening as leaving something old behind. No wonder people find themselves going around and around.

The first step is to realize we're spinning. The next is to decide on what side of the revolving door we want to live. Then, we need to let go of the door and exit. As frightening as it may be, we may find that we're longer dizzy or sick.

Espresso Shots:

1. *In what area of your life are you caught in a revolving door?*

2. *What is it about letting go and getting out that frightens you?*

3. *What would it look and feel like to be on the other side of the revolving door?*

MULTIPLYING CANDLES

"Add your light to the sum of light." —Leo Tolstoy

If I were to light a candle and place it on a table, there would be one candle burning in the middle of the room. If I were to ask ten people to join me with candles of their own, and each were to take the flame from my candle and use it to light their own, would the light somehow multiply? The light from one candle would spread. The one flame would now shine from ten other candles. Imagine what would happen if each took their candle and found ten more. The light from my one candle would multiply again . . . and again . . . and again.

This kind of multiplication lesson is profound when applied to the spiritual life. One person imagines providing homes for people, others join in, and soon you have Habitat for Humanity! It can be as simple as paying for the coffee of the person behind you in line, making a point of encouraging someone with a spoken or written word, or defending someone when they're not in the room to defend themselves. Candles come in all shapes and sizes, but I believe the light is the same.

Regardless of what candle you light, the light can spread from yours to others and brighten the world.

Espresso Shots:

1. *In what way have you brought light into the world?*
2. *Have you ever seen that light multiply?*
3. *In what way can you light a candle and share its light today?*

WAIT

Certain words can carry enormous weight. A word can keep one person up all night, while having no effect on someone else. For me, one of the most challenging words is wait. I've always traveled quickly and expected life to keep up. I suspect that is the reason I find Advent the most challenging season in the church.

The weeks leading up to Christmas are designed to prepare our hearts and minds to go to Bethlehem. Despite what stores tell us, Christmas does not come on the Friday after Thanksgiving (or earlier). It comes on December 25, and until that day, we are to wait. Like a child who sees a package wrapped and under the tree, I often experience waiting as torture.

Those who are not wired as I am tell me there's much to be gained from waiting. It allows them to prepare, to get their heads and hearts ready to receive. They even have the nerve to tell me that what they receive means more when they wait for it.

On the rare occasions I have followed their advice, I have found that waiting reminds me that it's not all about me, that it's up to the giver, not the recipient. The anticipation heightens my appreciation for the gift that's coming and for the giver, who's kind enough to think of me. Waiting also sharpens my attention to the gift and allows me to see and feel it in ways I wouldn't have had I rushed in and unwrapped it whenever I wanted.

I guess the church knew what it was doing when it created Advent. I guess God knew what he was doing when he sent his amazing gift.

Espresso Shots:

1. *How hard is it for you to wait to open a present or be patient for something to come?*

2. *In what way can you see wisdom in waiting?*

3. *What can you do in these days to sharpen your attention so that you can see and feel Christmas with renewed appreciation?*

A REMARKABLE WOMAN

She was a remarkable woman. Only thirteen years old, or so, but that's not what made her special. She was wise beyond her years, but that didn't make her remarkable, either. She had found a wonderful, upstanding young man to marry, but that was common in the day. She gave birth to a child, but that didn't make her extraordinary, nor did the way she cared for that child and stayed close to him throughout his life. She even stood and watched that child die an awful death, but not even that made Mary a remarkable woman.

When she was young, before she was married, an angel came to Mary and told her she would bear a child even though she had never been with her future husband in that way. Astonishing, for sure.

But what made her remarkable, what truly set young Mary apart, was one simple word: Yes. She said yes to God, and that's what made her truly remarkable.

Espresso Shots:

1. *Why do you think God chose Mary?*
2. *In what ways did she prove to be an amazing choice?*
3. *Have you ever said yes to God?*

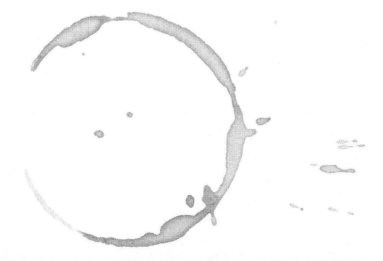

COMMON DENOMINATORS

In math class, we were taught how to find the common denominator. When presented with multiple fractions, the way to begin working with them is to find the common denominator, the number below which they have in common. It was a lesson I used that semester, but I picked it up again when I became a minister.

I was a school chaplain, and when I first arrived, I was overwhelmed by all the different people. There were teachers and administrators, mothers and fathers, children and adolescents, boys and girls, families who were financially comfortable and others who were struggling. Some were popular and others sat alone. Some who coasted to an A and others who crawled to a C.

It wasn't until I remembered that math lesson from years before that I learned how to serve the community: find the common denominators.

No matter a person's age, we're all children. Despite all the ways we try to create a facade, deep down we all wonder if we are good enough. As happy as our faces look, we all have sadness within. As certain as we may appear, we all have doubts. As self-centered as we can be, we all want to touch someone else's life.

Jesus was the master at finding common denominators. He didn't care about a person's status, occupation, or reputation. He saw only lost children of God searching for home.

In the end, that's our common denominator.

Espresso Shots:

1. *When have you found a common denominator with someone who seemed different from you?*

2. *How does finding a common denominator change a conversation or relationship?*

3. *How can you learn to find common denominators on a regular basis?*

LETTING GOD IN

Once I was diagnosed as dyslexic, my teachers changed the way they taught me. A dyslexic has a short circuit between the two halves of the brain, which causes them to reverse or turn letters and numbers upside down. My teachers began using tools that engaged my different senses, in hopes that one of the senses would get through unaltered. Put another way, they used my senses to get the lessons in me.

I was reminded of this teaching strategy while Christmas shopping recently. I saw decorations lining the road and decorating the stores. I heard the music playing, along with bells from the Salvation Army volunteers, and I smelled cider bubbling in the back of a clothing store. I rubbed my hands through the soft Christmas sweaters and ate more than a few Christmas cookies in a kitchen store. Through my senses, Christmas found its way into me.

The church has known this teaching method for centuries. With spectacular spaces and stained-glass windows, the buildings dazzle our eyes. With music, it opens our ears. With incense and flowers, it awakens our noses. With polished wood and velvet cushions, it invites our hands to join the worship, and with communion it lets us taste God's presence.

During this Christmas season, in particular, and the spiritual journey, in general, I invite you to open your senses and let God in.

Espresso Shots:

1. _Of all your senses, which one do you use the most often, and which is the most powerful?_

2. _In what ways do you use your senses to let God in?_

3. _How can you learn to use more of your senses in your spiritual life?_

A CHRISTMAS PARABLE

Two children ran down the stairs eager to open their Christmas presents. The first ran to the tree and grabbed every present with his name on it. He piled the packages by his seat and began ripping the paper with an insatiable appetite. He looked to see what the box said was inside and offered a quick thank you to his parents or Santa before moving on to the next package.

His sister took her time. She took one present at a time and opened it with care. She not only saw what the box said but also opened and explored the gift inside before moving on. Looking at her parents, she said how much she loved each present.

His Christmas was over in a flash. Looking at the pile of gifts and mangled wrapping paper, he felt sad because Christmas was over.

Her Christmas lasted all day. Looking at her opened presents, she felt like Christmas was just beginning.

Espresso Shots:

1. *Do you run or walk through life?*

2. *Do you rip open the wrapping of each moment then move on, or do you take your time?*

3. *How can you learn to receive your life (each moment, person) like a gift?*

THE ODDS

"May the odds be ever in your favor." —*The Hunger Games*

I've never been one to play the odds. Either I'm not smart enough to figure them out, or I don't like living a calculated life. Sometimes though, I look at people who know the odds and live a life according to them, and I'm envious. When a sudden bill arrives, they are ready with the necessary cash. When someone dies unexpectedly, their house is in order. When the economy tanks, they have positioned themselves to weather the storm.

Not playing the odds has made my life more difficult than it needed to be, but it has helped me in living a spiritual life. It seems everything Jesus taught challenged the odds. It was as if he wanted to challenge every form of logic or common sense the world had to offer. No wonder many who met him walked away shaking their heads.

What nonsense, they must have said to one another. I wonder if that was the whole point. To follow an itinerant preacher from Galilee, to sell all that you had, to take your place at the end of the line goes against everything the world teaches. No wonder so many walked away. No wonder church pews have so much space.

Playing the odds requires cleverness. Defying the odds requires faith.

Espresso Shots:

1. *How calculated is your life?*
2. *In what ways or areas do you live by faith?*
3. *How can you learn the balance being as wise as serpents and innocent as doves?*

MAKING ROOM

"Move over," the child said, hoping to squeeze into the back seat with his cousins. "No room," was their united chorus.

"Hold the elevator," the woman shouted as she ran toward the closing doors. "Sorry, no room," was all she heard before they closed.

"Do you have a room?" asked the weary fiance'. "No, sorry," the innkeeper replied. "You can sleep in the stable if you want."

We learn early on what it feels like when there's no room. Eager to join, we find closed doors, which leave us feeling invisible and rejected. We're tempted to knock and try again, but the door rarely opens, and the response is always the same.

I remember hearing about Joseph and Mary looking for room as a child. I couldn't believe the innkeeper wouldn't make room, especially given who was asking. Why didn't God do something? Instead, the couple settled in the stable, and Mary gave birth to Jesus there.

This is the first of countless times of people closing the door to Jesus—in biblical days and through the ages. We may couch our responses with regret, but still we make no room. *I would, but I have a million other things to do. I have one room, but I need to save it for (fill in the blank). I would, but what would the neighbors say?*

Our excuses are as plentiful as God's requests. Maybe this Christmas, we'll find room.

Espresso Shots:

1. *When has God come to you seeking room in your life?*
2. *If you said no, what reason did you offer?*
3. *How can you find room this season?*

RECONCILED

The child didn't know what he was doing. Shopping with his father, he saw a shiny red truck that would go well with his other cars at home. He slipped it into his jacket, and it wasn't until the two were having dinner that the father realized what had happened. He tried not to overreact but explained the boy would need to go back to the store, apologize, and return the truck. There were tears, but the father assured his son he loved him and everything would be okay.

The store owner accepted the boy's apology and placed the truck back on the shelf, and both the father and son returned to the car feeling relieved. "It's Christmas," the son exclaimed as he saw the promised snow had begun to fall, and the two drove home in silence.

That is, until the boy started singing his favorite Christmas carol. He had learned it in church and grew to love it while watching *A Charlie Brown Christmas* cartoon. It said everything the father hoped the son would one day understand about what had happened at the store—and what happened on that Christmas long ago. Instead of trying to explain, he just let his son sing:

> *Hark! The herald angels sing*
> *Glory to the newborn King*
> *Peace on earth and mercy mild*
> *God and sinners reconciled.*

Espresso Shots:

1. *In what surprising ways has the Christmas message come to you?*

2. *What does it mean that God and sinners were reconciled?*

3. *Watch* A Charlie Brown Christmas *in its entirety. You might even sing along.*

BEHIND THE CURTAIN

Every Christmas season, we went to a special party at a neighbor's house. Like other parties, many people attended, and food and drink abounded. What made this party unique was that each year, the hosts would gather the guests into the spacious living room to retell the Christmas story and sing carols. I knew the story but liked hearing it again. I also loved the carols but was always embarrassed to sing—that is, until my sister showed me the wide windowsills behind the large, thick curtains. She crawled behind one, and I another, and in the safety of that space, we both sang freely. I felt connected to God as I listened to the story. I felt an intimacy with God as I sang.

The memory of being behind the curtain is as comforting to me as it is disappointing. I savor the safety I found there and delight in my finding a place to sing out loud. But why did I need such a place? Why was I so embarrassed to sing?

I can see that I long for wide windowsills still, places where I will feel safe to sing out loud. My struggle is to live in front of the curtain, where everyone can see me and be brave enough to sing where everyone can hear.

Espresso Shots:

1. *What was one of your happiest Christmas memories?*
2. *Were you/are you embarrassed to sing?*
3. *Find a way to come out from behind the curtain and speak about your faith.*

CHRISTMAS IS A GIFT

Their Christmas card was displayed on a table in the hallway and unopened gifts with their names on them lay under the tree when the phone call came and changed Christmas forever. "There's been a tragic accident," the voice on the other end sputtered. "Everyone in the airplane was killed." Time stopped in an instant, memories of what was being said blurred; confusion and panic overwhelmed. The family in the Christmas card was gone. The gifts would never be opened.

I think of this family every December. It reminds me how precious life is and how everything can change in an instant. It helps me remember what's important when the seasonal festivities take over.

Hopefully I can remember it when someone calls at an inconvenient time or the line is long at the cash register.
Hopefully I can remember it when bills arrive or when my children are fighting over who opens their gifts first.
Hopefully I can remember it when I'm stressed over creating the perfect meal and when I am lonely and feeling sorry for myself.

Hopefully, I can remember that Christmas is promised to no one. All that's wonderful and challenging about it is wrapped in the same package. It may be my last, or someone I love may not be here next year. With newfound appreciation, I want to open my heart and arms as wide as I can and receive this Christmas like the gift it is.

Espresso Shots:

1. *What is it about Christmas that gets in the way of your receiving it as a gift?*
2. *What would you do differently if you knew it was your (or someone else's) last Christmas?*
3. *How can you open your heart and arms more this Christmas?*

GIFT GIVING

I'm a gift giver. It's how I was taught to express love. Giving gifts fills my soul in ways other love languages do not. Like a puppy, I shake when I find the perfect gift and am so excited that I often end up giving the gift early. Sometimes watching someone open a present is more exciting for me than actually opening the present is for them. When I leave something anonymously at someone's doorstep, it's all I can do not to hide in the bushes and watch.

There are dangers that come with being a gift giver. Someone might not like the gift you give, they might not want a gift at all, or, worst of all, they might expect your generosity, which takes away it being a gift in the first place. For gift givers, such reactions can create sadness and a little resentment. When that happens, I try to remind myself that the reaction is not the point: giving the gift is.

I can't help but think God knows what it's like. After all, God is the biggest gift giver there is. His generosity knows no bounds, and the variety of expressions is as countless as the stars. How do we receive God's gifts? Do we receive the gifts with a grateful heart? Do we decide whether a gift is to our liking? Do we take such generosity for granted? Like me hiding in the bushes, what will God see when we open the door and see the gift at our doorstep?

Espresso Shots:

1. *Do you enjoy giving gifts?*
2. *Have you ever given a gift that was not appreciated?*
3. *How did it make you feel? Do you think God knows that feeling?*

HOLY DISRUPTIONS

I often wish life was smooth and void of all disruptions. I secretly believe I would be happier if life was consistent and predictable. This desire and belief have led me to work on creating a predictable life, but, without fail, something comes along and changes my neat and tidy life.

Life as it is described in the Bible is no different. Just when things are going in a certain direction, something happens that changes everything. No matter what the people may be looking for, disruptions come.

Just when a young woman is about to be married, an angel appears.

Just when shepherds are keeping watch over their flocks by night, a heavenly chorus begins singing.

Just when you think a wedding feast is over, there's new wine.

Just when you think Jesus is bringing peace on earth, tables get turned over.

Just when you think the special night is over, Judas arrives with soldiers.

Just when you think the story is over, the tomb is empty.

Disruptions one and all, and yet through them, life is transformed. Disruptions awaken, challenge, and inspire us, even if we don't understand or like them. In fact, like our lives, disruptions can become holy.

Espresso Shots:

1. *Identify a disruption in your life that became holy.*

2. *Why do you think disruptions are necessary and/or effective?*

3. *How can we learn to see disruptions as holy?*

COLORFUL FLAMES

I once believed my sister had magic powder hidden somewhere in our living room. Each time we made a fire, she'd tell me to close my eyes. When she told me to open them again, the flames of the fire were an assortment of colors. When she wasn't around, I searched the living room for her magic powder but never found it. Only years later did I learn she used newspaper comics to create the colorful flames.

I was reminded of that childhood memory while staring at the flames in the fireplace this morning. I love this quiet time before others awaken. It allows room for my soul to breath before the day begins. Whether sitting in silence or reading, it is a time to focus on God and the life I've been given. Remembering my sister's trickery, I recalled how I once believed there was a magic spiritual powder that made life colorful. When no one was looking, I searched the world for such powder. Fortunately, just as I realized there was no magic powder and God was no magician, I learned to notice colors in the flames of my life. With the eyes of faith, we can see the reds, greens and purples swirling around the world in which we live.

That's magic enough for me.

Espresso Shots:

1. *When you were young, what did you think about God?*
2. *In what ways did your faith grow up?*
3. *With eyes of faith, can you see God at work in colorful ways?*

LET THE RUMPUS BEGIN

As Advent makes its final approach, and Christmas comes into view, I feel like the main character in Maurice Sendack's classic, *Where the Wild Things Are*.

"And now," cried Max, "Let the wild rumpus start!" The tree is up and decorated, presents bought and wrapped, and the annual traditions are in motion. It's time to enjoy the rumpus with all its twists and turns.

I loved Christmas as a child but enjoying it as an adult has become a challenge. The fundamental reason it's become a struggle is not because of the change in Christmas, but the change in me. It's the twists and turns or, as Max would say, the rumpus. I come to these final days with expectations—that the season will be magical, everyone will be happy and say kind things, people will arrive on time and add to the lively conversation, and everyone will sing carols unreservedly. After years of frustration and disappointments, I've learned these are just future resentments because no person, place, or season can live up to my expectations.

Uncle Billy, or Aunt Susie, drinks too much, Mrs. Stimpson keeps going on about her late husband's tragic death at ninety-four, and children look for the next gift before the paper from the last one has hit the floor. I cling to what I think Christmas should be, but it's hard to receive all that Christmas is when my hands are clinched tight. My problem is that I see Christmas as something I create, I orchestrate, and I control. Standing like a conductor in front of musicians, I expect everyone to play their parts perfectly, the way I've heard them in my mind, and it never happens that way.

Rather than bemoaning that fact, I need to let Christmas come as it will, as the gift it is. I need to open my hands and shout, "Let the rumpus start!"

Espresso Shots:

1. *Has your view of Christmas changed over the years?*
2. *What expectations get in the way of your enjoying Christmas fully?*
3. *In what way could you unclench your fist and let Christmas come as it will?*

ROOM FOR DOUBT

Poor guy. All Thomas wants to do is believe, and now he's the one remembered for doubting. Doubting Thomas, we call him, and yet he's not all that different from you or me.

Jesus is arrested and sentenced to death. The disciples fear they would be next, but a few days after Jesus' death Thomas hears Jesus is alive. It sounds too good to be true, especially after watching all that has happened, so Thomas says he will only believe if he sees Jesus, scars and all, for himself. In fact, he doesn't just want to see Jesus, he wants to put his fingers into the wounds.

I can't blame Thomas. Believing would be so much easier if we could see the evidence or, better yet, touch it. Believing without seeing is something we did when we were little, but we grew out of it. Trusting came naturally as children, but we grew up.

Unfortunately, with all we gained by growing up, we lost just as much, maybe more. No longer do we believe without seeing, trust without verifying, love without proof.

Thomas helps me understand that not seeing makes the believing more powerful, the trust more exceptional, and the love more authentic. Instead of removing our doubt, we need to make room for it, for the darkness of doubt can make our faith shine brighter.

Espresso Shots:

1. *How good are you at believing without seeing proof?*
2. *How do your doubts accentuate your faith?*
3. *How can you learn to live a life of faith while still possessing doubts?*

DON'T TRUST THE BOX

The box with his name on it under the tree taunted him throughout December. He could see the name of the store though the thin paper: Cosby's, a famous hockey store in New York City. He wondered what it might be. Skates? A helmet? It didn't matter. He'd have something to impress the kids at school, something from the store where his brother got all his equipment.

"Okay, you may open it," his mother said after he'd been squirming all morning.

He ran to the tree and went straight to the box he'd been waiting to open for a month. The paper didn't stand a chance against his enthusiasm, and pieces were still floating in the air as he lifted the top of the box. In it was a painting his mother had done in a recent painting class.

He tried to hide his disappointment. To this day, he can't recall anything else he received that Christmas. The painting eventually hung in his room, where he stared at it from his bed. He grew to love the painting. He took it with him to college. When he moved into his first apartment, the painting was the first thing he hung on the wall. The painting was like having a piece of his mother with him. It got him through the time he was laid off and when his daughter was in the hospital. Now, with his mother gone, the painting meant even more.

The painting was never something he expected, but it ended up being all he ever wanted.

Espresso Shots:

1. *Were you ever surprised by a gift wrapped in a misleading box?*
2. *Did you ever receive a gift that you grew to appreciate over time?*
3. *In what way was Jesus' birth a surprise, then and now?*

STOCKINGS

In the food chain of stockings, it's nothing special, but something deep within stirred when my mother recently sent me my childhood stocking. Opening some long-ignored Christmas box, she found this relic of Christmas past and decided to send it to her middle-aged little boy. Like few other objects, it carried me back to the mornings of rushing to the fireplace in my parents' room at first light where my stocking hung, farthest on the right.

Such time travel can lead to stifling nostalgia, but it can also awaken the child within. Remembering when life wasn't so complicated, when what was in my stocking was my greatest concern, renews my soul. To feel again the joy and happiness that is uniquely Christmas can clean debris from my spiritual receptors.

Jesus once said that to receive the kingdom of God, we are to become like children. The lesson made little sense when I was a child, but its wisdom is undeniable now that I am older. I hear it as if for the first time when I look at the moth-eaten stocking now hanging on our mantle.

So, bring on the lights… turn up the carols… and hold on tight to the people and traditions that speak to your heart! Go back in time, to when you were a child, if only for a moment. Stop squinting at the world with cynicism and open your eyes wide with hope. Let down your burdened shoulders and dance about the room. Race your children to Christmas morning, where all we need to know is hanging on the mantle.

Espresso Shots:

1. *What object represents your childhood Christmases most?*
2. *What were you like on Christmas morning?*
3. *Describe what Christmases were like in great detail to someone, and ask them to do the same.*

A MATTER OF HEART

I learned an important lesson about Christmas from an unexpected source, a painting. I painted it for my daughter and was taking a last look before wrapping it and putting it beside the tree. There was something about the painting that "worked," as artists say. I looked beyond the elements of composition, contrast, and color and enjoyed the painting.

On the wall of my studio is another painting that doesn't work. Its lines are crooked, perspectives wrong, and colors slightly off. All I see is what's wrong with the painting, and it leaves me restless and agitated. When a painting works, it draws you closer. You look beyond the details and enter. When it doesn't, every detail drives you crazy, and you want to walk away.

I sometimes have Christmases that work, and others that do not. When Christmas works, I'm drawn in and look beyond the details and enter. When it doesn't, the details get in the way, and I'm left feeling agitated. Some years, I don't notice the traffic, overplayed music, and rush to get everything done. It's like I'm dancing with God in everything I do. Other years, the traffic and noise are all I see. It's like I'm stepping on God's toes during the dance and want to sit this one out.

I've come to see that it's not the painting or the season but the heart with which I receive them. When my heart is centered on what really matters, I enter into the season in a profound way and walk closer to the one it seeks to celebrate. When my heart is distracted and unfocused, I only see the details and miss the point.

The condition of my heart draws me in or pushes me away. It's that way with paintings. It's that way with Christmas.

Espresso Shots:

1. *When do the details draw you toward Christmas, and when do they push you away?*
2. *In what ways does your heart dictate how you receive Christmas?*
3. *How can you open your heart and enter into Christmas this year?*

THE MANGER

"This will be a sign for you: you will find a child wrapped in bands of cloth and lying in a manger." —*Luke 2:12*

It was an unlikely place to find God. A palace or throne would have made more sense, and yet making sense doesn't seem to be God's chief concern. So, the manger it was. They wrapped the child and placed him on the straw. I'm sure the animals in the stable were confused. It was where they went to eat. Now there was a baby lying there.

Of the many images of Christ in the world, lying in the manger is among the most profound. His ministry had not begun, but his life among us had. Like Mary and Joseph, the shepherds and kings must have looked at Jesus in the manger with awe. It is a moment that not only spoke of God's presence but also the world's hunger. It was true way back then and is still true today.

We live in a world that is starving to death. Despite all that we possess, there's a hunger within us all. We hunger for something more, and it is only fitting that the one to bring what we are starving for is found in a manger.

May we gather close and see in the child lying there, the longing of our hearts, the answer to our prayers, and the food for our souls.

Espresso Shots:

1. *In what ways is your soul hungry?*
2. *What do you see when you look into the manger?*
3. *How can that child fill your deepest hunger and the hunger of the world?*

SHEPHERDS

"In that region there were shepherds living in the fields, keeping watch over their flock by night." —Luke 2:8

The shepherds preferred the outdoors. Given how the others in society looked down on shepherds, they were more comfortable among sheep.

They were minding their own business, so when the angel came looking for them, they must have been frightened and confused. "We're sure you're mistaken," they must have wanted to say. "You must be looking for some others." But the angel sought them. *The Messiah has come. Go to Bethlehem and meet him for yourselves.*

I wonder what the shepherds talked about as they made their way to the city of David. Did they think they were being sent on a wild goose chase? Were they tempted to turn back?

When the innkeeper pointed them to the stable out back, I'm sure they wondered if they were being dismissed, once again. But still, they plowed ahead. Once in the stable, a place where they would have felt particularly at home, they saw the babe lying in a manger.

"Of course," they must have said as they looked at the child, "this makes all the sense in the world." God with us means God with all of us. I'm sure the shepherds felt valued in a way they never had. It made them the first to join the heavenly chorus: "Glory to God in the highest heaven, and on earth peace to those on whom his favor rests."

Espresso Shots:

1. *What do we learn about Christ that he is made known to the shepherds first?*
2. *How were the shepherds uniquely qualified to see Jesus?*
3. *What does God-with-us mean today?*

SHEPHERDS AND KINGS

"On entering the house, they saw the child with Mary his mother; and they knelt down and paid him homage. Then, opening their treasure chests, they offered him gifts of gold, frankincense, and myrrh." —Matthew 2:11

After months on the road searching for a sign, the kings were delighted to see the star shining over Bethlehem. I'm sure they nudged their camels in hopes of picking up the pace. They would soon see the messiah, the one they had been sent to find. Climbing down and grabbing their gifts, the kings walked toward the stable with reverence. Lowering their heads and removing their crowns, they entered only to see others had arrived before them. *Shepherds, of all people,* the kings must have grumbled. In the social food chain at the time, shepherds were low, and they were high. They probably wanted to mention the social faux pas but stayed quiet. Instead, the wisemen knelt beside the others and presented their gifts.

For more than two thousand years we have lived in that same tension. With reverence, we search for Jesus, and we celebrate finding him. The problem comes when we see others already there. They may look different, come from a different background or social standing, and part of us wishes Jesus was here for us, and for people like us, only. The truth lies within the story as it has been passed along for centuries. The Word became flesh and dwelt among us. Not just some of us, but all of us. May this be the Christmas we celebrate like never before. May we take off our crowns, if we have any, and kneel beside one another as we worship the one who made us brothers and sisters once and for all.

Espresso Shots:

1. *Do you identify with the shepherds or kings?*
2. *In what ways have you been guilty of thinking Christ belongs to you, and people like you, alone?*
3. *In what way can you kneel beside another this Christmas and worship the one who came for us all?*

$5 POSTERS

Lying around the child were gifts of all shapes, sizes, and values. It had been a good Christmas, one where she received almost all she asked for and a few surprises, as well. There was a painting done just for her, her grandmother's earring made into a necklace, and a jewelry box, but it was the $5 poster of a boy band that excited her most.

Although her reaction to the poster was completely age-appropriate, it was a vivid reminder of how often the things we value are not the most impressive or expensive. Like my daughter, I wanted things as a child that must have made my parents scratch their heads.

I wouldn't be surprised if that's how God feels all the time. We're given countless gifts daily, and yet they so often fall to the side, ignored by us. With sunsets painted across the sky, we choose to watch a game on TV. With trails to hike and beaches to explore, we choose a gym with monthly payments. New acquaintances are picked over family dinners, and movies over conversations.

Although I love watching sports and movies, I need to make sure that I am valuing the things that matter. I need to trim the sail of my spiritual vessel and plot a revised course, as a sailor friend likes to say. That could mean staying in for dinner, playing games with my kids, or finding an hour for time alone in nature. Such moments always make me grateful. Such moments remind me what's really valuable.

Espresso Shots:

1. What was something you valued, or had to have, that you now see was not as valuable as you thought?

2. In what ways are you still missing the things of significant worth in your life?

3. What would it take to recalibrate your heart so you hold tight to what really matters?

PUTTING CHRISTMAS AWAY

One of the saddest sights is a discarded Christmas tree lying in the gutter, waiting to be carried away. With strands of tinsel waving in the breeze and a forgotten ornament clinging for dear life, the tree sits like a spiritual hangover on the side of the road. Some are taken to the curb within minutes of opening the last present; others make it to Epiphany, but eventually all the trees that were bought with great enthusiasm and put up with care are discarded so that people can return to their usual routines.

Too often, what we do with Christmas trees is also what we do with Christmas itself. Our focus on Christ's birth and joy at the thought of God being with us is as temporary as the season itself. Christians were right to set aside a day to recall the wonder of Christmas, but it led to us putting the moment in a box that we open once a year. The incarnation and wonder of God's presence among us is so outrageous that no box can contain it, no day can capture it, and no season can fully express its significance.

I have always adored Christmas. The music, decorating, and story itself stir my heart like no other time of year, and yet I struggle with how to keep my heart open. Like everyone else, I put Christmas out on the curb when I am done with it. Somehow, I need to learn how to keep Christmas alive after the trees are gone, the decorations put away, and music silenced.

Espresso Shots:

1. *What are your favorite Christmas traditions?*
2. *How quickly do you remove your tree and box up your decorations?*
3. *In what ways could you keep Christmas alive after you put the decorations away?*

LEGACY

Whether we want to or not, each of us will leave a legacy of some sort when we're gone. Some people know this and spend every waking hour working on their legacy. It might be to leave a fortune to children, a name on a building, or a renowned reputation. Others don't give it a thought, but they will leave a legacy, too. Given the inevitability of leaving a legacy, we would do well to look at what our legacy will be. Despite our best intentions, the legacy we intend is not always the legacy we leave.

There once was a minister who sought nothing more than to leave an impressive legacy. At first, he thought the way he'd do so was by climbing the ecclesiastical ladder and becoming a leader in the church. When it became clear he'd not be able to climb as high as he wanted, he sought to make his parish his legacy. After years of growing his parish and building an expansive campus, a fire destroyed it all. In the time he had left, he gave up his obsession with his legacy and worked with the people to rebuild the parish. No longer able to do everything on his own, he turned to his parishioners, who found gifts and talents they never knew they had. When he died, no building bore his name, no fortune amassed, but the parish had discovered a faith they never knew. It was quite a legacy.

Espresso Shots:

1. *How much do you think about your legacy?*

2. *What is your greatest hope, and fear, about your legacy?*

3. *How can you leave a meaningful legacy with the time you have left?*

PROGRESS NOT PERFECTION

The hats are ready, along with the confetti, and it would be tempting to run toward the new year with little or no thought about the year that is drawing to a close. Tomorrow will be here soon enough. Today is a special day, one in which we remember the spiritual journey is about progress, not perfection.

New Year's Eve can be one of the most depressing days of the year, if we let it. We come to the end of the year with regrets and unmet resolutions. Only when I joined the folks in 12-step recovery did I learn to stop beating myself up for not doing things perfectly. "It's enough not to drink for twenty-four hours," my first sponsor said when I showed him my ambitious goals for sobriety.

Since then, I've learned to stand back and appreciate whatever progress I made during a day, week, month, or year. Whether in my family, work, or spiritual life, there's always something to be thankful for. No doubt, there are things I wish I had done, but today is the day to give thanks for what I did accomplish. Unmet goals can wait for the new year. Now is the time to be grateful for all the ways we've grown or stumbled in the right direction.

One of my favorite sayings from recovery circles seems a fitting prayer for the close to the year and as the final words in this collection of meditations. I offer it with love and gratitude for coming along with me on this journey:

I'm not what I want to be.

I'm not what I'm gonna be.

But, thank God, I'm not what I used to be.

ABOUT THE AUTHOR

A graduate of Taft School and Hamilton College, Chip Bristol also holds a master's in divinity from Virginia Theological Seminary and a master's in fine arts in creative writing from The New Hampshire Institute of Art.

Years in school ministry have prepared him well for this creative and accessible collection of spiritual meditations. He lives in Greensboro, North Carolina, with his wife, Louise, and their combined family.

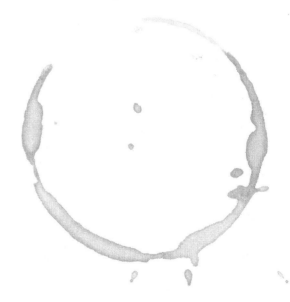

Made in the USA
Columbia, SC
10 March 2023

13505223R00207